Criminal Profiling

Criminal Profiling provides a thorough and up-to-date overview of profiling in criminal justice.

By focusing on different styles of profiling—whose underpinnings rely on behavioral and geographical theories—it is designed to provide police and others in criminal justice with an understanding of the consistency of behavior at the crime scene, the consistent nature of criminal motivations, how criminals work in familiar geographic areas, and how to construct a timeline of events. Profiling attempts to generate an identifiably consistent personality pattern based on principal character traits inferred from behavior at the crime scene, leading to the predictability of future criminal behavior. The three main types of profiling used in criminal justice—crime scene analysis (FBI profiling), investigative psychology, and geographic profiling—are explained and analyzed, and the essential role of victimology and case linkage is emphasized. Special consideration is given to three primary assumptions—behavioral consistency, behavioral distinctiveness, and homology—that underlie the effectiveness of different approaches to criminal profiling.

Practical and approachable, this book brings together the theory and practice of criminal profiling. It is suitable for students in Criminal Profiling and other investigative courses, and equips both future and present investigators with the tools to use profiling principles to their fullest advantage.

Kevin Borgeson, Ph.D., is an Associate Professor of Criminal Justice and Research Fellow at the Center for Holocaust and Genocide Studies, Salem State University.

Rebecca C. Kendall, Ph.D., is an Associate Professor in the Department of Sociology and Criminal Justice at Curry College in Massachusetts.

Stephanie Cappadona, Ph.D., is an Associate Professor in the Department of Sociology and Criminal Justice at Curry College in Milton, Massachusetts.

Criminal Profiling

Applied Theories

Kevin Borgeson, Rebecca C. Kendall, and Stephanie Cappadona

Routledge
Taylor & Francis Group
NEW YORK AND LONDON

Designed cover image: DedMityay via Getty Images

First published 2026
by Routledge
605 Third Avenue, New York, NY 10158

and by Routledge
4 Park Square, Milton Park, Abingdon, Oxon, OX14 4RN

Routledge is an imprint of the Taylor & Francis Group, an informa business

ISBN: 978-1-032-43229-8 (hbk)
ISBN: 978-1-032-42834-5 (pbk)
ISBN: 978-1-003-36630-0 (ebk)

DOI: 10.4324/9781003366300

Typeset in Times New Roman
by SPi Technologies India Pvt Ltd (Straive)

I would like to dedicate this book to two special people in my life: Liz Wood, my partner in crime, and my son-in-law, Adam Campbell. Liz, your guidance and valuable insights help my work tremendously—especially in grounded theory. Without you, these theories would never have seen the light of day: thank you. You are the world's best partner and one of the best social scientists I have met. Keep inspiring me!

Adam Campbell, your insight into the mental illness of serial offenders has been some of the most valuable insight I have ever received in understanding serial offenders. Your assessments of their criminal origins have helped me tremendously in understanding their violent nature— the world needs more clinicians and theoretical thinkers like you!

Contents

About the Authors

Binneh S. Minteh is an assistant professor of Criminal Justice at Salem State University. He is a former Gambian Armed Forces First Lieutenant. He attended the Turkish Land Forces Command School in Istanbul and the Turkish Gendarmerie Officers School in Ankara. He was the Gambia National Gendarmerie training school commander, where he taught courses on National Security, Police and Society, Intelligence, Leadership, and Terrorism and Counterterrorism. He immigrated to the United States in 1997 as a refugee. Dr. Binneh Minteh has published on terrorism and counterterrorism, social movements, police and society, organized crime, cybercrime, cyberspace and cybersecurity. His research interests include terrorism and counterterrorism, cybercrime and cybersecurity, social movements, peace and security studies, organized crime, and police and society.

Kevin Borgeson, Ph.D., Associate Professor of Criminal Justice and Research Fellow for the Center for Holocaust and Genocide Studies, Salem State University, earned his BA from Bridgewater State College and his Ph.D. from Northeastern University. His major areas of interest are serial offenders, profiling, hate crimes, and right-wing domestic terrorism. He is the author of several books, including Routledge's *Terrorism in America* (2018) and *Skinhead History, Identity, and Culture* (2017), both coauthored with Robin Maria Valeri.

Nicholas Stone is an assistant researcher and collaborator with Dr. Borgeson. He has a bachelor's degree in Criminology from Stonehill College and a master's degree from Salem State University. He has written on and researched hate, extremism, hate crimes, terrorism, and criminal profiling.

Rebecca C. Kendall, Ph.D., is an Associate Professor in the Department of Sociology and Criminal Justice at Curry College in Massachusetts. Dr. Kendall earned her doctoral degree in criminology and justice policy from Northeastern University and her master's degree in forensic and counseling psychology from William James College. Her policy and research interests are in the area of violence and victimization, with a specific focus on sexual offending, intimate partner violence, human trafficking, and the relationship between victimization and delinquency. Dr. Kendall has clinical experience doing mental health treatment and assessment with incarcerated male offenders.

Stephanie Cappadona, Ph.D., is an Associate Professor in the Department of Sociology and Criminal Justice at Curry College in Milton, Massachusetts. She holds a Master of Science in Criminal Justice and a Ph.D. in Sociology, with a concentration in Violence and Conflict, from Northeastern University in Boston. Dr. Cappadona's teaching and research are deeply rooted in the principles of social justice and human rights. Her interdisciplinary expertise informs a wide range of courses, including Social Theory; Sociology of Violence; Criminology; Justice and Human Rights Advocacy; Hate Crimes and Hate Groups; and Youth, Crime, and Justice.

Acknowledgments

This book was one of the most thought-provoking journeys of my academic career. Along the way, several people listened to my theories of criminal behavior and gave valuable feedback. I would like to thank Robin Valeri immensely—you are, without a doubt, one of the best criminal psychologists out there, and it has been a wonderful journey exploring many of the various theories in social psychology with you. I have known you for 25 years, and you are truly a great friend and co-author.

Other people that listened to me over the past year and have given valuable opinions are James Bacigalupo and Nick Stone. Both of you started out as students with me—now you are both colleagues and friends. Your knowledge in the field of criminology is vast and groundbreaking—I have taught you well, young Jedis—keep blazing your academic trails, you have a lot to offer the criminal justice and criminology community.

Introduction

A well-established maxim in criminology is that a relatively small number of people are responsible for the overwhelming number of violent crimes being committed in society. This suggests that many of these are serial crimes—a pattern of crimes repeatedly being committed by an individual or group of perpetrators. If law enforcement can identify these patterns, along with various characteristics of the offenders and the time and space in which the crimes are occurring using a criminal profile, it may prove beneficial to detecting the offender. The sooner a serial offender can be identified, the sooner the crimes and social and personal harms that accompany them can be reduced. While research by social scientists on serial offenders tends to focus on serial murder, serial killers actually have the fewest victims of any serial offender. For instance, while the average serial killer has eight victims, the serial arsonist has, on average, over 30 incidents and is one of the least studied types of offenders. Profiling thus has applications beyond serial murder and can be applied to most cases with an unknown offender.

Profiling attempts to generate a consistent personality pattern based on principal character traits inferred from crime scene behavior, lending themselves to the predictability of future criminal behavior. The investigative technique is not necessarily intended to identify a specific offender of the crime under investigation. Instead, it is intended as a tool to assist investigators with characteristics of the type of person who could be responsible for the crime; provide geographical parameters to narrow the residence, work, or other base location of the offender; facilitate case linkage; or narrow a suspect list.

Several assumptions go into the process of criminal profiling. First, profiling assumes behavioral consistency, meaning that crime is believed to be an extreme form of non-criminal activity. It is likely that an offender's criminal behavior reflects variations in ordinary day-to-day interpersonal activities. Second, profiling assumes behavioral distinctiveness, meaning there will be variations between offenders in the way they commit an offense. Finally, profiling assumes homology, or that offenders that display similar behavior will possess similar characteristics.

Many believe criminal profiling is a new investigative method developed in America during the last part of the 20th century. And while criminal profiling largely came into the popular social consciousness in the 1980s, historical writings demonstrate various rudimentary forms of criminal profiling have been used around the globe for hundreds of years. More contemporary use of the process of profiling has been conducted on Hitler, the "Mad Bomber," the Lindbergh baby kidnapper, and the Boston Strangler, to name just a few. It has only been in the last 50 years that scholars have modified various criminal profiling methods, and these techniques continue to be debated, revised using scientific means, and empirically tested.

DOI: 10.4324/9781003366300-1

With its use over the years, different profiling methodologies based on the assumptions stated above have been developed. There are four main types of profiling used in criminal justice: Crime Scene Analysis (FBI profiling), Investigative Psychology (IP), Geographic Profiling (GP), and Behavioral Evidence Analysis (BEA).[1]

Crime Scene Analysis (CSA) is the style of profiling developed by several Federal Bureau of Investigation (FBI) special agents in the 1970s. CSA is based on the assumption that a person's behavior at the crime scene can reveal characteristics about the type of person who would commit that specified crime. With its foundations in the social sciences, crime scene, victim, and other forensic information are collected and assessed to develop a criminal profile. This type of profiling is formulated on an organized and disorganized dichotomy. An organized offender is intelligent and forensically aware of what they are doing and does not leave much evidence at the crime scene(s). On the other hand, a disorganized offender does not plan out their offenses and is thus prone to leaving behind evidence. CSA has several criticisms, the two major ones being the lack of a theoretical foundation and the lack of empirical evidence to demonstrate the utility of the profiling technique.

IP was developed by David Canter in the late 1980s based on the need for a more structured, systematic approach to applying psychological concepts to crime investigation. Canter developed his approach to offender profiling based on his background as a psychologist and thus grounded it in the scientific method of investigation, building a style of profiling he believed overcame the pitfalls of the FBI method. IP is not an entirely new discipline; rather, it applies existing psychological research and theory to the investigative process. IP is not without criticisms. For instance, the methodology is heavily laden with statistical analysis and can be difficult to comprehend. Another drawback to a research-based profiling approach is the low frequency of more extreme types of violence. Canter, in recent years, has turned to GP and moved away from inferential analysis of behavior, focusing on the geographic location of offenders who have committed crimes.

Kim Rossmo invented GP in the late 1980s based on the premise that offenders operate in environments familiar to them. Most of our lives focus on our residency as our focal point (like our jobs, friends, etc.) in our everyday interactions. With the location of residence being the tying element in our lives, GP assumes that criminals commit crimes in proximity to where they live. Living environments are valid in cases like arson where the perpetrator usually lives within a two- to three-mile radius from the first two to three crimes committed. This type of profiling cannot give the exact location of where an offender lives, but may provide an approximate area in which to look. GP is useful for police because it allows them to concentrate in central areas and not waste vast resources searching places the offender is unlikely to reside or work.

Another type of profiling, BEA, was developed by Brent Turvey in 1991 while completing his undergraduate/graduate degree at the University of New Haven in Connecticut. BEA was developed from what Turvey believed were shortcomings of Investigative Analysis—the main drawback he believed was the underrepresentation of forensic evidence used in investigating of serial crime. BEA's cornerstone is the role of forensic science in determining details of unknown offenders. The profile constructed via this method does not determine characteristics of offenders (unless forensic evidence is found) but instead describes the forensic facts of the case to generate a profile of offenders. Because Turvey's methodology is not based on psychological characteristics, it is controversial in the criminal justice field because most law enforcement agencies in the United States and Europe use either IP or CSA, which have a heavy emphasis on psychological theories.

This book provides a basic overview of the historical development, various methodologies, and uses of criminal profiling. Some outstanding features of this book include the history of profiling, a discussion of the theories and concepts that compose the different types of profiling, and an overview and applicability of the various profiling methods, including detailed assumptions needed for each type to be effective. The current book includes chapters on the four primary types of profiling (i.e., CSA, GP, IP, and BEA), victimology, criminological theories of crime, and several distinct types of crimes (i.e., violent paraphilic crimes, violent non-paraphilic crimes, and cybercrimes). By focusing on different styles of profiling—whose underpinnings rely on behavioral and geographical theories—the current book can help criminal justice professionals:

- Understand the consistencies in crime scene behavior
- Construct a timeline of events
- Understand the consistency of criminal motivations
- Understand why criminals work in familiar geographic areas

Extant books on criminal profiling typically cover one or more specific types of profiling (IP, BEA, CSA, or GP) and discuss how to develop a profile in that discipline. The primary purpose of the current book is not how to construct an offender profile but to compare the core theories and concepts that make up each type of criminal profiling. In addition, while most existing books on criminal profiling focus almost exclusively on serial killings or paraphilic cases, this book includes a chapter on the use of criminal profiling in serial criminal cases that do not contain a sexual component. Recently, criminal profiles have been developed to determine patterns in criminal cases of arson, bullying, stalking, and hate crimes. These crimes are typically serial in nature and provide a basis for determining criminal patterns of behavior. Investigators have begun to recognize the utility of establishing patterns of crimes other than homicides to determine the type of individual committing those other types of serial crimes.

All crimes have some degree of underlying motive—the challenge lies in determining how a complex array of factors came together to drive offending. At times, criminal motivation will only be known by the offender themselves, and it will be up to investigators to piece together evidence after the crime(s) have occurred to elucidate patterns and attempt to identify an offender. Research into criminal motivation and risk factors for criminality can highlight who is most at risk for engaging in delinquent behavior. Findings from this large body of literature can help investigators narrow down a suspect pool, link cases, and develop geographical parameters. While there will never be a simple answer to the question of why people commit crimes, advances in the types of criminal profiling discussed here will continue to move the field forward.

Note

1 It should be noted there is debate in the field about whether BEA is an original, distinct methodology of profiling.

1 History of Criminal Profiling

Stephanie Cappadona

> Wild Animals never kill for sport. Man is the only one to whom the torture and death of his fellow creature is amusing in itself.
>
> —James Anthony Froude (1818–1894)

Introduction

Until the Age of Enlightenment, myths, demons, and monsters routinely were created in cultures as an attempt to explain shocking, odious, and violent behavior. Witches, werewolves, and vampires were frequently blamed for horrific murders, especially of children "since only a supernaturally and bestially malevolent being could possibly be responsible for killings of such savagery" (Miller, 2014, p. 2). It was difficult for people to comprehend that one of their community members could be responsible when a heinous crime occurred. The dastardly deed would often be ascribed to either an "outsider" (i.e., someone who was not like them) or to a supernatural force or monster.

Homicide has existed as long as more than two people have inhabited the same space on Earth. Whether committed by an individual, group, or state, homicide involves a variety of motivations—some clearly discernible, while others may, at least initially, be ambiguous. The impetus for deliberately taking the life of another human can be, in its most basic sense, attributed to some form of conflict, the source of which can typically be attributed to love, jealousy, money, greed, vengeance, and hate (Sears, 1991). Regardless of motivation and responsible party, the result of homicide is waves of anguish and destruction for the survivor, friends, family, and community. When homicides are of the serial type, the devastation increases exponentially. Serial homicides comprise only about 1% of all homicides in the United States but receive an inordinate amount of attention (Keatley et al., 2018). Even with such a small number of American homicides attributed to serial killers, there are nonetheless numerous friends, coworkers, and loved ones affected and forever changed. Yet, somehow, in the wake of such devastation, there inevitably emerges a bizarre fascination when the homicide is suspected of being committed by a serial killer.

Reasons for the morbid interest in serial homicide may stem from the viciousness and heinousness of these killings—*what type of human could do this to another*? Another is the mysterious assailant, the fact that someone could be responsible for this type of hunting of other humans, or the seemingly indiscriminate nature of the act. In America, this morbid fascination with serial killing is even more pronounced when that series of murders is motivated by sexually sadistic behavior.

Sexually sadistic multiple murderers sometimes become infamous pseudo-celebrities; those with a high body count or a "good story" gain this status in American popular culture.

DOI: 10.4324/9781003366300-2

Serial killers have become a hot commodity. Interested individuals can choose from a plethora of true crime podcasts, video documentaries, books, Halloween costumes, comic books, mugshot photos on t-shirts, trading cards, and the like. Interest in such serial killers does not lie merely in product consumption. This allure extends to the study of multiple murderers as well. Many professors who teach college-level criminology courses have undoubtedly heard from students about their interest in becoming a criminal profiler, likely at the FBI. Similarly, criminal justice and psychology students inevitably express interest in forensic science and criminalistics. Most of these students are under the misconception that they will be responsible for the entire investigative process, from collecting and processing evidence, searching for the killer, conducting interviews and interrogations, and convicting the murderer. They may even believe that the scientific evidence will swiftly lead to a dark, disturbed serial killer. Misinformation regarding this type of occupation is compounded by media sensationalism and Hollywood myths of serial killers—particularly concerning the profiling of serial crimes.

It is important to note what criminal profiling means and how it is distinguished from *racial profiling*. Racial profiling can refer to how law enforcement assesses an individual to determine if that person may have engaged in criminal activity. As identified by the Ontario Human Rights Commission,

> (r)acial profiling is different from criminal profiling. Racial profiling is based on stereotypical assumptions because of one's race, colour, ethnicity, etc. Criminal profiling, on the other hand, relies on actual behaviour or information about suspected activity by someone who meets the description of a specific individual.
>
> (Ontario Human Rights Commission, n.d., para 2)

That is *not* the profiling that is covered in this chapter. The only use of race in criminal behavioral profiling is that of a statistical value, not prognostic, as research has repeatedly demonstrated that violent crime tends to be intra-racial (Pinizzotto & Finkel, 1990).

Criminal profiling, as discussed here, uses crime scenes and behavioral evidence as the basis for determining the type of individual who may be responsible for a heinous series of crimes. Criminal profiling will not lead law enforcement directly to the responsible individual(s). Rather, it is a tool to be used in conjunction with other investigative methods to narrow the search for a suspect and indicate to investigators the type of individual who could be responsible for a specific crime.

The chapter begins by defining criminal profiling and relevant terms. Next, the chapter reviews the history and development of various approaches to profiling. The latter half of the chapter addresses four specific types of criminal profiling: CSA, IP, GP, and BEA.

What Is Criminal Profiling?

Definition

An array of labels and descriptions exists for the process of criminal profiling. In its most rudimentary form, a criminal profile is described by Geberth (1996) as:

> An educated attempt to provide the investigative agencies with specific information as to the type of individual who would have committed a certain crime … with the objective … to provide the investigator with a personality composite of the unknown suspects that will aid apprehension.
>
> (pp. 710–711)

The purpose of the criminal profile is to provide law enforcement with information about the offender that may be used to determine the type of person or persons who would commit the multiple murders. This could be offender demographics, personality characteristics, and possible motives for multiple homicides if they can be linked to either a single person or a pair of murderers (Norris, 2014). Criminal profiling as used by law enforcement in serial criminal cases has historically been termed *criminal behavioral profiling* but has also been called *offender profiling, psychological profiling, offender analysis, behavioral profiling, profiling, criminal personality profiling, or investigative profiling* (Kocsis, 2006; Norris, 2014). *Criminal profiling* will be used as an umbrella term throughout this chapter.

Criminal profiling has its roots in the social sciences, specifically behaviorism and psychology. This type of profiling—observing traits and behaviors to determine an outcome—has historically been implemented in various settings, including the military (Pinizzotto & Finkel, 1990), consumer product advertising (Sheth, 1985), and even in veterinary medicine by animal care specialists (Hart & Miller, 1985). It is well known that mass advertising campaigns have used basic theories of psychology and behaviorism to induce potential consumers to buy products since the early part of the 20th century.

In the field of law enforcement, criminal profiling has been used in hostage negotiations and to assist with investigations of serial crimes such as arson, rape, and homicide (Webb, 2013).

Douglas and Burge (1986) state that when law enforcement acquires knowledge of a barricaded suspect's basic behavioral and personality characteristics, it can inform techniques for effective outcomes and not provoke erratic or violent behavior in the suspect. However, not all criminal cases can benefit from criminal profiling. When this is the case, Ainsworth (2001) suggests that trained profilers can provide interrogation questions and techniques to detectives. As stated by Webb (2013), profilers alternately can "establish probable cause for search warrants, assist prosecutors relative to prosecutive strategies, and possibly provide testimony as a witness for the prosecution or as an expert witness during the sentencing phase of the trial" (p. 21). When a clear motive for homicides is not apparent, and standard investigative processes don't produce results, alternative investigative techniques may prove fruitful. A criminal profile is not intended to replace traditional police investigations but to complement the work of experienced, skilled detectives.

Criminal profiling may prove essential during a serial criminal investigation by steering it toward the correct path to identify the perpetrator (Woodworth & Porter, 2000). Investigators endeavor to identify multiple murderers as early in their series of murders as possible. Murder is like any other behavior; practitioners may improve their skills over time, and early mistakes can provide a clue to the identity of the unknown perpetrator (Morton et al., 2014). When a criminal profile can narrow the suspect list, seasoned detectives have a better opportunity to locate the individual before the crimes spiral further out of control and claim more victims. As stated earlier, serial crimes are very rare compared to other violent crimes, but they can terrorize an entire geographic location where the crimes occur. Likewise, members of certain groups can be terrified if a specific one has been targeted. Communities find themselves on "high alert" as the next target could ostensibly be anyone. For example, during the suspected serial murders of "The Boston Strangler" during the early 1960s in the Boston area, the *Chicago Tribune* reported that:

> Few women set out on the street alone, day or night. Many arranged to spend their nights together, alternating at each other's homes. Families set up telephone checks, several times a night, on daughters, mothers, or sisters who lived alone. Locks, door chains, guard dogs, and weapons were bought faster than they could be stocked.
>
> (Boston Globe 2021, Boston Strangler Recalled, para 5)

Serial crimes are challenging for investigators because they typically occur between strangers, not friends, family, or associates. When the motive is not obvious and a relationship between the offender and target cannot be immediately determined, the crime may be more difficult to solve. Even innovative investigators may require the assistance that a criminal profile can provide. Criminal profiles have been employed both when the offender is known and when one is not known, as in a serial crime. When done by trained professionals, a profile can provide personality and behavioral characteristics to point law enforcement in the correct direction to locate their suspect. Profiles may provide valuable information about the known suspect to assist with hostage negotiations, interviews, and interrogation strategies (Douglas et al., 1986). Further, suppose the profiler can discern certain characteristics about the known individual from their behavior and the situation. In that case, a criminal profile can provide crucial information about conducting the negotiations more effectively to resolve the situation safely.

Rationale for Using Criminal Profiling Techniques

The criminal profile is often considered more art than science (Canter, 2004; Kocsis & Palermo, 2007; Holmes & Holmes 2009). The foundations for developing a criminal profile stem from the social sciences. Forensic psychiatrists and psychologists have viewed behavioral characteristics through personality theories in their attempts to establish the connection between comparable behaviors in analogous situations (Norris, 2014). While theories in the behavioral sciences cannot be treated as "laws" like theories in the physical sciences, they can provide a more comprehensive understanding of human behavior due to their interdisciplinary nature (Bartol & Bartol, 2013). A frequently stated maxim in the social sciences is that past behavior predicts future behavior. Harris et al. (2016) state that because personality traits tend to be stable over time, behavior—criminal or not—is the expression of one's personality traits and is also relatively stable. Previous research in this area suggests support for the stability of individuals' personalities and behavior over time and space (Weisbuch et al., 2010; Miller, 2014). Egger (2002) affirms the consistency of serial criminal behavior by explaining that if patterns of behavior can be deciphered, personality traits associated with that criminal behavior can be determined.

Albarracin and Wyer (2000) explain in their study of the cognitive effects of previous behaviors on future behaviors, "the consistency of a person's behavior over time is the result of personality and motivational factors that are common to the situations in which the behavior occurs" (p. 5). Most individuals have the ability to evaluate the consequences of their behavior and the agency to modify future behaviors in similar situations. Analyzing evidence from crime scenes can determine the linkage of cases to the same perpetrator. As proclaimed by German psychiatrist Karl Berg (1938) following his interview with German serial killer Peter Kurten, "[w]here a series of crimes are committed, the same technique inevitably suggests the same criminal. That is an old aphorism in criminology" (p. 45). Kurten, infamously known as "The Vampire of Dusseldorf," admitted to the brutal murder of at least nine men, women, and children in Germany between February and November 1929. Through examination of the homicide evidence, and despite the change in the murder weapon from knife to hammer, Dr. Berg meticulously describes the facts connecting all nine murders in his book *Sadist*. During interviews with the psychiatrist before his execution, Kurten admitted that he had changed his method of killing "to keep up the appearance of a plurality of criminals" (1938, p. 170). This was the serial killer's attempt to confuse investigators.

Predicting future criminal behavior based on past criminal behavior may appear to be an oversimplification. However, human behavior is dichotomous—simultaneously complex and simplistic.

A serial offender may continue criminal behavior, especially if it was previously successful—the individual did not face negative consequences such as being apprehended and convicted—and the behavior may be repeated in comparable situations and motivations.

Behavior is an essential element of personality. In psychology, behaviorism is a theoretical perspective that posits that an individual's behavior results from the previous consequences of behavior in equivalent environments. Behavior analysis is concerned with "understanding, describing, and predicting behavior … analyzed in terms of interactions between behavior itself and the environment" (Sloane, 1992, para 3). With basic behavioral principles and the implementation of behavior analysis, certain personality traits and behavior characteristics can be determined for the composition of a criminal profile.

Investigators cannot expect a criminal profile to lead them directly to their suspect in a serial crime case. That mythos only exists in works of fiction. Woodworth and Porter (2000) maintain that the purpose of a criminal profile in a serial case is not to solve the case by miraculously naming a suspect. The authors posit that profiling can assist in serial criminal investigations by placing the search for the perpetrator on the correct path. This is critical as serial crimes, especially adult offenders and perpetrators of sexual violence, often escalate their criminal violence over time (Hewitt & Beauregard, 2014). An accurately constructed profile may facilitate criminal apprehension before the crimes spiral further out of control and claim more victims.

When developing a criminal profile, another essential component is inferential reasoning. The three main types of logical inferential reasoning used in criminal profiling include inductive, deductive, and abductive (Carson, 2009). The three are not distinct types of reasoning, but as suggested by Petherick and Brooks (2021), they exist at discrete locations along a spectrum. Stated another way, they represent different stages of examination. The authors explain these stages as

> beginning with various hypotheses about what has occurred or that may be true (induction), and through the scientific method we falsify each conclusion until we are left with the best possible explanation (abduction) or only one that is based on universal laws or principles and cannot be falsified (deduction).
>
> (p. 695)

Inductive reasoning occurs when an inference is concluded from known facts or statistical probabilities to reach a likely conclusion. The inductive argument goes from the specific to the general. To illustrate, Carson (2009) provides an example by describing a hypothetical crime scene: a body is left bleeding from a wound, and a knife covered in blood lies near the body. Using inductive reasoning, the conclusion may be that the bloody knife at the scene is the murder weapon. If the remaining evidence supports that inference, then inductive reasoning was effective in determining a conclusion. But suppose that upon further examination of the crime scene and the autopsy report, it is discovered that the bloody knife near the body is inconsistent with the wounds inflicted. Or maybe the blood on that knife was not human, but instead animal blood. Suppose the murder victim was cutting up an animal to eat, and an intruder came in and used a different style of knife to stab the victim, taking the knife with them. The original inferential hypothesis was incorrect. In this hypothetical, if investigators rely on known facts or previously acquired knowledge to the exclusion of other evidence, the conclusion will likely be wrong. Investigators must also be aware of their biases and interpretations of evidence (Carson, 2009). Due to the complexity of human behavior, a trained profiler must use all evidence in a case, while being acutely aware of their own biases that could impact their inferences while composing a profile.

The second type of reasoning is deductive, which is "based on universal laws or principles and cannot be falsified" (Petherick & Brooks, 2021, p. 695). This is precisely why Carson (2009) cautions that deductive reasoning may prove of limited use in criminal profiling. Human behavior can be quite complex, and there are few universal truths concerning criminal behavior. The deductive approach to criminal profiling begins with a more general statement or theory, supported by specific observations to reach a conclusion. If the premises are true, then the conclusion must be true. Petherick and Brooks (2021) state that deductive arguments contain inductive arguments because the thesis begins with general statements. In the case of criminal profiling, these would be general statements about the behavior or the evidence in the case that necessarily leads to the specific case under investigation. A profiler may develop an initial theory of what happened at a crime scene, based on their established knowledge of other cases—the inferential reasoning. However, if the totality of evidence, some of which may contradict the initial hypothesis, is not considered, the analysis and resulting criminal profile may be inaccurate.

The final type of reasoning is abductive. Carson (2009) discusses how this type of reasoning is less understood than the other two and is rarely mentioned in the field of law enforcement. In abductive reasoning, observations are made and a hypothesis—the most likely one—is created. It begins with incomplete or partial observations and proceeds to the most plausible conclusion, which is often the case with many crime scenes if there is no witness or camera to recount the details to law enforcement. Investigators study the scene and draw the most likely conclusion. However, if a crime scene is staged and novice investigators are unfamiliar with the signs of staging, their abductive conclusion could misdirect the investigation. Maybe they infer that the crime scene was a robbery and sexual assault "gone wrong" by an unknown offender, that led to murder. Their conclusion could be based on the removal of the target's clothes before a complete autopsy of the deceased. When, in fact, a more seasoned investigator could have easily determined the clothes were removed to make the crime scene look like a sexual assault, and that the target was killed by someone close to them.

With a rationale for the application of a profile established, the remainder of the chapter will provide a brief history of criminal profiling generally and delve into each profiling technique's history, development, and processes. The four types of profiling techniques employed in law and social sciences include CSA, IP, GP, and BEA.

History of Criminal Profiling

Historical Origins

Contemporary criminal profiling did not develop from a single individual, organization, or geographic location. As is true with any history, the history of profiling and its various methods were influenced by the time and place, including varying degrees of advanced social science principles. A brief overview of the evolution of criminal profiling is provided below.

The actual origins of profiling are somewhat elusive. Turvey (2012) posits that some of the earliest recorded uses of profiling were "made by the anti-Semitic scholar Apion to the Roman Emperor Caligula in 38 CE … [which] involves the demonization of Jews … [with the] 'blood libel'; or false accusation of ritual killing" (pp. 3–4). He further notes that it is this inferential use of "crime-related characteristics" that identifies this description as not only an early use of profiling but also of false accusations. Nearly 2,000 years later, the blood libel, along with many other myths, was prejudicially used against Jewish people around the world.

Another historical period when false allegations, intentional or unintentional, were used against a group of people was the perceived witch hunts in Europe between the 15th and 18th centuries and early New England in the 17th century (Bartol & Bartol, 2013). The infamous

Malleus Maleficarum, or *The Hammer of Witches*, was written by two German scholars of theology and Inquisitors, Jakob Springer and Heinrich Kramer (i.e., Institoris) (Schuyler, 1987). Pope Innocent VIII appointed the pair "to do their best for the purification of the faith and the suppression of witchcraft ... [I]t's advocacy of the suspension of rules of evidence and other safeguards of law led to the torture and executions of thousands" (p. 20). The manual has been noted as "one of the first systematic approaches for identifying and making inferences about supposedly guilty individuals" (Woodworth & Porter, 2000, p. 243). The book is essentially composed of the misogynistic conjecture of witches' sexual exploits with demons and the theft of mortal men's penises. The book is comprised of three main parts: the first uses religious doctrine and theory to substantiate the existence of witchcraft; the second details the magic used by witches to lure their victims and how to resist them; the third contains proscribed legal procedures to be used against witches (Smith, 2002). The majority of the modern world views these persecutions as misguided, ridiculous, and gender biased. They illustrate how, even in the 15th century, a systematic attempt was made to identify perceived criminals or enemies (witches) through behaviors and physical characteristics.

Tarin Will, a researcher of Scandinavian Studies, proffered a more controversial view of the historical use of criminal profiling (Konieczny, 2012). From early 13th-century Icelandic literature studies, Will knew that the Viking people, like most societies, were troubled by community members who exhibited antisocial and violent behaviors. They made the connection between physical attributes and violent behavior. More specifically, certain physical characteristics were thought to be indicative of high levels of testosterone, which has been associated with aggressive behavior. Vikings recorded the physical characteristics of these individuals in what Dr. Willis referred to as "mugshots" and believed that "In this sense, they were perhaps the first to begin criminal profiling" (Konieczny, 2012, p. 5). Like others throughout history, Viking society was concerned with individuals or groups whose behavior did not follow acceptable social norms, and they sought to identify who would be a threat to their existence.

Contemporary History of Criminal Profiling

Cesare Lombroso, known as the Father of Criminology, was a 19th-century Italian medical doctor whose meticulous studies of criminals influenced the positivist school of criminology. He is credited with "what is widely considered the first attempt toward scientific theory in criminological thought" (Tibbetts & Hemmens, 2010, p. 189). Trained in the legal and medical fields, he assessed his theories utilizing observations and hypothesis testing. Positivism grew out of the classical school of criminology, which attributed criminal behavior to an individual's free will and pleasure-seeking. The positivist school of criminology considered "all kinds of behavior, especially criminal, on biological, psychological, and sociological variables" (p. 192). He, like the Vikings, focused on physical traits as a clue to an individual's behavior.

Lombroso's book *The Criminal Man*, published in 1876, theorized that through the study of human physical characteristics, one could identify criminals. During his examination of the skull of a local thief, Giuseppe Villella, Lombroso

> Noticed a median occipital depression at the spot where there should have been a projection due to the insertion of the cerebral falx ... this characteristic ... indicated ... the persistence of ancestral 'atavistic' characteristics in Villella's cranium. The criminal was biologically linked to inferior animals. His deviance was thus the consequence of his constitution ... the phenomenon of criminality [was] possibly the product of arrested development at a more primitive mental state.
>
> (Mazzarello, 2011, p. 98)

Despite Lombroso's contribution to the field of criminology, today criminologists reject the notion of physical characteristics as indicative of criminal behavior.

No longer relying on *physical* characteristics to denote criminality, investigators scrutinize the crime scene to gain knowledge of the perpetrator's non-criminal and criminal behavior. Knowledge gained from a crime scene exposes behavioral characteristics that may assist in prioritizing suspects (James & Nordby, 2009). Patterns of repeated actions can provide information regarding behavior and motivation but would be much more difficult for a single criminal offense, or crimes that cannot be linked together. For a solitary act of crime, evidence could be lacking, and motivations for behavior may appear "senseless." Even when the criminal behavior seems random, it may not be. No crime is senseless to the perpetrator—to them, the behavior has significant meaning. Therefore, with repeated, similar crimes, if the connection can be established, the totality of evidence from more than one crime scene may assist in providing a motive.

One of the earliest modern profiles was that of Adolf Hitler by Dr. Walter Langer. The U.S. Office of Strategic Services requested psychiatrist Langer to provide a psychological profile of Adolf Hitler during World War II (Egger, 2002; Holmes & Holmes, 2009; Pinizzotto & Finkel, 1990). Agents hoped that by getting into the mind of the dictator, they could more effectively predict his behavior and strategic military moves during the war, and interrogations after the war if he was taken into custody. Through interviews and research conducted by his assistants, Dr. Langer composed a psychological profile of Hitler that contained eight possible outcomes for Hitler and the war (Holmes & Holmes, 2009). When Hitler committed suicide, it confirmed one of the predicted outcomes from the profile. In fact, it was the most likely outcome in Langer's profile.

A second prominent profile was produced by Dr. James Brussel when he was consulted by the New York City Police Department in 1956 to assist them in locating the "Mad Bomber" (Holmes & Holmes, 2009). Someone had been detonating bombs in public spaces around the city since 1940. None had yet died, but 16 people had been injured. The police began to recognize a pattern of increasing sophistication in the serial bombings, which necessitated their request to the psychiatrist. Dr. Brussel studied the crime scene photos and angry rants in letters the bomber mailed to local newspapers and proclaimed the offender was, among other traits, a paranoid schizophrenic. The profile was published in local newspapers, and a Consolidated Edison employee scoured through the company's employee files and found the name George Metesky. Metesky was a former Consolidated Edison employee who blamed the company for an injury he received in 1931 while on the job. He exhausted his unemployment compensation and was subsequently let go. The first bomb, accompanied by a note, exploded at Consolidated Edison (Holmes & Holmes, 2009). Police investigated and found Metesky to be a disgruntled former employee who believed the company was to blame for his tuberculosis, which he thought to be caused by fumes from a furnace blast at work (Cannell, 2017). Dr. Brussel's criminal profile identified the personality characteristics investigators should focus on in determining a likely suspect. He also predicted that the suspect would dress in a double-breasted suit. Metesky changed into a double-breasted suit when the police arrested him at his home. The analysis offered by the psychiatrist did not, nor was it intended, to name a suspect. However, the published criminal profile led the Consolidated Edison employee to search the personnel records and report George's name to law enforcement. The criminal profile provided by Dr. Brussel steered the investigation down the right path so law enforcement could narrow their focus and locate the serial bomber more quickly.

With the history established, the remainder of this chapter will discuss four types of profiling—CSA, IP, GP, and BEA.

Crime Scene Analysis

CSA is likely the profiling with which the general population has the greatest exposure, as it is the type that generally appears in movies and television. Crime scene profiling, or analysis, as defined by Bartol and Bartol (2013), "is the process of identifying cognitive tendencies, behavioral patterns, motivation, emotional dispositions, and demographic variables of an *unknown offender* based on characteristics and evidence gathered at the scene of the crime" (p. 16). The FBI has referred to this type of profiling as criminal investigative analysis (Federal Bureau of Investigation, n.d.; Homant & Kennedy, 1998; Norris, 2006). Norris states that criminal investigative analysis is intended to encompass "not only profiling, but other services such as indirect personality assessment, equivocal death analysis, and trial strategy" (2006, p. 32). According to the FBI's Behavioral Analysis Units (BAU), their special agents provide law enforcement a criminal investigative analysis consisting of the following: information on an offender's motivation, victim selection, sophistication level, actions, relationship to that particular crime, and the sequence of events (Federal Bureau of Investigation, n.d.).

While it cannot reveal a specific individual responsible for the crime, CSA can narrow the list of suspects by assisting investigators in focusing attention on a certain personality type. A trained profiler scrutinizes crime scene photos and autopsy reports to uncover any indicators suggesting the type of individual who committed the crime (Ainsworth, 2001). Through careful observation, information can be analyzed with "some subjective descriptions of the demographic, motivational, behavioral patterns, and psychological features" (Bartol & Bartol, 2013, p. 16). Through the identification of behavioral and personality characteristics, law enforcement can prioritize certain suspects for interviews. Investigators should always keep an open mind, thoroughly examine all suspects in a case, and allow the evidence to guide the investigation.

Historical Development of CSA

Early applications of CSA, before being more formalized, occurred in prominent serial homicide cases around the world, like the Whitechapel Murders, "The Vampire of Dusseldorf" Peter Kurten, and the "Mad Bomber" George Metesky. For instance, in 1888, the London Metropolitan Police requested the assistance of their police surgeon, Dr. George B. Phillips, for a series of murders in Whitechapel. After a thorough examination of the Whitechapel murder victims' bodies, Phillips was one of the first to suggest that the murderer had some anatomical knowledge. Dr. Phillips examined the evidence and "attempted to create a reconstruction of various crime scenes and describe the wounds of the victims to gain a greater insight into the offender's psychological makeup" (Woodworth & Porter, 2000, p. 244). Another London doctor, Thomas Bond, was also consulted on the Whitechapel multiple murders. Like Dr. Phillips, Dr. Bond examined the bodies and forensic evidence to develop a sketch of the likely murderer. He determined the murders were related, but a crucial component of the crime differed from Dr. Phillips. Dr. Bond concluded that the murderer "had no medical training or knowledge of anatomy, despite the killer's extensive cutting and mutilation of his victims" (Bonn, 2017, para. 6). Since the Whitechapel serial killer was never definitively identified, it remains unknown if either Dr. Phillips or Dr. Bond constructed accurate profiles. However, this remains one of the first contemporary applications of CSA.

The systematic use of CSA in law enforcement investigations of serial crimes is attributed to the FBI's Behavioral Science Unit (BSU), now the BAU. The unit was established in 1972 in response to an increase in homicides, particularly stranger homicides, in the United States (Ramsland, 2011). At the FBI Academy in Quantico, Virginia, a catalyst for the more methodical use of crime scene profiling was an Applied Criminology course taught at the Academy by Agent Howard Teten. He drew on the expertise of the famous Dr. Brussel and Special Agent Patrick Mullany to advance the approach of using crime scene evidence to determine the motive and personality of the offender. Ramsland (2011) describes how Teten "developed a hypothesis that in certain types of homicides, you'd be able to determine the kind of person you were looking for by what you could see at the crime scene" (p. 24). While this was not a novel technique, Teten attempted to build upon past profiling procedures. He assessed the evidence in solved cases, composed a profile, and "checked" his work by comparing his profile to the convicted offender. As Ramsland recounts, he repeatedly gathered sexual homicide cases from the local police departments to compose his practice profiles. In essence, he was rehearsing and refining his method.

Through a grant from the National Institute of Justice (NIJ), FBI special agents initiated the Criminal Personality Research Project to gather data in an attempt to form a classification system for offenders in serial homicide cases (Jenkins, 1994). The FBI model of CSA, a model they term criminal investigative analysis, continued to evolve through the contributions of Special Agents Ressler and Douglas. They, along with other agents, interviewed 36 convicted serial murderers during the 1980s to determine what, if any, characteristics they held in common. For example, do serial offenders who rape, torture, mutilate, and strangle their targets have any similar personality or behavioral characteristics, or childhood and familial experiences such as physical, sexual, or verbal abuse? It was believed that if the special agents uncovered similar patterns of behavior and history, they could then devise a classification system to assist other investigators in serial homicides. In the 1980s, agents also studied "rapists, child molesters and abductors, and arsonists … [and] described and identified critical characteristics of these crimes. These characteristics initially were used for profiling techniques" (Douglas, Ressler et al., 1992, p. ix). The result of these comprehensive criminal studies was the *Crime Classification Manual* (CCM). The authors specify four reasons for the manual:

> [T]o standardize terminology within the CJ field, [t]o facilitate communication within the criminal justice field and between criminal justice and mental health, [t]o educate people in the criminal justice system and the public at large to the types of crimes being committed, [and] [t]o develop a database for investigate research.
>
> (1992, p. x)

One of the outcomes of the FBI sexually sadistic serial killer research was an organized and disorganized dichotomy included with numerous other crimes in the CCM (Petherick & Brooks, 2021). The distinctions and similarities of the dual taxonomy of serial killers will be discussed in more detail in a later chapter.

From their vast education and investigative experiences, agents at the FBI's BSU analyzed their collected research data. Agents endeavored to validate the technique of their criminal profiling. Part of this attempt was to demonstrate the use of a version of the scientific method to counter claims that they engaged in guesswork and relied solely on intuition. Douglas, Ressler et al. (1986) describe the stages of the profiling process to be similar to that used by clinicians when making a diagnosis and treatment plan; specifically, "data are collected and assessed, the situation reconstructed, hypothesis formulated, a profile developed and tested, and the results reported back" (p. 405). The authors describe their technique of criminal profiling in six steps:

1 *Profiling Input Stage*—complete crime scene information, including social and political environmental factors; victim information; and forensic information such as toxicology and autopsy reports.
2 *Decision Process Models Stage*—this is where the organization of information takes place: homicide type and style; primary intent of the murderer; victim and offender risks; escalation, time, and location factors.
3 *Crime Assessment Stage*—assessment of whether the crime scene was staged or not, motivation, and other crime scene dynamics.
4 *Criminal Profile Stage*—contains demographics, physical characteristics, habits, beliefs, and values, pre-offense behavior leading to the crime, and post-offense behavior.
5 *Investigative Stage*—the constructed report is presented to the appropriate law enforcement agency.
6 *Apprehension Stage*—at this stage, investigators attempt to interview the suspect upon arrest, and attempts are made to validate the profile and its process.

Despite attempts to provide a more methodological approach to crime scene profiling, this approach has several criticisms discussed below.

Criticisms of CSA

Two main criticisms of the CSA approach to serial crime profiling are the lack of theoretical foundations on which the technique is based and the lack of objectivity by the profiler (Woodworth & Porter, 2000; Verde & Nurra, 2010). Evaluating the CSA technique is more difficult without a specific, testable theory driving it and with subjective evaluations of the evidence.

Empirical evidence to evaluate the CSA technique has produced contradictory results (Canter, 2004; Kocsis & Palermo, 2016). This is likely due to disparities in methodologies and varying definitions and terms in the field of profiling. One such criticism maintains that a lack of evidence for "offender homology" likely renders criminal profiles that rely on "trait-based" methods unsound. With differing terminology, even within the same discipline, it is problematic for those who attempt to develop a typology for serial criminal behavior. Canter (2004) asserts that numerous studies have attempted to pinpoint similarities of traits to bolster the homology argument for serial offenders, but most have been unable. However, he also points to other studies of professional profilers who have found statistically significant levels of accuracy.

In one such study, Pinizzotto and Finkel (1990) used a personality profile to investigate the accuracy and process differences between profilers and non-profilers. Of interest in this study was whether a criminal personality profile could be developed of the individual likely responsible for a sex crime and one for a homicide. Researchers used closed police cases to determine which group was more accurate in identifying the features of an offender from crime scene information. It should be noted that since the cases were closed, the perpetrator was known, and the accuracy of the predictions for both groups could be verified based on a determination of how closely the predictions matched the alleged offender arrested for the crime. The authors state that the psychological profile "focuses attention on individuals with personality traits that parallel traits of others who have committed similar offenses" (Pinizzotto & Finkel, 1990, p. 216). Through examination of the crime scene, the goal of CSA was to discover the type of person responsible for the serial crime. As discussed earlier in the chapter, it is not intended to identify a specific individual who committed the crime. Rather, it is an attempt to determine personality and behavioral traits that are associated with individuals who have committed analogous crimes. Pinizzotto and Finkel (1990) believe that

> through close examination of the crime scene one is able to extrapolate certain relevant psychological material that leads to a profile ... the forensic investigator will let the entire crime scene, including the victim, tell, in effect, what *kind* of person committed this act.
> (p. 216)

They concluded from the results of their study that the professional profilers were, in fact, more precise than non-profilers concerning sex crimes. But this accuracy was not found with homicide offenses. With such contradictory findings, more research is required to form a definitive conclusion.

CSA is not a tool that can be used in all crimes. When law enforcement pursues an unknown offender and enough case evidence is available to construct a profile, CSA may provide useful assistance by focusing on suspects who possess certain characteristics or providing alternative avenues for investigators to explore (Woodworth & Porter, 2000). While typically used in serial crimes like arson, rape, and homicide, CSA has been expanded for use in terrorism (Silke, 2001) and organized crime investigations (Woodworth & Porter, 2000).

Investigative Psychology

The field of IP encompasses much more than criminal profiling. Youngs and Canter (2006) describe it as

> A framework for the integration of a diverse range of aspects of psychology into all areas of criminal and civil investigation. It is concerned with all the forms of criminality that may be examined by the police, from arson and burglary to murder, rape, or even terrorism.
> (p. 322)

The IP approach to criminal profiling developed out of the inevitable search for a technique that represented a more rigorous scientific approach to profiling (Salfati, 2021). The IP profiling technique is attributed to British Psychologist Dr. David Canter, who stresses the importance of psychological theories and scientific research. His model is continually "increasing the sample size on which the ruminations are based ... conducting research and using rigorous methodologies to expand knowledge ... [t]herefore the conclusions are still inductive but based in more empirically robust evaluations" (Petherick, 2006 p. 39). Kapardis (2017) posits that the IP profiling technique is not concerned with a suspect's motivation for committing the crime, Instead, it seeks to uncover patterns of criminal behavior by using a research-based approach. He, like Canter, believes that IP can assist law enforcement in a variety of crimes.

The distinction between CSA and IP is highlighted by Bartol and Bartol (2013) in that "*scientific* crime scene profiling began in the United Kingdom, while clinically based crime scene profiling began in the United States ... [and] it is also important to stress that both methods have value" (emphasis in original, p. 62). Both criminal profiling approaches rely on analyzing behavior at the crime scene during the commission of the crime. However, Egger (2002) argues that the Canter Model of IP relies more on victim information than CSA. Another distinction can be made between the two models because IP is said to ground the profile in psychological theory, whereas the CSA model is not based on a particular theoretical perspective. Finally, the IP model requires the use of empirical evidence and not inferences or objective investigative experience (Woodworth & Porter, 2000).

Canter (2004) defines IP in much broader terms than purely a profiling technique. He proposes that psychology as a discipline should include more than profiles for serial offenders, and instead "include the effective utilisation of police information, through interviews and from police records, as well as the study of police investigations and decision support systems" (p. 7). Essentially, he suggests that IP should be applied to all areas of a law enforcement investigation.

Historical Development of IP

Canter first became involved in investigative work when his expertise was requested by British law enforcement. Bartol and Bartol (2013) describe how the Metropolitan Police requested Canter's assistance in the early 1990s while working on a particularly frustrating case of serial rapes, perpetrated by "The Railway Rapist." These crimes would escalate and eventually become rape murders, which is what necessitated outside expert assistance. With his vast experience in studying human behavior and environmental psychology, Canter believed he could develop a criminal profile to help law enforcement determine who was responsible for the crimes. He provided police with a "profile of 17 personality traits and behavioral characteristics, plus several environmental clues" (Bartol & Bartol, 2013, p. 63). While the profile did not locate the offender(s), it did provide helpful information for the investigators to locate the offender's home location. His profile successfully identified numerous behavioral characteristics similar to the actual offender's.

Three pillars form the foundation of IP: information retrieval from the crime scene for analysis; decision making by the investigators must be methodological and free of bias; and an analysis of criminal behavior, which includes the use of proper models of behaviors committed during the crime and offender characteristics (Salfati, 2021). The elements of crime scene information, characteristics, and actions of the offender are similar to CSA but attempt to make the profile more reliable by adding the investigator's objectivity, not inferences from subject perspectives. While one cannot be completely free of biases, IP stresses the importance of analyzing a crime without prejudgment or conjecture. By determining characteristics of the criminal behavior and CSA, it may be possible to understand the nature and motivations for the crime. If a classification system can be identified, it may further benefit the IP criminal profiling method.

Criticisms of IP

Petherick and Brooks (2021) note a fundamental issue with IP regarding empirical research. For those analyzing serial sexual murders, because these crimes are comparatively rare, there is a real deficiency of cases from which to draw data. Constructing an appropriate profile may be more difficult without robust research on extreme or ultra-violent crimes.

As with any profiling technique, the profile is only as good as the data used to construct it. If the information used to create the profile is flawed, the resulting profile and any investigative decisions will be flawed (Ainsworth, 2001). Another criticism of IP is similar to that of the CSA method. Both profiling methods use inductive reasoning (Petherick, 2006).

Where different motivations may exist for similar behaviors, this may lead to the profiler misconstruing the actual motivation for the crimes and leading investigators in the wrong direction.

Geographic Profiling

GP is the third type of criminal profiling discussed in this chapter. Like other criminal profiling techniques, GP will not identify an offender. It can prioritize suspects and pinpoint possible residences or workspaces by utilizing crime event locations. This is particularly useful in serial crimes where law enforcement can be inundated with information about the crime. GP is a tool that analyzes patterns of crime locations to determine where an offender lives, works, or spends a significant amount of time. Rossmo (2000) explains this profiling technique is based on determining spatial patterns and the hunting practices of offenders, especially in serial violent crimes. As an example, Miller (2014) recalls how a criminal profiler was asked to assist a marine biologist in studying shark behavior. By analyzing the data, they determined that sharks patiently stalk their intended prey. They do not blindly or randomly grab whatever is in front of them. Instead, the sharks "[are] lurking out of sight … hunt strategically … [and] they prefer prey animals that are young and alone … like their human counterparts, learn from experience and improve on their hunting technique over time" (p. 2). Human predators, particularly serial offenders, hunt their intended prey, just as animal predators. Similarly, by analyzing a criminal offender's geographic activity, GP can determine the most likely location of the offender.

The theoretical foundation of GP is based on the principle of "distance decay" which states criminal offenders choose to commit crimes in areas closest to home (Norris, 2014). According to this principle, offenders are believed to commit fewer crimes farther from their home base. Norris proffers this is based on the "assumption that not only do criminals prefer to operate in areas in which they are familiar with, but also the areas where they offend share distinct overlap with the places they attend as noncriminals" (p. 11). Suppose in a serial crime, the offender maintains a stationary home base. With careful analysis, GP may elicit valuable information concerning that place. By understanding information regarding the offenders' pattern of movements, the GP acts as a "detailed mapping of crime locations, patterns, and trends" (Kapardis 2017, p. 746). Humans repeat successful behaviors and exist in spaces where they are knowledgeable and comfortable. Offenders' physical movements and locations can be central to the offender's choice of victim. Humans are creatures of habit, and serial offenders exhibit behaviors similar to non-offenders, by operating in their comfort zone. Offenders may alter these patterns if it becomes necessary to be successful with their criminal behavior (Geberth, 1996).

Historical Development of GP

The current use of GP employs computer software technology to develop the profile, but the notion of determining patterns to reveal geographic location is not new. From ancient celestial bodies to global maritime locating, global positioning systems (GPS) in some forms have allowed for the discovery of information about the world. Immense technological and scientific advancements over the last few decades allow for technique refinement to ensure accuracy and for GPS applications to various uses. GP in criminal serial cases derives from several sources discussed below.

One contribution to the evolution of GP came out of Chicago, Illinois, around the turn of the 19th century. Rapid industrialization and urbanization presented the city with a myriad of social problems, such as increased crime and delinquency. Scholars at the University of Chicago endeavored to understand the reciprocal relationship between residents and geographical space. Robert Park viewed the city through the lens of an urban sociologist. He studied the relationship between humans, social structures, and institutions. His key notion was the view of the city as a growing organism, shaped by human behavior. Park et al. (1925) suggested that the natural areas (the community) provided institutions to socialize residents as a form of social control. His colleague, Ernest Burgess, built upon this notion with the Concentric Zone theory, which divided the city into five different zones to examine the sociodemographic variables in each zone (Park et al. 1925). Sociologists at the University of Chicago, Shaw and McKay, then expanded the work of Park and Burgess to study the environmental influences on human behavior. Using the Concentric Zone theory, they applied spatial mapping to plot the location of the occurrence of juvenile delinquency in 1930s Chicago (Cullen et al., 2014). The results of their spatial analysis indicated that regardless of the ethnic group occupying the space over the years, the juvenile delinquency rate was consistent in the residential area closest to the industrial inner city. The researchers concluded that the characteristics of the geographical space, not the individual, contributed to the delinquent behavior (Shaw & McKay, 1942). These findings further support the accepted belief that serial killers, like the majority of criminal offenders, do not typically travel too far from home to commit their crimes (Snook et al., 2007).

Canadian scholars Patricia and Paul Brantingham built on previous research in the field with their investigations of crime patterns to determine the spatial distribution of crime. The Brantinghams suggested earlier criminological research was lacking in attempts to explain criminal differences in spatial patterning by the variety in offending. Rather, they argued that opportunities, not criminal motives, drive crime locations. Crime results from opportunistic circumstances that play a role in the geographical choice of crime space (Brantingham & Brantingham, 1981). Through their research, they proffered the notion that all individuals have "an 'activity space' related to the areas in which we live, work, and play and that this activity space produces a discernible pattern of movement around the city" (Webb, 2013, p. 33). The Brantinghams' studies in environmental criminology influenced Canadian criminologist and former Detective Dr. D. Kim Rossmo's work on GP.

Rossmo, inspired by the works of the Brantinghams, developed a technique that utilizes spatial data related to the "crime scene locations to provide a statistical estimate of the probable residence or base of operations of an unknown offender" (Woodworth & Porter, 2000, p. 254). Rossmo (2012) defined his technique of GP as "a criminal investigative methodology that analyses the locations of a connected series of crime to determine the most probable area of offender residence" (144). He suggests that the principal reason for this type of profiling was to assist law enforcement with information management and analysis. Stemming from environmental criminology, his technique emphasizes the interactions between the environment and the individual. As the author indicates, the theories of crime patterns, rational choice, and routine activities, which influence environmental criminology, "form the basis for understanding the target patterns and hunting behaviour of criminal predators through the microlevel dimensions of offender, victim, crime, and environment" (p. 145).

Criticisms of GP

One criticism of GP is its reliance on offender proximity to the crime scene (Van der Kemp & van Koppen, 2007). For example, an offender who purposely commits crimes outside their familiar spaces, or an offender well known in their community, may choose another location for their crimes to avoid suspicion or detection. A second issue with using GP in serial crime cases is the possibility that an offender may stray from their routine, or one that does not adhere to a typical routine (Van der Kemp & van Koppen, 2007). For example, transitory offenders, whether unhoused or traveling for work or the military, have the opportunity to commit their crimes over a vast amount of space. Or a truck driver picks up a target in one state, drives across numerous states, commits murder, and disposes of the body in a distant jurisdiction. Additionally, Kocsis and Palermo (2007) suggest that GP could be less effective in cases where offenders commit crimes near their place of work and residence (which may be located in opposite directions), offenders who amass victims' bodies in their residence, or offenders who dump or bury them and victims are not yet found. The further lament the lack of regulation and certification in the field of GP. They note the variations in terminology across disciplines and differences in methodology or computer software. The authors suggest that criminal profiling limits its growth process when trained profilers do not unify and work together to better the field by defining shared terminology, credentials, and training.

Behavioral Evidence Analysis

The final profiling technique discussed in this chapter is what Turvey (2023) refers to as BEA. He defines the method as "an evidence-based form of criminal profiling that requires analysis of forensic evidence, forensic victimology, offender modus operandi, and offender motive in each individual criminal incident" (p. 153). BEA is similar to the FBI model in that it investigates the serial perpetrator's behavior by analyzing evidence left at the crime scenes. But as Turvey clarifies, it differs from CSA because BEA is deductive, not inductive. BEA analyzes the forensic evidence for the case where a profile is constructed. It does not base the profile on other similar groups of cases or statistical probabilities, as does CSA. Petherick (2006) states that since BEA uses deductive reasoning, in addition to the scientific method, it "will not make a conclusion about an offender unless specific physical evidence exists suggesting a particular characteristic" (p. 46). With BEA, the profiler does not infer any knowledge. Rather, a large part of this type of profiling is analyzing the physical evidence and its relation to the crime and then reconstructing the crime scene. Whereas CSA would infer characteristics of the offender from previous similar offenses, BEA analyzes the evidence based only on the evidence presented at a given crime scene.

Historical Development of BEA

BEA is one of the more recently advanced criminal profiling processes and emerged out of the search for a more scientific approach to criminal profiling. Turvey (2012) developed and refined this profiling technique based on forensic science and physical evidence. BEA has a comparable methodological progression to CSA—using evidence from the crime scene and behavioral principles. BEA is multidisciplinary, including influences from criminology, psychology, psychiatry, and forensic science.

An important component of BEA includes using deductive reasoning, wherein the case evidence is evaluated using only available evidence. BEA does not use past patterns of criminal behavior to determine what has occurred in a different (however similar) criminal case. A profiler using BEA to develop a profile should treat each case individually. The profile is not constructed with the inferences of statistics that occurred in other cases with similar behaviors and crimes. Instead, characteristics of the crime and offender are determined through analysis of the existing evidence, and conclusions are drawn on actual evidence, not probabilities taken from similar cases.

There are two phases to the BEA method of criminal profiling. Phase I is the investigative phase, and Phase II is the trial phase (Turvey, 2012). Phase I, the investigative phase, consists of analysis of forensic evidence. Using this analysis may assist law enforcement in linking similar crimes and determining the likelihood of escalation in serial crimes. Phase I also involves prioritizing suspects and working with investigators on interrogation and interview techniques. Phase II, the trial phase, is intended to assist investigators and prosecutors with case preparation. Some goals of this phase include the determination of the criminal offender's motives, including "insight into offender fantasy and motivations ... [and] evaluating the nature and value of forensic and behavioral evidence" (p. 127). He states that Phase II, the trial phase, is only applicable in a criminal case when a suspect can be identified.

Petherick and Brooks (2021), in their description of BEA, differ from Turvey in that they discuss four stages of the process: forensic analysis, victimology, crime scene characteristics, and offender characteristics. A profile is constructed by gathering and examining all the evidence from the crime. In the first stage, forensic analysis involves examining the evidence and reconstructing the crime scene. With this information, a profiler can determine what and how the behavior occurred. Next is the victimology stage, which includes information such as basic personal information, like the age, sex, and occupation of the victim. It is also necessary to include any routines the victim had, hobbies, or other activities that may be useful in identifying when and how the victim was chosen. Next is the third stage, where the profiler scrutinizes the crime scene information. The authors further describe the qualities such as establishing "the distinguishing features of the crime scene, including the method of approach and attack, the method of control, location type, nature and sequence of any sexual acts, materials used, precautionary acts and verbal activity" (p. 701). Finally, the last stage in composing the BEA is the offender characteristics. Information gathered from the other stages assists the profiler in determining offender characteristics like personality and behavioral traits, including level of criminal sophistication and possibly motive in the crime(s).

Criticisms of BEA

While the BEA profiling method is relatively recent, Chifflet (2015) does put forth one criticism of the BEA profiling technique. He suggests that BEA profiling, while not dependent on previous similar cases or statistical probabilities like CSA, nevertheless depends on the assertion of a motivational typology (e.g., an offender who commits a specific crime is anticipated to maintain certain personality traits). That is, speculation regarding motive based on the type of offender is dependent on an unproven theory. And conclusions drawn regarding the offender characteristics and victimology are also grounded in sound, but unproven theory.

Conclusion

Despite continual innovations in methods and types of criminal profiling, critics of the process remain. Sears (1991) believes profiles to be too simplistic and overly general to be of any significant worth to investigators. The concern is that instead of helping to focus the investigation on a suspect, it might direct law enforcement toward the wrong offender. Additionally, Petherick (2006) points out that if the original inferences or statements of physical evidence are incorrect, then the investigator will be led astray, and the profile only contributes to the misuse of resources, lost time, and misidentification of suspects.

Chifflet (2015) proffers two critiques of criminal profiling: the lack of scientific validation for the theories that underlie criminal profiling; and the lack of consensus concerning validity measures. The contention is that while deductive approaches profess not to use group studies to generalize to a specific case, they do use inferences for types of offender motivation to commit the crime. He points to the lack of measurement validity in the various profiling techniques and states that there is no consensus on which part of the profiling process would best be used to assess the profiling or profiler validity (e.g., utility of the profile, skills of the profile). So, due to variation in determining how to measure the validity of the process effectively, Chifflet (2015) declared "the validation research is highly fragmented and often fails to convincingly demonstrate [it] stands as a sound discipline" (p. 244).

Finally, Turvey (2023) provides the critique that with such variety in definitions and approaches to constructing a profile, the lack of training in behavioral sciences or social sciences, variety across disciplines used as the foundation for the criminal profile, no uniformity for technique, method, and the lack of consistency across law enforcement agency and country, the discipline of criminal profiling will continue to be viewed as dubious.

The current chapter has provided a brief overview of four criminal profiling techniques. CSA, IP, GP, and BEA are all criminal profiling methods with foundations in logical reasoning. CSA, also known as the FBI model (which they term criminal investigative analysis), uses crime scene evidence and inductive logic to determine the probable likelihood that a particular type of individual would be responsible for the crimes. IP relies on psychology to learn the personality of one most likely to be the suspect of a particular crime. GP uses computer software to determine possible locations of an unknown suspect's residence by analyzing spatial patterns related to the crime(s) committed. BEA uses crime scene evidence and victimology to reconstruct the crime and determine offender characteristics.

In conclusion, early accounts of criminal profiling were diagnostic evaluations (DEs) composed by psychologists or psychiatrists. While similar approaches are used in modern profiles, the search for scientifically based techniques to improve on former methods continues. Criminal profiling has evolved as a technique from the contributions of a variety of interrelated disciplines in criminology, sociology, ecology, psychology, and psychiatry. Much of the criticism that criminal profiling suffers from is reasonable. To date, there is no consensus on terminology, technique, or training to develop a profile. Some methods of criminal profiling are grounded in theory and use the scientific method to improve empirical evidence for a technique, but others are not.

Criminal profiling is an ever-evolving process, with each emerging technique built on the former (Norris, 2014). Ainsworth (2001) claims the

> [a]dvancement of any technique relies on careful study of what has worked and what has not worked in the past. An understanding of *why* some approaches have been more successful than others is also essential if profiling is to move forward.
>
> (p. 13)

All four techniques of criminal profiling discussed in this chapter have advantages and disadvantages. As with any research in the social sciences, none of the methods discussed is ideal in and of themselves. Scholars in the field should continue to test and make modifications as necessary to ensure the most reliable profiling techniques to assist investigators.

References

Ainsworth, P. (2001). *Offender Profiling and Crime Analysis*. Routledge. https://archive.org/details/offenderprofilin0000ains/page/6/mode/2up

Albarracin, D., & Wyer, R.S. (2000). The cognitive impact of past behavior: Influences on beliefs, attitudes, and future behavior. *Journal of Social Psychology*, *79*(1), 5–22.

Bartol, C.R., & Bartol, A.M. (2013). *Criminal and Behavioral Profiling*. Sage Publications.

Berg, K. (1938). *The Sadist*. Acorn Press. https://archive.org/details/b20442166/page/44/mode/2up?ref=ol&_autoReadAloud=show&view=theater

Bonn, S.A. (2017). Jack the ripper identified: Unmasking jack the ripper more than 130 years after he vanished. *Psychology Today*, https://www.psychologytoday.com/us/blog/wicked-deeds/201401/jack-the-ripper-identified

Boston Globe. (2021, August 10). *Boston Strangler Recalled*, Chicago Tribune, https://www.chicagotribune.com/1992/09/30/boston-strangler-recalled/

Brantingham, P.J., & Brantingham, P.L. (1981). *Patterns of Crime*, Sage Publications https://archive.org/details/patternsincrime0000bran/page/396/mode/2up

Cannell, M. (2017). Unmasking the mad bomber: When James A. Brussel used psychiatry to think like a criminal, he pioneered the science of profiling. *Smithsonian Magazine*, April. https://www.smithsonianmag.com/history/unmasking-the-mad-bomber-180962469/

Canter, D. (2004). Offender profiling and investigative psychology. *Journal of Investigative Psychology and Offender Profiling*, *1*, 1–15.

Carson, D. (2009). The abduction of Sherlock Holmes. *International Journal of Police Science & Management*, *11*(2), 193–202. https://doi.org/10.1350/ijps.2009.11.2.123

Chifflet, P. (2015). Questioning the validity of criminal profiling: An evidence-based approach, *Australian & New Zealand Journal of Criminology*, *48*(2), 238–255.

Cullen, F.T., Agnew, R., & Wilcox, P. (2014). *Criminological Theory: Past to present: Essential readings*. Oxford University Press.

Douglas, J.E., & Burgess, A.W. (1986). United States Department of Justice, Criminal Profiling: A Viable Investigative Tool Against Violence Crime, *Federal Bureau of Investigation Law Enforcement Bulletin*, *55*(12), 9–13.

Douglas, J.E., Burgess, A.W., Burgess, A.G., & Ressler, R.K. (1992). *Crime Classification Manual*. Jossey-Bass, Inc.

Douglas, J.E., Ressler, R.K., Burgess, A.W., & Hartman, C.R. (1986). Criminal profiling from crime scene analysis. *Behavioral Sciences & the Law*, *4*(4), 401–422.

Egger, S.A., (2002). *The Killer Among us: An Examination of Serial Murder and its Investigation*. Prentice-Hall.

Federal Bureau of Investigation (n.d.). Law enforcement resources, behavioral analysis. https://le.fbi.gov/science-and-lab/behavioral-analysis

Geberth, V.J. (1996). *Practical homicide investigation: Tactics, procedures, and forensic techniques* (3rd ed.). CRC Press, Inc.

Harris, M.A., Brett, C.E., Johnson, W., & Deary, I.J. (2016). Personality stability from age 14 to age 77 years. *Psychology and Aging*, *31*(8), 862–874. https://doi.org/10.1037/pag0000133

Hart, B.L., & Miller, M.F. (1985). Behavioral profiles of dog breeds. *Journal of the American Veterinary Medical Association*, *186*(11), 1175–1180.

Hewitt, A., & Beauregard, E. (2014). Offending patterns of serial sex offenders: Escalation, de-escalation, and consistency of sexually intrusive and violent behaviours. *Journal of Investigative Psychology and Offender Profiling*, *11*, 57–80. https://doi.org/10.1002/jip.1407

Holmes, R.M., & Holmes, S.T. (2009). *Profiling Violent Crimes: An Investigative Tool*. Sage Publishing.

Homant, R.J., & Kennedy, D.B. (1998). Psychological aspects of crime scene profiling. *Criminal Justice and Behavior*, 25(3), pp. 319–343.

James, S.H., & Nordby, J.J. (2009). *Forensic Science: An Introduction to Scientific and Investigative Techniques* (3rd ed.). CRC Press.

Jenkins, P. (1994). *Using Murder: The Social Construction of Serial Homicide*. Aldine De Gruyter.

Kapardis, A. (2017). Offender-profiling Today: An Overview. *Essays in Honour of Nestor Kourakis*, Sakkoulas Publications.

Keatley, D.A., Golightly, H., Shepard, R., Yaksic, E., & Reid, S. (2018). Using behavior sequence analysis to map serial killers' life histories. *Journal of Interpersonal Violence*. *36*(5–6), 2906–2928. https://doi.org/10.1177/0886260518759655

Kocsis, R.N. (2006). *Criminal profiling: Principles and practice*. Humana Press.
Kocsis, R.N., & Palermo, G.B. (2007). Contemporary problems in criminal profiling. In Kocsis and Palermo (Eds.), *Criminal Profiling: International Theory, Research, and Practice*, 327–345.
Kocsis, R.N., & Palermo, G.B. (2016). Criminal profiling as expert witness evidence: The implications of the profiler validity research. *International journal of law and psychiatry*, *49*(Pt A), 55–65. https://doi.org/10.1016/j.ijlp.2016.05.011
Konieczny, P. (2012). Vikings were 'first to begin criminal profiling.' *Medieval Warfare*, *2*(6), 4–5.
Mazzarello, P. (2011). Cesare Lombroso: An anthropologist between evolution and degeneration. *Functional Neurology*, 26(2), 97–101.
Miller, L. (2014). Serial killers: I. Subtypes, patterns, and motives. *Aggression and Violence Behavior*, *19*, 1–11.
Morton, R.J., Tillman, J.L., & Gaines, S.J. (2014). Serial murder: Pathways for investigations. *Justice Department, Federal Bureau of Investigation*, 1–78.
Norris, G. (2006). "Criminal Profiling: A Continuing History". In W. Petherick (Ed.), Criminal Profiling Methods, Serial Crime: Theoretical and practical issues in behavior profiling (1–14, 2nd ed.). Elsevier.
Norris, G. (2014). The Evolution of Criminal Profiling: From Whitechapel to Quantico and Beyond. In Wayne Petherick (Ed.), *Profiling and Serial Crime: Theoretical and Practical Issues* (pp. 3–14). Elsevier.
Ontario Human Rights Commission, (n.d.) *What Is Racial Profiling? Fact Sheet*. Ontario Human Rights Commission. https://www.ohrc.on.ca/en/what-racial-profiling-fact-sheet#:~:text=Racial%20profiling%20is%20based%20on,description%20of%20a%20specific%20individual
Park, R.E., Burgess, E.W., & McKenzie, R.D. (1925). The city: Suggestions for investigation of human behavior in the urban environment. In M. Janowitz (Ed), *The Heritage of Sociology Series*. University of Chicago Press.
Petherick, W. (2006). *Criminal Profiling Methods, Serial Crime: Theoretical and practical issues in behavior profiling* (pp. 31–52, 2nd ed.). Academic Press.
Petherick, W., & Brooks, N. (2021). "Reframing criminal profiling: A guide for integrated practice," *Psychiatry, Psychology, and the Law*, *28*(5), 694–710. https://doi.org/10.1080/13218719.2020.1837030
Pinizzotto, A.J., & Finkel, N.J. (1990). Criminal personality profiling: An outcome and process study. *Law and Human Behavior*, *14*(3), 215–233.
Ramsland, K. (2011). Howard Teten: An FBI visionary. *The Forensic Examiner*, *20*(2), 22–27.
Rossmo, D.K. (2000). *Geographic Profiling*. CRC Press.
Rossmo, D.K. (2012). Recent developments in geographical profiling. *Policing*, *6*(2), 144–150.
Salfati, C.G. (2021). Investigative Psychology. In J.M. Brown & M.A.H. Horvath (Eds.), *The Cambridge Handbook of Forensic Psychology* (pp. 54–68, 2nd ed.). Cambridge University Press. https://www.cambridge.org/core/books/cambridge-handbook-of-forensic-psychology/EFC2698F64484ADA7CB13D7D368E5368#fndtn-information
Schuyler, J. (1987). The "Malleus Maleficarum" and Baldung's "Witches' Sabbath". *Notes in the History of Art*, *6*(3), 20–26.
Sears, D.J. (1991). *To Kill Again: The Motivation and Development of Serial Murder*. Scholarly Resource Books.
Shaw, C.R., & McKay, H.D. (1942). *Juvenile Delinquency and Urban Areas*. University of Chicago Press.
Sheth, J.N. (1985). History of consumer behavior: A marketing perspective. https://www.jagsheth.com/marketing-theory/history-of-consumer-behavior-a-marketing-perspective/
Silke, A. (2001). Chasing Ghosts: Offender Profiling and Terrorism. In D.P. Farrington, C.R. Hollin, & M. McMurran (Eds), *Sex and Violence: The Psychology of Crime and Risk Assessment*. Routledge.
Sloane, H. (1992). What is behavior analysis? *Classic Essay, Behavior Services of the Rockies*. https://www.bsotr.com/pdf/What%20Is%20Behavior%20Analysis.pdf
Smith, M. (2002). The flying phallus and the laughing inquisitor: Penis Theft in the 'Malleus Maleficarum.' *Journal of Folklore Research*, *39*(1), 85–117 https://www.jstor.org/stable/3814832
Snook, B., Eastwood, J., Gendreau, P., Goggin, C., & Cullen, R. (2007). Taking stock of criminal profiling: A narrative review and meta-analysis. *Criminal Justice and Behavior*, *34*(4), 437–453.
Tibbetts, S.G., & Hemmens, C. (2010). *Criminological Theory: A Text/Reader*. Sage Publishing.
Turvey, B. (2012). *Criminal profiling: An introduction to behavioral evidence analysis* (4th ed.) Elsevier, Academic Press.
Turvey, B. (2023). *Criminal profiling: An introduction to behavioral evidence analysis* (5th ed.) Elsevier, Academic Press.

Van der Kemp, J., & van Koppen, P. (2007). Fine-tuning Geographical Profiling. In R. Kocsis (Ed.), *Criminal profiling: International theory* (pp. 347–360). Humana Press.
Verde, C., & Nurra, A. (2010). Criminal profiling as a plotting activity based on abductive processes. *International Journal of Offender Therapy and Comparative Criminology*, *54*(5), 829–849
Webb, D. (2013). *Criminal profiling: An introductory guide*. CreateSpace Independent Publishing Platform.
Weisbuch, M., Slepian, M.L., Clarke, A., Ambady, N., & Veenstra-VanderWeele, J. (2010). Behavioral stability across time and situations: Nonverbal versus verbal consistency. *Journal of Nonverbal Behavior*, 34 (1), 43.
Woodworth, M., & Porter, S. (2000). Historical foundations and current applications of criminal profiling in violent crime scene investigations. *Expert Evidence*, *7*, 241–264. https://doi.org/10.1023/A:1016655103536
Youngs, D.E., & Canter, D.V. (2006). Introducing Investigative Psychology. In *Psychology and Law* (pp. 321–342). Juta & Co Ltd.

2 Motivation and Theories

Rebecca C. Kendall

Introduction

Attempting to understand the complex interaction of a wide array of factors that motivate individuals to commit crime is an arduous undertaking that has challenged criminologists, sociologists, and psychologists for years. Despite the public's seemingly insatiable curiosity about all things related to crime and criminals, there is no simple answer as to why people commit crime. Although it would be easier to believe so, there is no single factor that accounts for all criminal behavior or even the deviance of one individual. One reason for this is the wide and diverse range of actions and behavior that constitute crime—for instance, explanations for why people commit serial homicide are unlikely to be identical to explanations for financial crimes. Additionally, we know that most people will eventually commit a criminal act at some point in their lives, so the notion of defining "criminals" as a subset of the population may be misleading.

Despite these challenges, attempting to understand the multifaceted reasons for deviant behavior is a worthwhile endeavor if for no other reason than the possibility of reducing and solving crime. While there is no single factor or theory that can be used to explain all crime, we can highlight factors that have been identified in the research to increase risk of offending. Given the extensive range of theories of crime, this chapter cannot cover all existing theories or risk factors. Rather, this chapter will provide an overview of different schools of thought regarding criminal behavior with a focus on those risk factors that are most relevant to the field of criminal profiling. These perspectives come primarily from sociology, criminology, and psychology. A more thorough overview of criminological theory can be found elsewhere (see, for instance, Akers & Sellers, 2009; Cullen et al., 2018).

This chapter begins with an overview of research on motivation for criminal offending. The latter part of the chapter examines different schools of thought for explaining criminal or deviant behavior, including developmental theories, biological theories, learning and situational theories, and personality theories. Within these overarching schools of thought will be a discussion of some of the most common factors for explaining offending, such as family factors, brain abnormalities and genetics, attachment issues, modeling, substance abuse, mental illness, and psychopathy.

Motivation for Criminal Behavior

Studies of criminal behavior have attempted to understand what factors influence an offender's motivation for committing crime as well as determine the extent to which motivation is consistent across offenses. This research can help investigators understand how to interpret behavioral crime scene evidence. In a recent study, Koegl and Farrington (2022) examined the motivations for criminal offending in 136 male inmates at a prison in Ontario, Canada. The most frequently endorsed motivations were pleasure/happiness (i.e., to feel happy or good),

DOI: 10.4324/9781003366300-3

sensation seeking (i.e., to experience fun, excitement, or thrills), escape (i.e., to avoid dealing with reality), substance use, and utilitarian. Sex offenders were more likely to commit crimes for reasons related to substance use, utilitarian motives, social influences, or preservation/protection. Drug offenses were mostly frequently attributed to substance use, social influence, or utilitarian motives. The most frequent motives for property offenses included redemption/honor, substance use, social influence, and utilitarian motives. Finally, the authors found that offenders with higher aggression scores were more likely to have motives for offending that included anger, jealousy, or hate, and power or control.

In a study of almost 800 college students in Iceland, Gudjonsson and Sigurdsson (2004) attempted to understand whether there are individual differences in motivation for offending that are related to personality variables. Results showed that almost three-quarters of students committed their most serious offense in the past year in the company of others, thus highlighting the importance of peer groups. Individuals who scored higher on a measure of antisocial personality traits were more likely to explain their motive for offending in terms of perceived provocations (such as taking revenge) and were more motivated by financial gain and excitement. External attribution of blame was highest for those who committed violent offenses and acts of deception and lowest for traffic violations and property offenses.

Theories of Criminal Behavior

There is no single cause or one-size-fits-all theory of offending that can apply to all crimes or criminals. In fact, Holmes and Holmes (2009) describe attempting to understand the reasoning behind criminal offending as often being "theoretically grounded guesses" (p. 54). This point may be disconcerting to those who seek to understand why criminals do what they do. While investigators and criminologists know this to be true, the public still searches for simple answers to the complex behavior that is criminal offending. One thing heard quite often, particularly in the aftermath of more grisly tragedies, is that the offender must be "evil." As Ainsworth (2001) points out, people use the term "evil" to find meaning in what seems like senseless, horrific acts. By labeling offenders as evil, it allows us to distance ourselves from their actions because the offender is viewed as inherently different from us. The problem is that the label of "evil" does not help us understand the behavior or its underlying motivation.

Rather than labeling offenders as simply "bad" or "evil," it is the undertaking of criminologists to identify factors empirically linked to offending and to develop theories to explain why some individuals engage in deviant or delinquent behavior while others do not. As social psychologist Kurt Lewin (1943) noted, all human behavior is impacted by complex interactions between internal factors within the individual and external factors within the environment. As such, criminal behavior is based on a complex interaction of factors. In addition, factors that promote crime may depend on the specific type of crime in question. For example, environmental explanations may be more pertinent to some types of offending, while individual explanations are more appropriate for others (Ainsworth, 2001). Criminologists today are less likely to look for one "cause" of crime, but rather to identify "risk factors" for crime. Just as scientists look for risk factors for disease within medicine, social scientists are now looking at risk factors for delinquency rather than individual root causes (Samenow, 2014).

Given the extensive range of theoretical explanations for criminal behavior, theories can be organized by their common traits and underlying assumptions about human behavior. The following sections will provide an overview of explanations for criminality with a focus on risk factors and theories believed to be most relevant to criminal profiling. This starts by reviewing developmental explanations for crime, which focus on the accumulations of risk factors across the life course. Second, we consider theories that link crime to one's biological makeup. Next, we examine how learning and situational factors, such as peer groups, influence criminality. Finally, we finish with a review of theories that focus on personality and psychological explanations for crime. It should be noted that while this chapter has grouped explanations into four general categories, there are many other ways to distinguish theories, and some theories or risk factors could be included in multiple sections.

Developmental Explanations of Crime

The developmental approach to understanding crime focuses on the life course as a trajectory that can encounter risk and protective factors along the way. Developmental theorists suggest that criminal behavior is attributed to accumulated risk factors during a child's development. For instance, the following risk factors and characteristics for youth violence have been identified by Centers for Disease Control and Prevention: individual factors (e.g., history of violent victimization), family factors (e.g., authoritarian childrearing attitudes), peer and social factors (e.g., association with delinquent peers), and community factors (e.g., diminished economic opportunities; see Table 2.1 for full list of risk factors). It is also

Table 2.1 Risk Factors for Perpetration of Crime

Individual Factors	
	History of violent victimization
	Attention deficits, hyperactivity, or learning disorders
	History of early aggressive behavior
	Involvement with drugs, alcohol, or tobacco
	Low IQ
	Poor behavioral control
	Deficits in social cognitive or information-processing abilities
	High emotional distress
	History of treatment for emotional problems
	Antisocial beliefs and attitudes
	Exposure to violence and conflict in the family
Family Risk Factors	
	Authoritarian childrearing attitudes
	Harsh, lax, or inconsistent disciplinary practices
	Low parental involvement
	Low emotional attachment to parents or caregivers
	Low parental education and income
	Parental substance abuse or criminality
	Poor family functioning
	Poor monitoring and supervision of children
Peer and Social Risk Factors	
	Poor academic performance
	Low commitment to school and school failure
	Association with delinquent peers
	Involvement in gangs
	Social rejection by peers
	Lack of involvement in conventional activities
Community Risk Factors	
	Diminished economic opportunities
	High concentrations of poor residents
	High level of transiency
	High level of family disruption
	Low levels of community participation
	Socially disorganized neighborhoods

Centers for Disease Control and Prevention – Risk and Protective Factors n.d. https://www.cdc.gov/aces/risk-factors/index.html

important to acknowledge that a nurturing or prosocial environment can protect against these risk factors. The following section examines several important developmental risk factors for crime, including.

Research on developmental factors that influence later offending is often based on longitudinal studies (studies that follow individuals over time). One of the most influential longitudinal studies of male delinquency is the Cambridge Study in Delinquent Development, which began collecting data in the 1960s. Findings from this research highlight a number of developmental factors associated with delinquency, including criminal parents and delinquent older siblings, lower economic status and larger families, presence of physical neglect by parents, living in low-quality housing, harsh parenting styles, behavior problems at school (e.g., impulsive, hyperactive, poor attention, risk taking), lower IQ scores, and lower academic scores (Farrington & West, 1990). Additionally, in those who became chronic offenders, antisocial behavior was demonstrated early in life. At age 10, those boys were described as impulsive, hyperactive, having low intelligence, and unpopular; at age 14, they were described as aggressive and had friends who were viewed as delinquent (Farrington, 1991, 1997).

Research suggests that there are different developmental pathways to crime, but serious and long-lasting deviance appears to emerge early in life. One of the leading theories of pathways to crime comes from developmental psychologist Terrie Moffitt. Moffitt's (1993) developmental theory proposes two distinct pathways to crime: the life-course persistent (LCP) offenders and the adolescent-limited (AL) offenders. Moffitt suggests that these two groups are fundamentally different from each other and will display different patterns of delinquent behavior.

According to Moffitt (1993), LCP offenders will have long and extensive criminal careers, as they begin engaging in delinquency at an early age and continue far into adulthood. Moffitt states that these offenders will engage in criminal activity across a wide variety of conditions and situations. The LCP offender is believed to develop neuropsychological deficiencies before or shortly after birth, which then puts the child in a disadvantaged position. Prenatal problems can include maternal drug use, maternal cigarette smoking, inadequate prenatal nutrition, exposure to toxins, brain insult during delivery, or heritable conditions. Postnatal problems can result from inadequate nutrition, harsh and inconsistent parenting, lack of stimulation or affection, and child abuse. These neurological problems can result in under controlled or difficult temperaments, delayed motor development, low intellectual functioning, poor verbal and execution function, and hyperactivity. During childhood, the LCP offenders show problems with their temperament, attention problems, and hyperactivity in early school years, and learning problems in later school years. Because they are often rejected by their peers, the LCP offenders miss the opportunity to develop prosocial interpersonal skills. These individuals also exhibit problems in a variety of life domains as they grow up, for instance, problems with substance abuse, depression, work failure, involvement with deviant peers, and risky sexual behavior. These offenders become trapped in an antisocial trajectory that is exacerbated by their social context, that often includes inadequate school, violent neighborhoods, and disadvantaged homes. Moffitt estimates that roughly 5–10% of juvenile offenders follow this high antisocial developmental trajectory, and they are almost exclusively male.

While LCP offenders commit a greater proportion of total crime, most juvenile offenders are described by Moffitt (1993) as AL offenders. The AL offenders typically begin offending during their adolescent years and desist from offending at around the age of 18; thus, they do not start as early or continue as long as the LCP offenders. For many AL offenders, the frequency and even the level of violence may be the same for both groups during the adolescent years—so, taking a snapshot of their delinquency during adolescence can make it difficult to distinguish between the two groups. It is suggested that the AL offenders will gravitate toward delinquent acts that symbolize adult privilege, such as drug and alcohol offenses, running away, and truancy. AL offenders are more likely to be motivated by the opportunity to leave home, go to college, or get a job, all of which are factors that will promote desistance from crime as they age. Because their antisocial behavior is often a response to situational cues, if the behavior is no longer reinforced or no longer perceived as beneficial, this group of offenders with desist from crime. Typically, the early life of the AL offender is different from that of the LCP offender—the AL child is more likely to have developed the skills needed to get along with others and succeed later in life. It is believed that most female offenders fit into the AL category.

Moffitt's developmental pathways have been validated in empirical research. For instance, Raine et al.'s (2005) research supports the connection between neurocognitive deficits and antisocial behavior. In studies of LCP offenders, they have been shown to commit on average 40 crimes each, including both violent and non-violent crime (Stattin et al., 2010), and have a higher-than-average number of convictions between the ages of 41 and 50 (Piquero et al., 2010).

Research on brain development and maturation has added to our understanding of why delinquency tends to peak during adolescence. According to neuropsychologist Laurence Steinberg's dual-systems model of risk-taking behavior (2008, 2009, 2010), brain development can explain risk-taking behavior in adolescence and early adulthood. According to the theory, the increased risk-taking and sensation seeking during adolescence, including drug and alcohol use, reckless driving, and sexual activity, is associated with immature self-regulation. However, as the brain continues to develop into the mid-20s, the areas of the brain responsible for self-regulation and self-control will mature, and most risk-taking behavior will decrease.

To a large extent, human behavior is shaped by experience and interactions with others. Family environment and relationships are of paramount importance for children and play a significant role in shaping how they develop. A large body of research has shown that crime is often more prevalent in certain families. For instance, the Cambridge study (Farrington & West, 1990) found that 38% of delinquent boys (compared to only 15% of non-delinquent boys) had a parent with a criminal record. However, there are many possible reasons why crime may be clustered in families. For instance, early biological explanations viewed criminality as being inherited, while more modern thinking views criminality as socially learned (Canter, 2017). Given the importance of family influences, researchers have studied the ways in which parenting styles and attachment can impact the development of delinquency.

A number of studies have examined the influence of parenting on adolescent delinquency, showing that some parenting styles and practices are associated with criminal behavior. Research has shown that lax, neglectful, erratic, inconsistent, and overly harsh parenting styles are associated with delinquency in youth (Canter, 2017). Specifically, an authoritarian parenting style (i.e., focus on control, punishment, and rigid rules) has been significantly linked with increased delinquent behaviors (Amran & Basri, 2020). Additionally, Jackson and Foshee (1998) found that lower levels of delinquency were associated with parenting that is more responsive to a child's needs and includes clear rules and expectations.

Research has shown some association between delinquency and growing up in a single-parent family (Bank et al., 1993). However, this finding may be due to other associated factors such as poverty, mental health problems, or the trauma of divorce. One possible explanation could be the inability of single parents to provide as much parental monitoring as two-parent households. Parental monitoring refers to parents' awareness of their children's activities (Bartol & Bartol, 2016). Research shows that parental monitoring has a strong negative association with antisocial behavior during childhood and adolescence.

Another area of research emphasizes the importance of parent-child attachments in the formation of delinquent behavior. According to Bowlby and Ainsworth's attachment theory, children form attachments with their caregivers between six months and two years of age. These early attachments with warm and caring adults help the child develop a sense of safety and security. In his study of juveniles, Bowlby (1944, 1946) found that delinquent children were more likely to have experienced six months or more of maternal separation within the first five years of their lives. Bowlby implied that maternal separation was viewed as a rejection and that the loss of a warm and caring attachment eventually leads to delinquency.

Biological Explanations of Crime

At large, biological theories focus on individual factors, either inherited or congenital, that are associated with an increased risk of engaging in criminal behavior (Canter, 2017). While we know criminal behavior is not attributed to one single gene, it may be partially explained by the overall effect of many genes combined (Hollin, 2013). One issue biological theories face is the broad nature of what is considered "deviant" and the wide range of behaviors considered "criminal." For genes to predispose one to crime, the question then becomes, what, exactly, is one predisposed to?

Although largely unpopular today in favor of socio-biological theories, early biological theories challenged prior assumptions that crime was caused by supernatural factors such as evil spirits. The emphasis on science in criminology started in the mid-1800s and provided a basis for what continues today. Early biological theories of behavior focused on the fact that certain individuals or groups tended to offend more than others, and theorists at the time focused on anatomical, physiological, or genetic abnormalities to explain criminality.

Cesare Lombroso is said to be the "father of criminology" and believed criminality could be linked to physical characteristics. Lombroso (1876) argued that criminals were less evolved humans and displayed abnormal physical characteristics such as an asymmetrical skull, large ears, flattened or crooked nose, high cheekbones, fat lips, and a large jaw. Despite Lombroso's influence on criminology, his theory of the biologically inferior criminal was refuted by subsequent research (e.g., Goring, 1913). Several other theorists shared a similar belief that the root of criminal behavior lay in the individual's physiology. For instance, Sheldon's (1941) theory of constitutional types proposed that crime is related to individual body type. Ectomorphs, described as thin and bony, were said to be introverted and restrained. Endomorphs, described as large and heavy, were presumably sociable and relaxed. And finally, mesomorphs, described as broad and muscular, were believed to be aggressive and adventurous. Criminals were suggested to be more mesomorphic and less ectomorphic.

Early biological theories eventually fell out of favor due to their singular focus on personal characteristics while largely ignoring environmental factors. Unlike the reductionist or deterministic theories from the 19th and early 20th centuries, modern biological explanations for crime are considered *socio-biological*, as they recognize that context and environment matter (Canter, 2017). Most contemporary criminologists do not focus solely on heredity as the only cause of crime and agree that biology alone cannot explain criminal behavior. Instead, much of the conversation now is on just how much of a role biology plays in criminal behavior (Holmes & Holmes, 2009). Based on recent scientific findings about genetics, neurology, and biochemistry, modern biological research seeks to find a link between biochemical factors (e.g., allergies, environmental conditions, diet), chromosomal abnormalities (e.g., abnormal number of Y chromosomes), hormones (e.g., testosterone), neurobiological factors (e.g., neurotransmitters), and crime.

Studies on the genetic influence of crime usually look at families, twins, and adoptees. Taken together, these studies appear to imply that somewhere between one-third and one-half of the variation between criminals and non-criminals can be attributed to genetic factors. However, it is still unclear what, exactly, is inherited.

One common empirical method for studying the etiology of crime is to examine the prevalence of crime within families. Family studies assume that if crime is inherited, criminal parents will be more likely to have criminal children. In the Cambridge Study of Delinquent Children, Osborn and West (1979) found that 13% of sons of non-criminal fathers were criminals themselves, compared to 40% of sons of criminal fathers. The finding that criminals are more likely to come from criminal families does not necessarily mean that criminality is inherited. Instead, parents who engage in criminal behavior may be more likely to encourage and reward other deviant behavior in their children and may also be at higher risk for other social factors, such as low income and certain neighborhood characteristics (Canter, 2017). Family studies are not able to provide conclusive results about the genetic and environmental influences on crime because they are unable to separate those sources of influence.

Another common empirical approach to studying the genetic etiology of crime is the study of twins. Twin studies compare monozygotic (MZ; identical and sharing almost the exact same genetic makeup) and dizygotic (DZ; fraternal and sharing roughly 50% of their genes) twins. The assumption in twin studies is that genetic influences can be implied when the concordance rate, or degree of similarity, between MZ twins is greater than that in DZ twins. Taken together, findings from twin studies suggest a greater concordance rate for criminality between MZ twins than for DZ twins, thus supporting the presence of a genetic influence. The Twins Early Development Study examined 13,000 pairs of twins and found that both genetic and environmental factors contributed to criminality—specifically, the social environment was shown to affect individuals at genetic risk for antisocial behavior (Oliver & Plomin, 2007; Trouton et al., 2002). In another study of twins, results from the Twin Study of Child and Adolescent Development (Lichtenstein et al., 2007) showed that genetic factors were more important for explaining early onset aggressive behavior in children.

While twin studies can provide more separation of genetic and environmental effects than family studies, this approach does not control for ways in which MZ twins may be treated more similarly than DZ. Some twin studies, however, compare MZ twins reared apart. Despite the utility of this approach, there are very few major studies that examine MZ twins reared apart due to the lack of twin pairs separated at birth, and even fewer that have criminal records. One study of 32 sets of MZ twins reared apart found some concordance in childhood conduct disorders and adult antisocial disorders, but it only accounted for 16% of variation between individuals. So, although genes were found to play a role in criminality, environment appeared to play a stronger role (Grove et al., 1990).

A third approach to studying the relative influence of genetic and environmental factors is adoption studies, which examine people who have been adopted and brought up by non-biological parents. Adoption studies investigate whether children adopted from criminal parents are more likely to be criminals themselves. This approach largely overcomes the limitations of family and twin studies because genetic and environmental effects can be separated. The assumption in adoption studies is that similarities between adoptees and their biological parents are viewed as estimates of genetic influence, while similarities between adoptees and their adopted parents are viewed as estimates of environmental influence (Tehrani & Mednick, 2000). In one study of over 1,000 adoptees, Hutchings and Mednick (1975) found that when the biological father was criminal, 21.4% of sons became criminals; when the adoptive father was criminal, 11.5% of sons became criminals. Further, when neither father was criminal, 10.5% of sons became criminals; when both fathers were criminals, the percentage of adoptees who themselves became criminals was 36.2%. These findings imply a modest genetic component to criminality but emphasize that the interaction between genetics and environment is most important.

While family, twin, and adoption studies must separate genetic and environmental factors from a complicated interaction of people and their social environments, other biological studies of crime are able to look directly at the individual's genetic makeup to determine the genetic influence on crime. Included in this body of research are cytogenetic studies that examine the role of chromosomal abnormalities in criminality. One chromosomal abnormality in particular, 47, XYY in which males have an extra Y chromosome, may be of interest for understanding criminal behavior (Canter, 2017). In men, having an extra Y chromosome is linked to characteristics such as lower intelligence, violent behavior, and above-average height. Some studies have found this condition to be related to an increased risk of engaging in criminal behavior (Witkin et al., 1976; Stochholm et al., 2012). Taken together, this research has shown a strong link between chromosomal mutations and criminality (Schram & Tibbetts, 2017).

Not all biological explanations of crime are genetic—some elements of one's biology develop in the womb, during birth, or after birth. Prenatal and postnatal exposure to toxins and environmental pollutants can have a negative influence on the brain. For instance, maternal substance use during pregnancy can cause a number of negative short-term effects (e.g., low birth weight, motor abnormalities, irritability, decreased behavioral regulation) and long-term effects (e.g., impulsivity, lower IQ scores, poor language development, and deficits in problem solving; Bartol & Bartol, 2016). Other biochemical factors that have been shown to be related to aggression and impulsivity include lead poisoning, hypoglycemia, low levels of serotonin, vitamin and mineral deficiency, allergic reactions, and food additives. Unfortunately, there is no easy way to establish the causality of these factors, given that most are also related to associated factors like socioeconomic status (Canter, 2017).

There is some evidence that the brains of people who commit crimes may be different than prosocial individuals. Studies have largely shown that damage to any part of the brain, but most particularly to the frontal or temporal lobes, increases the risk of future criminal behavior (Schram & Tibbetts, 2017). Specifically, brain damage has been shown to be related to aspects of one's social and emotional functioning, including aggressive and antisocial behavior (Bryant et al., 1984). Raine et al. (2000) found a smaller amount of prefrontal gray and white matter in brains of people diagnosed with antisocial personality disorder (ASPD) than those who do not engage in violence. There is also some evidence that the brains of psychopaths differ from non-psychopaths. For instance, research has consistently shown that psychopathy is associated with decreased activity in certain areas of the brain (i.e., right laterobasal amygdala, dorsomedial prefrontal cortex, lateral prefrontal cortex) and increased activity in other areas of the brain (i.e., fronto-insular cortex on both hemispheres; Poeppl et al., 2019).

Learning and Situational Explanations of Crime

By the early to mid-1900s, theorists were shifting away from internal explanations of behavior to focus on social and situational factors. While biological theories assume individuals are predisposed to criminality, learning theories suggest that criminal behavior is learned through the same processes that all human behavior is learned. People learn rules, morals, and values through interaction, or socialization, with others. In general, it is proposed that people will repeat behavior, including criminal behavior, that is rewarded or reinforced and avoid behavior that is punished.

One of the first to apply the concept of learning to criminal behavior was Edwin H. Sutherland, whose differential association theory (1947) dominated sociology and criminology until the 1980s. According to the theory, criminal behavior is acquired through interaction with others. Specifically, the importance is on who we associate with, how frequently, how personally and meaningful the associations are, and how early they occur in our lives. Sutherland proposes that throughout our interactions with others, we learn definitions (or values) that are either favorable or unfavorable to the law, and people will become delinquent if they are exposed to an excess of definitions unfavorable to the law. Thus, it is the messages we receive about criminal behavior, not solely the contact with deviant others, that will influence whether we commit crime. Sutherland also posits that prosocial individuals can provide subtle messages favorable to law violation if they suggest that cheating and law violation are acceptable in certain circumstances. For instance, parents may themselves be law-abiding but convey the message that it would be acceptable to break the law in certain circumstances. One important aspect of differential association theory is that criminals are not seen as having different needs or values than non-criminals (Canter, 2017).

A limitation of differential association theory was that Sutherland did not specify precisely how learning occurs (Schram & Tibbetts, 2017). In order to more clearly define how criminal behavior is acquired, Burgess and Akers (1966) reformulated Sutherland's theory to include more concepts from behavioral psychology, including reinforcement and imitation. Akers (1998) then modified the theory into its current form, known as social learning theory. The theory includes four main concepts: differential association, definitions, differential reinforcement, and imitation. Almost identical to Sutherland's original concepts, differential association refers to the interaction with others who engage in certain behavior, and definitions include one's own attitudes attached to behavior, including either approval or disapproval. Differential reinforcement refers to anticipated future rewards and punishment. And finally, imitation refers to engagement in a behavior after observation of a similar behavior, particularly if that behavior is rewarded. Akers suggests that observational learning will occur mostly within families and that models perceived to be more respected and significant will be more influential on one's own behavior.

American psychologist Albert Bandura furthered our understanding of learning principles by incorporating the notion that individuals learn new behavior simply by observing others. Bandura's research on modeling/imitation showed that learning can take place with almost no amount of conditioning (or response) to a given behavior. Thus, we learn many of our values and behavior by simply mimicking what we see others do. In his now-famous "Bobo Doll" (a blow-up plastic doll) experiment, Bandura et al. (1961) divided child participants into three groups to watch a 5-minute film depicting an adult verbally and physically abusing an inflatable Bobo Doll. One group of participants observed the adult model in the video being rewarded, the second group saw the model being spanked and verbally reprimanded, and the third group saw the model receive neither punishment nor reward. After watching the video, the children were given 10 minutes of free play alone with the doll. Results showed that the group that saw the adult model being rewarded for aggressive behavior showed the most aggression toward the doll, and the group that saw the adult model being punished showed the lowest amount of aggression toward the doll. Additionally, boys were shown to be more likely to be aggressive than girls. Bandura's research on modeling has important implications for criminality. Specifically, that criminal behavior and attitudes can be learned by imitating behavior observed by one's models, particularly if the model is rewarded for the behavior, and that behavior can be learned through symbolic models, such as media, movies, and video games. While parents are likely to be the most significant models in a child's life, one's peer group becomes more important as they approach adolescence.

Criminological research has consistently shown that delinquent youth often have delinquent peer groups. In fact, studies show that association with a delinquent peer group is a significant predictor of initiation, frequency, maintenance, desistance, and types of individual antisocial behavior (McGloin & Thomas, 2019). For instance, in their landmark study of 1,000 delinquent and non-delinquent male youth in Boston, Glueck and Glueck (1950) found that 98% of delinquent youth also had delinquent peer groups (compared to only 7% of the non-delinquent youth). In addition, Pratt et al.'s meta-analysis of 133 studies (2010) found that association with other delinquent peers was a robust correlate of crime. In fact, Pratt and colleagues found the effect of delinquent peers on crime to be comparable to or stronger than other well-established correlates of crime. War (2002) suggests the reason for the peak in delinquency during adolescence is due to the significance of peer groups during that time. It is unclear, however, if youth are influenced and learn to be delinquent through interaction with delinquent peers (a peer influence perspective) or whether delinquent youth specifically seek out other delinquent peers (a peer selection perspective). Gallupe et al.'s (2019) meta-analysis of research on the relationship between delinquent peers and personal offending behavior found support for both the peer influence and peer selection perspectives. Thus, it appears that adolescents are both influenced by the delinquency of their friends and also tend to choose friends with similar involvement in offending.

While association with delinquent peers is sure to influence one's own delinquency, peers can also impact individual criminality in other ways. Peer rejection is one of the strongest predictors of later involvement in serious and long-lasting criminal behavior (Cowan & Cowan, 2004; Dodge, 2003; Trentacosta & Shaw, 2009). In fact, peer rejection can occur early in one's life—research shows that even by the age of five, children who display overly aggressive, disruptive, inattentive, and argumentative behavior are often excluded by peers (Dodge & Pettit, 2003; Patterson, 1982). Peer rejection can also exacerbate antisocial behavior in those already displaying aggression. Finally, peer rejection can have a cascading effect, causing poor academic performance, which puts one at further risk of developing delinquent behavior (Buhs & Ladd, 2001; Dodge & Pettit, 2003).

Some researchers suggest that anybody could potentially engage in antisocial behavior given the right circumstances. This body of research suggests that more emphasis should be placed on situational factors that precipitate criminal behavior. One situational factor that can impact whether one engages in deviant or delinquent acts is the presence of an authority figure. Yale psychologist Stanley Milgram's (1963) seminal study of authority demonstrated that people would obey an authority figure that instructs them to inflict pain on another person. In the study, each participant was paired with another "participant," who was actually a confederate of the researcher. The participant and the confederate were each assigned a role, either as a "teacher" or a "learner" (the participant was always assigned the role of the teacher). The research participant and confederate were then split into two rooms, and the participant was tasked with "teaching" the confederate a list of word pairs. When the confederate made a mistake, an experimenter in the room with the participant teacher instructed them to administer a shock to the learner. Results showed that two-thirds of the participants obeyed the experimenter's order and administered the maximum shock levels. Participants were less likely to obey the researcher if they had more physical, visual, and auditory contact with the victim. Interestingly, the closer the researcher got to the participant, the more likely they were to obey the order. Milgram theorized that people begin to see themselves as an agent for carrying out another's wishes, so the person believes they are no longer acting of their own accord.

Psychologist Philip Zimbardo's research has demonstrated the importance of another situational factor known as deindividuation. The concept of deindividuation refers to the process in which people feel they are disguised or subsumed by a group and cannot be identified (Bartol & Bartol, 2016). For instance, in large crowds or large groups, people tend to lose their sense of individuality, remove their controls, and neutralize their internal moral restraints. The feeling of anonymity can lead to a loss of personal identity in which one believes they can no longer be singled out and held accountable for their own behavior. In his car experiment, Zimbardo (1969) left one new car on the street in Palo Alto, California, and another new car on the street in Manhattan, New York, to see which car was more likely to be looted. Findings showed that within 26 hours, the car in Manhattan was stripped of all its valuable parts. Surprisingly, it was not delinquents who looted the car but rather just regular citizens and even some families. Conversely, the car in Palo Alto was left untouched. Zimbardo suggested it was the anonymity of the New York residents that made them believe they would not get caught.

In the infamous Stanford prison experiment, Zimbardo created a mock prison in the basement of the psychology building at Stanford University (Haney et al., 1973). He recruited volunteers and broke them into two groups: prisoners and guards (and there were no apparent personal differences between the groups). After the experiment began, the participant prisoners were treated like prisoners (e.g., handcuffed, fingerprinted, booked) and the participant guards were treated like guards (e.g., given uniforms and sunglasses to encourage deindividuation). The experiment eventually got out of control within the first few days and had to be ended because the prisoners displayed significant depression, crying, and confusion. Roughly one-half of the guards abused their power and became brutal and demeaning to the prisoners. The study demonstrated that almost anyone can be made to do almost anything when placed in a psychologically compelling situation. It also extended the concept of deindividuation to include situations beyond just crowds and include factors such as wearing a disguise, a mask, or, in the case of the Stanford "prison guards," a uniform.

Personality and Psychological Explanations of Crime

The final section of this chapter examines explanations for crime that focus on an individual's personality traits or psychological state. While many psychological explanations also have developmental, biological, or social underpinnings, the primary focus of the explanations discussed in this section is on the thought processes and personality styles of offenders. Explanations discussed here include theories about personality traits, cognitive factors, mental illness, substance abuse, and psychopathy.

Some theories suggest that features of normal personality can be related to offending (Canter, 2017). It is believed that some personality characteristics are specifically associated with violent crimes, and although not always empirically tested, these are widely supported by those working in the field (e.g., law enforcement, profilers). For instance, violent offenders are typically thought to be aggressive, withdrawn, argumentative, isolated, antisocial, suspicious, and paranoid (Holmes & Holmes, 2009). In addition, Glueck and Glueck (1950) found that delinquents were more likely to be extroverted, vivacious, impulsive, less submissive to authority, more socially assertive, and to lack self-control.

The most widely cited personality theory of crime is Eysenck's (1977) theory of three underlying dimensions of personality: neuroticism-emotional stability, extraversion-introversion, and psychoticism-normality. Each of these dimensions of personality is viewed as a continuum, with most people falling somewhere in the moderate range on all three dimensions.

Eysenck argues that those who engage in antisocial behavior will be high in neuroticism, extraversion, and psychoticism.

Another theory of personality, the three-factor model, proposes three dimensions of personality: positive emotionality (i.e., tendency to experience positive emotions), negative emotionality (i.e., tendency to experience negative emotions), and constraint (Tellegen & Waller, 2008). Research has provided empirical support for the relationship between negative emotionality, low constraint, and crime (Caspi et al., 1994; Agnew et al., 2002). This suggests that people who commit crimes may view the world as a hostile or threatening place and have limited constraint to control over their impulses.

The personality trait Machiavellianism has also been shown to be high in many criminals (Paulhus & Williams, 2002). The concept of Machiavellianism, inspired by Italian prince Niccolò Machiavelli's 1532 book *The Prince*, describes the type of person who exploits the weaknesses of others for their own gain (Christie & Geis, 1967). It is no surprise that offenders tend to manipulate and take advantage of the perceived weaknesses or failings of others.

Studies have also examined the relationship between aspects of interpersonal cognitive and crime. For instance, in their general theory of criminality, Gottredson and Hirschi (1990) propose that criminals lack self-control and have a lowered ability to delay gratification. Locus of control is another cognitive factor that has been linked to offending. Locus of control refers to whether one believes they internally control their own behavior or whether their behavior is the result of external factors such as fate or persons in authority. Research suggests that offenders tend to provide explanations for their behavior that focus on external control rather than personal factors (Hollin, 2013). Finally, social perspective taking is our ability to see something from another person's perspective and is consequently linked to empathy. Studies of offenders have shown them to have lower levels of empathy and more limited perspective-taking (Jolliffe & Farrington, 2004).

Not all people who commit crimes lack remorse for their actions. In fact, most people who engage in delinquent behavior are still partially committed to the dominant social order and likely feel some amount of guilt for their behavior. Therefore, offenders must find ways to rationalize (or neutralize) their actions. Sykes and Matza's (1957) techniques of neutralization theory suggests that these techniques help them justify or excuse their behavior and are likely learned and supported by the person's social group (e.g., peers, parents). Some common justifications or excuses for delinquency include denial of responsibility (e.g., it is not my fault), denial of injury (e.g., no one got hurt), denial of the victim (e.g., they had it coming), condemnation of the condemners (e.g., law enforcement is corrupt), and appeal to higher loyalties (e.g., I did not do it for myself).

When offenders commit atrocious acts, it is common for the public to assume they must be mentally disordered, but the relationship between mental disorder and crime is not easy to untangle (Canter, 2017). There are multiple explanations for any empirical link established between mental disorder and criminality, including that the two share a common etiology. For example, trauma could be a precursor to both mental illness and offending (Hollin, 2013). It is also important to note that offenders with mental illness may be more likely to be caught, arrested, and plead guilty. Additionally, the high prevalence of mental illness among prisoners found in the research may reflect symptoms that developed after incarceration and thus may not actually be a cause of their offending.

Despite these cautions, there is certainly a link between some mental illnesses or specific symptoms and criminal behavior. The American Psychiatric Association's Diagnostic and Statistical Manual (DSM)—5th Edition is used by most mental health practitioners in the United States. The DSM-V defines mental disorder as "a syndrome characterized by clinically significant disturbance in an individual's cognition, emotion regulation, or behavior that reflects a dysfunction in the psychological, biological, or developmental processes underlying mental functioning" (American Psychiatric Association, 2013). There are many disorders in the DSM that can range from the milder side to the more serious, and not all mental disorders are associated with criminal behavior. There is a wide range of disorders that constitute mental illness, but the broad classes of mental disorder that will be discussed here are most relevant to offending and include psychotic disorders, personality disorders, conduct disorder, and substance abuse-related disorders.

In one survey of American male prisoners, Silver et al. (2008) found that mental illness was linked to violent and sexual offenses, in that the crimes committed by those with mental illness were more deviant and included younger victims. In some instances, specific symptoms of mental illness play a role in the offending behavior—for instance, for those with schizophrenia, hallucinations and persecutory delusions can relate to serious offending (Taylor et al., 1996). In one study of 26 homicidal (either completed or attempted homicides) children in Florida, Myers et al. (1995) found that 96% of participants met criteria for a DSM-III-R disorder at the time of the crime. The most frequent disorders and symptoms among the sample were conduct disorder (84%); substance abuse disorder (45%); history of psychotic symptoms (71%) with paranoid ideation being the most common followed by auditory hallucinations; and suicidal ideation (52%), with 14% having at least one past suicide attempt.

For some individuals, symptoms of psychotic disorders are tied to criminal behavior. Psychosis is not a diagnosis in itself, but rather a cluster of symptoms related to disturbances in psychological functioning. Psychosis is present in disorders such as schizophrenia, bipolar disorder, and other psychotic and mood disorders. Schizophrenia typically involves the breakdown of thought patterns, emotions, and perceptions. Some literature suggests that schizophrenia among men and women is associated with increased risk of both non-violent and violent offenses, including homicide (Hodgins, 2008; Silverstein et al., 2015). In a Swedish cohort study of 8,891 men and 4,951 women, Fazel, Grann et al. (2009a) found that the most common types of crime committed by people with schizophrenia were physical assault, threats, and harassment. A systematic review of 20 studies examining the relationship between schizophrenia and violence found an increased risk of engaging in violent behavior among those with schizophrenia compared to the general population, and that comorbid substance abuse significantly increased the risk of violence (Fazel, Gulati et al., 2009b).

Personality disorders are a class of disorders that include persistent issues regulating emotions and relating to others or an enduring pattern of engaging in behavior that deviates significantly from expectations of one's culture. These disorders are pervasive and inflexible, stable over time, and generally have an onset in adolescence or early adulthood (American Psychiatric Association, 2013). The personality disorder most commonly associated with criminality is ASPD. ASPD includes a pervasive pattern of disregard for and violation of the rights of others. A diagnosis of ASPD is common in forensic settings. While the prevalence of ASPD in the general population is roughly 3% for males and 1% for females, the prevalence is estimated to be anywhere from 30% to 50% in correctional settings (Bartol & Bartol, 2016).

Conduct disorder has similar features to ASPD but is only diagnosed in children. Conduct disorder refers to a repetitive and persistent pattern of behavior that violates the rights of others and social norms (e.g., aggression to people or animals, destruction of property, deceitfulness or theft; American Psychiatric Association, 2013). Among youth in the juvenile justice system, conduct disorder is one of the most common mental health diagnoses. Childhood onset (before age ten) is strongly associated with violent behavior throughout adulthood for males and females. Children with conduct disorder are often rejected by their peers because of their aggressive behavior; peer rejection prevents them from learning how to appropriately interact socially, and they are forced to use aggressive means to get their needs met (Bartol & Bartol, 2016).

Substance use disorders are a category of mental disorders that refers to a pattern of symptoms caused by using a substance despite its negative effects. The relationship between drugs and crime usually falls into one of three categories. First, drug-defined crimes involve the sale and/or possession of an illegal substance. Second, drug-related crimes involve violent behaviors induced by the effects of a drug or illegal activity that is motivated by continued drug use. Finally, crimes associated with drug use involve illegal activities that may have occurred while a person was under the influence of an illegal substance, but those activities were not a direct result of the drug use (Schram & Tibbetts, 2017).

Higher rates of substance abuse have been found among offenders than the general population (Fazel et al., 2006; Glaze & Palla, 2005; Karberg & James, 2005). Additionally, research has shown a high prevalence of alcohol use during the commission of offending (Felson et al., 2007; Felson & Staff, 2010). For instance, in a review of 23 studies from nine countries, researchers found that 37% of perpetrators of homicide were intoxicated during the commission of the crime (Kuhns et al., 2014). In a sample of 13,000 people arrested in 2013, marijuana was the most frequently used drug (at 82.9%), followed by methamphetamines (62.9%), opiates (50.0%), and cocaine (38.2%; Office of National Drug Control Policy, 2014). One study found that the odds of engaging in criminal behavior were 2.79 times greater for drug abusers than for non-drug users (and six times greater for crack users specifically; Bennett et al., 2008).

While psychopathy is not recognized as a mental illness in the DSM, it is considered a personality disorder most associated with criminality. In addition, while ASPD (as defined in the DSM-V) and psychopathy share similar features, they are not the same and include two separate sets of criteria to make a diagnosis. Psychopaths demonstrate a variety of behavioral and neurophysiological characteristics that differentiate them from other groups of individuals, and there is some evidence of a genetic component to psychopathy (Tuvblad et al., 2014). Psychopaths account for less than 5% of the adult population but are responsible for some of the most violent crimes (Hare, 1996, 1998). Within the adult prison population, the prevalence rate of psychopathy is between 15% and 25% for males and less than 15% for females (Bartol & Bartol, 2016).

Physician Hervey Cleckly was a pioneer in the study and conceptualization of psychopathy. Cleckly (1941, 1982) identified what he believed were 16 characteristics of the typical psychopath. Robert Hare (2003) furthered this work and developed his conceptualization and measurement of psychopathy based heavily on Cleckly's writing. Hare's conceptualization was meant to be more applicable to psychopaths in male prisons and forensic/psychiatric populations. Some of Hare's items are similar or the same as Cleckly's items, but Hare also added additional items. Hare's 20-item Psychopathy Checklist Revised (PCL-R) is the most popular tool for assessing psychopathy. Items on the PCL-R include characteristics such as impulsivity, lack of guilt or remorse, irresponsibility, callous/lack of empathy, and criminal versatility (see Table 2.2 for a list of all items on the PCL-R).

Research from scores on the PCL-R suggests that psychopathy is multidimensional, and there are thought to be at least two dimensions. In the two-factor model, factor one represents the interpersonal and emotional components of psychopathy (e.g., lack of remorse, callousness, and manipulation of others), and factor two is reflective of the antisocial lifestyle (e.g., poor planning, impulsiveness, need for stimulation). There is some suggestion that factor one is more closely linked to biopsychological factors and associated with predatory

Table 2.2 Items on the Psychopathy Checklist—Revised

Glib/superficial charm	Promiscuous sexual behavior
Grandiose self-worth	Early behavioral problems
Need for stimulation/proneness to boredom	Lack of realistic long-term goals
Pathological lying	Impulsivity
Conning/manipulative	Irresponsibility
Lack of guilt or remorse	Failure to take responsibility for own actions
Shallow affect	Many short-term marital relationships
Callous/lack of empathy	Juvenile delinquency
Parasitic lifestyle	Revocation of conditional release
Poor behavioral controls	Criminal versatility

violence, and that factor two is more closely linked to environmental factors and impulsive violence (Bartol & Bartol, 2016). A four-factor model of psychopathy has been supported across diverse samples, including male and female offenders, different ethnic and cultural groups, and young and old offenders. The four-factor model includes the interpersonal factor (e.g., lying and conning behavior), impulsive lifestyle factor (e.g., irresponsible behavior, sensation seeking, impulsiveness), affective factor (e.g., shallow affect, lack of remorse), and antisocial tendencies (e.g., crime and other antisocial behavior; Bartol & Bartol, 2016).

Violence committed by psychopaths appears to be more instrumental, dispassionate, and predatory, and more likely to be motivated by greed, vengeance, anger, retribution, or personal gain (Hare, 1999). Sexual offenses committed by psychopaths tend to be more brutal, unemotional, sadistic, and violent, and more likely to include victims who are strangers (Porter et al., 2003; Hare et al., 2000).

Conclusion

All crimes have some underlying motive—the challenge lies in determining how a complex array of internal and external factors came together to propel offending. At times, criminal motivation will only be known by the offender themselves, and investigators may only hope to gain insight into the motive after the crime has been committed. However, research into criminal motivation and risk factors for criminality can provide a better understanding of who is most at risk for engaging in delinquent behavior. Findings from this large body of literature can help lawmakers develop policies that prevent crime and aid investigators in solving crimes when they occur. While there will never be a simple answer to the question of why people commit crimes, advances in hard and social sciences will continue to move the field forward.

References

Agnew, R., Brezina, T., Wright, J.P., & Cullen, F.T. (2002). Strain, personality traits, and delinquency: Extending general strain theory. *Criminology*, *40*, 43–72.

Ainsworth, P.B. (2001). *Offender profiling and crime analysis*. Routledge.

Akers, R.L. (1998). *Social learning and social structure: A general theory of crime and deviance*. Northeastern University Press.

Akers, R.L., & Sellers, C. (2009). *Criminological theories: Introduction, evaluation, and application* (5th ed.). Oxford University Press.

American Psychiatric Association. (2013). *Diagnostic and statistical manual of mental disorders* (5th ed.). American Psychiatric Association.

Amran, M.S., & Basri, N.A. (2020). Investigating the relationship between parenting styles and juvenile delinquent behaviour. *Universal Journal of Educational Research*, *8*, 25–32.

Bandura, A., Ross, D., & Ross, S.A. (1961). Transmission of aggression through imitation of aggressive models. *Journal of Abnormal and Social Psychology*, *63*, 575–582.

Bank, L., Forgatch, M.S., Patterson, G.R., & Fetrow, R.A. (1993). Parenting practices of single mothers: Mediators of negative contextual factors. *Journal of Marriage and Fmaily*, *55*, 371–384.

Bartol, C., & Bartol, A. (2016). *Criminal behavior: A psychological approach* (11th ed.) Pearson.

Bennett, T., Holloway, K., & Farrington, D.P. (2008). The statistical association between drug misuse and crime: A meta-analysis. *Aggression and Violent Behavior*, *13*, 107–118.

Bowlby, J. (1944). Forty-four juvenile thieves. *International Journal of Psychoanalysis*, *25*, 1–57.

Bowlby, J. (1946). *Forty-four juvenile thieves: Their characters and home-life*. Bailliere, Tindall & Cox.

Bryant, E. T., Scott, M. L., Tori, C. D., & Golden, C. J. (1984). Neuropsychological deficits, learning disability, and violent behavior. *Journal of Consulting and Clinical Psychology*, *52*(2), 323.

Buhs, E.S., & Ladd, G.W. (2001). Peer rejection as an antecedent of young children's school adjustment: An examination of mediating processes. *Developmental Psychology*, *37*, 550–560.

Burgess, R.L., & Akers, R.L. (1966). A differential association-reinforcement theory of criminal behavior. *Social Problems*, *14*(2), 128–147.

Canter, D. (2017). *Criminal psychology* (2nd ed.). Routledge.

Caspi, A., Moffitt, T.E., Silva, P.A., Stouthamer-Loeber, M., Krueger, R.F., & Schmutte, P.S. (1994). Are some people crime-prone? Replications of the personality-crime relationship across countries, genders, races, and methods. *Criminology*, *32*, 163–196.

Centers for Disease Control and Prevention (n.d.). Risk and protective factors. https://www.cdc.gov/child-abuse-neglect/risk-factors/index.html#:~:text=Risk%20factors%20are%20characteristics%20that,perpetrating%20child%20abuse%20and%20neglect

Christie, R., & Geis, F.L. (1967). *Studies in machiavellianism*. Academic Press.

Cleckly, H. (1982). *The mask of sanity*. Mosby.

Cleckly, H. (1941). *The mask of sanity: An attempt to reinterpret the so-called psychopathic personality*. Mosby.

Cowan, P.A., & Cowan, C.P. (2004). From family relationships to peer rejection to antisocial behavior in middle childhood. In J.B. Kupersmidt & K.A. Dodge (Eds.), *Children's peer relations: From development to intervention* (pp. 159–178). Psychological Association.

Cullen, F.T., Agnew, R., & Wilcox, P. (2018). *Criminological theory: Past to present* (6th ed.). Oxford University Press.

Dodge, K.A. (2003). Do social information-processing patterns mediate aggressive behavior? In B.B. Lahey, T.E. Moffitt, & A. Caspi (Eds.), *Causes of conduct disorder and juvenile delinquency* (pp. 254–276). Guilford Press.

Dodge, K.A., & Pettit, G.S. (2003). A biopsychological model of the development of chronic conduct problems in adolescence. *Developmental Psychology*, *39*, 349–371.

Eysenck, H. (1977). *Crime and personality* (2nd ed.). Routledge and Kegan Paul.

Farrington, D.P. (1991). Anti-social personality from childhood to adulthood. *The Psychologist*, *4*, 389–394.

Farrington, D.P. (1997). Human development and criminal careers. In M. Maguire, R. Morgan, & R. Reiner (Eds.), *The Oxford Handbook of criminology* (2nd ed.) Oxford University Press.

Farrington, D.P., & West, D.J. (1990). The Cambridge study in delinquent development: A long term follow up of 411 London males. In G. Kaiser & H.J. Kerner (Eds.), *Criminal personality, behavior, life history*. Springer-Verlag.

Fazel, S., Bains, P., & Doll, H. (2006). Substance abuse and dependence in prisoners, A systematic review. *Addiction*, *101*, 181–191.

Fazel, S., Grann, M., Carlstrom, E., Lichtenstein, P., & Langstrom, N. (2009a). Risk factors for violent crime in schizophrenia: A national cohort study of 13,806 patients. *Journal of Clinical Psychiatry*, *70*, 362–369.

Fazel, S., Gulati, G., Linsell, L., Geddes, J.R., & Grann, M. (2009b). Schizophrenia and violence: Systematic review and meta-analysis. *PLOS Medicine*, *6*, 1–15.

Felson, R.B., Burchfield, K.B., & Teasdale, B. (2007). The impact of alcohol on different types of violence incidents. *Criminal Justice and Behavior*, *34*, 1057–1068.

Felson, R.B., & Staff, J. (2010). The effects of alcohol intoxication on violent versus other offending. *Criminal Justice and Behavior*, *37*, 1343–1360.

Gallupe, O., McLevey, J., & Brown, S. (2019). Selection and influence: A meta-analysis of the association between peer and personal offending. *Journal of Quantitative Criminology*, *35*, 313–335.

Glaze, L.E., & Palla, S. (2005). Probation and parole in the United States, 2004. In *Bureau of justice statistics bulletin*, November. U.S. Department of Justice.

Glueck, S., & Glueck, E. (1950). *Unraveling juvenile delinquency*. Harvard University Press.

Goring, C. (1913). *The English convict*. Patterson Smith.

Gottredson, M.R., & Hirschi, T. (1990). *A general theory of crime*. Stanford University Press.

Grove, W.M., Eckert, E.D., Heston, L., Bouchard, T.J., Segal, N., & Lykken, D.T. (1990). Heritability of substance abuse and antisocial behavior: A study of monozygotic twins reared apart. *Biological Psychiatry*, *27*(12), 1293–1304.

Gudjonsson, G.H., & Sigurdsson, J.F. (2004). Motivation for offending and personality. *Legal and Criminological Psychology*, *9*, 69–81.

Haney, C., Banks, W.C., & Zimbardo, P.G. (1973). Study of prisoners and guards in a simulated prison. *Naval Research Reviews*, *9*, 1–17.

Hare, R.D. (1996). Psychopathy: A clinical construct whose time has come. *Criminal Justice and Behavior*, *23*, 25–54.

Hare, R.D. (1998). Psychopathy, affect, and behavior. In D. Cooke, A. Forth, & R. Hare (Eds.), *Psychopathy: Theory, research, and implications for society* (pp. 105–138). Kluwer.

Hare, R.D. (1999). Psychopathy as a risk factor for violence. *Psychiatric Quarterly*, *70*, 181–197.

Hare, R.D. (2003). *The hare psychopathy checklist-revisited* (2nd ed.) Multi-Health Systems.

Hare, R.D., Clark, D., Grann, M., & Thornton, D. (2000). Psychopathy and the predictive validity of the PCL-R: An international perspective. *Behavioral Sciences & the Law*, *18*, 623–645.

Hodgins, S., Cree, A., Alderton, J., & Mak, T. (2008). From conduct disorder to severe mental illness: Associations with aggressive behaviour, crime and victimization. *Psychological Medicine*, *38*, 975–987.

Hollin, C.R. (2013). *Psychology and crime: An introduction to criminological psychology*. Routledge.

Holmes, R.M., & Holmes, S.T. (Eds.). (2009). *Profiling violent crimes: An investigative tool* (4th ed.). Sage.

Hutchings, B., & Mednick, S.A. (1975). Registered criminality in the adoptive and biological parents of registered male criminal adoptees. In *Proceedings of the annual meeting of the American psychopathological association* (No. 63, p. 105).

Jackson, C., & Foshee, V.A. (1998). Violence-related behaviours of adolescents: Relations with responsive and demanding parenting. *Journal of Adolescent Research*, *13*, 343–359.

Jolliffe, D., & Farrington, D.P. (2004). Empathy and offending: A systematic review and meta-analysis. *Aggression and Violent Behavior*, *9*, 441–476.

Karberg, J.C., & James, D.J. (2005). *Substance dependence, abuse, and treatment of jail inmates, 2000*. Bureau of Justice Statistics.

Koegl, C.J., & Farrington, D.P. (2022). Advancing knowledge about motivations for criminal offending. *Victims & Offenders*, *17*, 313–334.

Kuhns, J.B., Exum, M.L., Clodfelter, T.A., Bottia, M.C. (2014). The prevalence of alcohol-involved homicide offending: A meta-analytic review. *Homicide Studies*, *18*, 251–270.

Lewin, K. (1943). Defining the field at a given time. *Psychological Review*, *50*, 292–310.

Lichtenstein, P., Tuvblad, C., Larsson, H., & Carlström, E. (2007). The Swedish Twin study of CHild and adolescent development: The TCHAD-study. *Twin Research and Human Genetics: The Official Journal of the International Society for Twin Studies*, *10*(1), 67–73.

Lombroso, C. (1876). *Criminal man*. Torin.

McGloin, J.M., & Thomas, K.J. (2019). Peer influence and delinquency. *Annual Review of Criminology*, *2*, 241–264.

Milgram, S. (1963). Behavioral study of obedience. *Journal of Abnormal and Social Psychology*, *67*, 371–378.

Moffitt, T.E. (1993). Adolescent-limited and life-course persistent antisocial behavior: A developmental taxonomy. *Psychological Review*, *100*, 674–701.

Myers, W., Scott, K., Burgess, A.W., & Burgess, A.G. (1995). Psychopathology, biopsychosocial factors, crime characteristics, and classification of 25 homicidal youths. *Journal of the American Academy of Child & Adolescent Psychiatry*, *34*, 1483–1489.

Office of National Drug Control Policy. (2014). *2013 annual report arrestee drug abuse monitoring program II*. Office of National Drug Control Policy.

Oliver, B.R., & Plomin, R. (2007). Twins' Early Development Study (TEDS): A multivariate, longitudinal genetic investigation of language, cognition and behavior problems from childhood through adolescence. *Twin Research and Human Genetics*, *10*, 96–105.

Osborn, S.G., & West, D.J. (1979). Conviction records of fathers and sons compared. *The British Journal of Criminology*, *19*(2), 120–133.

Patterson, G.R. (1982). *Coercive family processes*. Castalia Press.

Paulhus, D.L., & Williams, K.M. (2002). The dark triad of personality: Narcissism, Machiavellianism, and psychopathy. *Journal of Research in Personality*, *36*, 556–563.

Piquero, A.R., Farrington, D.P., Nagin, D.S., & Moffitt, T.E. (2010). Trajectories of offending and their relationship to life failure in late middle age: Findings from the Cambridge Study in Delinquent Development. *Journal of Research in Crime and Delinquency*, *47*, 151–173.

Poeppl, T.B., Donges, M.R., Mokros, A., Rupprecht, R., Fox, P.T., Laird, A.R., Bzdok, D., Langguth, B., & Eickhoff, S.B. (2019). A view behind the mask of sanity: meta-analysis of aberrant brain activity in psychopaths. *Molecular Psychiatry*, *24*, 463–470.

Porter, S., Woodworth, M., Earle, J., Drugge, J., & Boer, D. (2003). Characteristics of sexual homicides committed by psychopathic and nonpsychopathic offenders. *Law and Human Behavior*, *27*, 459–480.

Pratt, T.C., Cullen, F.T., Sellers, C.S., Winfree Jr., L.T., Madensen, T.D., Daigle, L.E., Fearn, N.E., & Gau, J.M. (2010). The Empirical status of social learning theory: A meta-analysis. *Justice Quarterly*, *27*, 765–802.

Raine, A., Lencz, T., Bihrle, S., LaCasse, L., & Colletti, P. (2000). Reduced prefrontal gray matter volume and reduced autonomic activity in antisocial personality disorder. *Archives of general psychiatry*, *57*(2), 119–129.

Raine, A. Moffitt, T.E., Caspi, A., Loeber, R., Stouthamer Loeber, M., & Lynam, D. (2005). Neurocognitive impairment in boys on the life-course persistent antisocial path. *Journal of Abnormal Psychology*, *114*, 38–49.

Samenow, S.E. (2014). *Inside the criminal mind*. Penguin Random House Company.

Schram, P.J., & Tibbetts, S.G. (2017). *Introduction to criminology: Why do they do it?* (2nd ed.) Sage Publishing.

Sheldon, W.H. (1941). *The varieties of temperament*. New York: Harper.

Silver, E., Felson, R.B., & Vaneseltine, M. (2008). The relationship between mental health problems and violence among criminal offenders. *Criminal Justice and Behavior*, *35*, 405–426.

Silverstein, S.M., Del Pozzo, J., Roche, M., Boyle, D., & Miskimen, T. (2015). Schizophrenia and violence: Realities and recommendations. *Crime Psychology Review*, *1*, 21–42.

Stattin, H., Kerr, M., & Bergman, L.R. (2010). On the utility of Moffitt's typology trajectories in long-term perspective. *European Journal of Criminology*, *7*, 521–545.

Steinberg, L. (2008). A social neuroscience perspective on adolescent risk taking. *Developmental Review*, *28*, 78–106.

Steinberg, L. (2009). Should the science of adolescent brain development inform public policy? *American Psychologist*, *11*, 739–750.

Steinberg, L. (2010). A dual systems model of adolescent risk-taking. *Developmental Psychobiology*, *52*(3), 216–224.

Stochholm, K., Bojesen, A., Jensen, A. S., Juul, S., & Gravholt, C. H. (2012). Criminality in men with Klinefelter's syndrome and XYY syndrome: a cohort study. *British Medical Journal open*, *2*(1), e000650.

Sutherland, E.H. (1947). *Principles of criminology* (4th ed.) Lippincott.

Sykes, G., & Matza, D. (1957). Techniques of neutralization. *American Sociological Review*, *22*, 664–670.

Taylor, P.J., Garety, P., Buchanan, A., et al. (1996). Delusions and violence. In J. Monahan, & H. Steadman (Eds.), *Violence and mental disorder: Developments in risk assessment* (pp. 161–181). University of Chicago Press.

Tehrani, J.A., & Mednick, S.A. (2000). Genetic factors and criminal behavior. *Federal Probation*, *64*, 24–27.

Tellegen, A., & Waller, N.G. (2008). Exploring personality through test construction: Development of the multidimensional personality questionnaire. *The SAGE Handbook of Personality Theory and Assessment*, *2*, 261–292.

Trentacosta, C.J., & Shaw, D.S. (2009). Emotional self-regulation, peer rejection, and antisocial behavior: Developmental associations from early childhood to early adolescence. *Journal of Applied Developmental Psychology*, *30*, 356–365.

Trouton, A., Spinath, F.M., & Plomin, R. (2002). Twins Early Development Study (TEDS): A multivariate, longitudinal genetic investigation of language, cognition and behavior problems in childhood. *Twin Research*, *5*, 444–448.

Tuvblad, C., Bezdjam, S., Raine, A., & Baker, L.A. (2014). The heritability of psychopathic personality in 14- to 15-year old twins: A multirater, multimeasure approach. *Psychological Assessment*, *26*, 704–716.

Warr, M. (2002). *Companions in crime: The social aspects of criminal conduct*. Cambridge University Press.

Witkin, H.A., Mednick, S.A., Schulsinger, F., Bakkestrom, E., Christiansen, K., Goodenough, D., Hirschhorn, K., Lundsteen, C., Owen, D., Philip, J., & Rubin, D. (1976). Criminality in XYY and XXY men. *Science*, *193*, 547–555.

Zimbardo, P.G. (1969). The human choice: Individuation, reason, and order versus de individuation, impulse, and chaos. *Nebraska Symposium on Motivation*, *17*, 237–307.

3 Assumptions of Criminal Profiling and Linkage Analysis

Kevin Borgeson and Nicholas Stone

Introduction

The topic of profiling has been debated in the criminal justice field for years, while some say it is an effective tool that aids in the investigation of serial crime, others say it is not. This chapter will look at the assumptions underlying the four main types of criminal profiling discussed in this book and lay out the importance of crime linkage analysis when doing a profile.

Motive, Modus Operandi (MO), and Signature

There is no such thing as a motiveless crime—all criminals are propelled for one reason or another to commit their crime. The issue of motivation is central to criminal profiling and any theoretical approaches to understanding criminal behavior. As Petherick and Turvey (2008) note, figuring out the motivation behind a particular crime is an important part of criminal investigation, prosecution, and sentencing because:

- It reduces the suspect pool to those individuals with a particular motive.
- It assists with the investigative linkage of unsolved crimes with a similar motive.
- Along with other class evidence (i.e., means, opportunity, associative evidence), motive can provide circumstantial bearing on offender identity.
- Along with other contextual evidence, motive can provide circumstantial bearing on offender's state of mind.
- Along with circumstantial evidence, motive can provide circumstantial bearing on whether a crime has actually occurred.

(p. 274)

When we talk about motive, it is important to note that an individual's motivation is typically not static—motivation can change and may be crime dependent. However, while offending is likely to change over one's life course as their experience grows and they undergo developmental changes, there will be some level of behavioral consistency (Canter & Youngs, 2003).

Although most people could probably give you their own definition of *motive*, it is surprisingly a difficult concept to adequately define. In addition, *motive* must be distinguished from other relevant but distinct terms used in the criminal justice field to describe an offender's criminal behavior or patterns of behavior, including *MO* and *signature*. Despite their similarity, these terms should not be used interchangeably.

DOI: 10.4324/9781003366300-4

While there have been different attempts to define the concept, for the purposes of this chapter, we will use Petherick and Turvey's (2008) definition of *motive*: "the emotional, psychological, and material needs that impel and are satisfied by behavior" (p. 276). Motive should be distinguished from the concept of *intent*, which Petherick and Turvey (2008) define as "the specific aim that guides behavior" (p. 276). Motivation for offending is different than justification or reasons, which may be given after the offending to explain one's own behavior (Koegl & Farrington, 2022). One's motive is influenced by both internal conditions (i.e., those that are derived from the individual) and external conditions (i.e., those that are derived from the environment). Additionally, both internal and external factors can be considered proximate (i.e., immediate) or pathological (i.e., long-term; Petherick & Turvey, 2008). An individual's motive can be difficult to ascertain because only the offender knows their motive; however, motive can be generally inferred from behavioral evidence (Leonard, 2001).

A related yet distinct concept is *MO*, a Latin term meaning *method of operating* (i.e., the manner in which the crime was committed; Turvey, 2008). The MO is essentially the "how" of a crime and includes all behaviors, either simple or complex, required by the offender to successfully carry out a crime (Hazelwood & Warren, 2003). According to Turvey (2008), the MO is important to criminal profilers because it can provide information about the offender, such as:

- A particular discipline, trade, skill, profession, or area of knowledge (criminal and non-criminal).
- Knowledge particular to the victim, suggesting contact, or a prior relationship.
- Knowledge particular to a crime scene, suggesting varying levels of familiarity (p. 311).

An offender's MO is dynamic and malleable and can develop over time as the offender learns (e.g., they learn what methods are most effective) or deteriorates (e.g., their mental state is deteriorating, or they are using substances; Hazelwood & Warren, 2003; Turvey, 2008).

The MO usually has three basic purposes. The first purpose the MO serves is to protect the offender's identity (e.g., wearing gloves or a mask). The second purpose of the MO is to help the offender successfully complete the crime (e.g., using a weapon to control the victim). Finally, the MO can help facilitate the offender's escape (e.g., using a stolen vehicle during the commission of the crime; Turvey, 2008, p. 311). A number of factors can influence the offender's MO, including the unavailability of a victim, response from the victim during the offense, or the interruption of an offense (Hazelwood & Warren, 2003).

The term *signature* is used in criminal investigation to refer to specific behaviors that offenders engage in because they serve some sort of psychological or emotional need (Turvey, 2008). Additionally, the signature can help investigators understand an offender's motive for the crime. The signature includes two distinct parts: the signature aspect and the signature behavior. The signature aspect refers to the emotional or psychological themes that are satisfied by the offense. The signature aspects can include themes of profit, anger or retaliation, reassurance or experimentation, assertiveness or entitlement, or sadism. The signature behavior includes the acts engaged in by the offender that are not necessary to commit the crime and thus suggest some underlying psychological or emotional need. Although conceptually distinct, it can be difficult to distinguish between MO and signature behaviors, and sometimes they are satisfied by the same behaviors (i.e., the same behavior satisfies an emotional need but is also a practical element of the crime). According to Turvey (2008, p. 326), signature behaviors often include the following criteria:

- Actions at the scene of the crime that take extra time to complete (not including behaviors that are part of the MO)
- They are not necessary to carry out the crime
- They involve the expression of a need or emotion
- Can include the expression of fantasy

In their study of the consistency of crime behavior during 347 sexual assaults committed by 69 serial sex offenders, Harber et al. (2012) found that offenders' level of consistency for crime-related behavior depended on the specific behavior, but overall, offenders appeared to re-evaluate and change their MO over time. There were several behaviors that showed more consistency across offenses, and offenders with longer crime series were more likely to behave consistently across the offenses. The offenders appeared to be consistent in whether they selected a residential area to encounter the victim and commit the crime, in targeting a victim who was alone at first contact, and the style of how they chose to approach the victim. Although not frequent, there was a high degree of consistency for whether the offender masturbated or engaged in exhibitionism during the offense. Finally, use of a weapon in the commission of the offending was not highly consistent across offending series.

In order to better understand the consistency of ritual and signature behaviors across a series of offenses, Schlesinger et al. (2010) examined the crime scene behaviors of 38 serial sexual homicide offenders. Findings showed that 97.4% of the offenders engaged in ritualistic behavior with at least two victims in their series of homicides. The most common ritual behaviors were penis penetration, binding, overkill, beating, and posing. While only 13.5% used the exact same ritual with every victim in the series, 83.3% engaged in ritual behaviors that were behaviorally similar to at least two victims. Additionally, 45.9% of offenders demonstrated evolution of their ritualistic behaviors across their series (e.g., engaging in more elaborate torture with subsequent victims), and almost half the sample experimented with a unique behavior at one or more crime scenes in their series. Results suggest that serial sexual homicide offenders engage in complex and varied behavior at crime scenes. The authors conclude that their findings did not support the idea that serial sexual homicide offenders leave unique "calling cards" at every crime scene—instead, while they engaged in some ritualistic behavior, they typically did not engage in the exact same behavior at every offense. However, while most of the rituals were not exactly the same, they were thematically and behaviorally similar and consistent.

One study of male adolescent sexual offenders set out to examine the relationship between the location of the crime and the offender's MO. Leclerc et al. (2008) sampled 103 adolescents between the ages of 13 and 17 in Quebec, Canada, who committed at least one sexual offense against a child younger than 12. The authors found that offenders who victimized both boys and girls were more likely to use a wider repertoire of strategies than those with only male or female victims. Additionally, the findings suggest that the location of the crime was related to MO strategy, and thus, offenders appear to use a cost-benefit analysis to determine which MO strategy will be the most successful in the moment.

Defining Linkage Analysis—Different Types of Linkage and Their Applications

Crime Linkage is the practice of connecting two or more criminal cases by analyzing the perpetrator's crime scene behavior and MO. Like all deductive crime investigation methods, variations of crime linkage exist for different applications. The United Kingdom defines two distinct methods of crime linkage, case linkage analysis (CLA) and comparative case analysis (CCA). CLA is when the hypothesis of multiple offenses being linked is presented to a crime analyst to determine whether they are truly linked. As an example, an investigator noticing similarities between four different murder cases targeting gay men may bring the opinion that they were committed by the same offender to an analyst to potentially establish a link. In the United Kingdom, this method is conducted by Behavioral Investigative Advisers. CCA involves actively trawling through databases for crimes that share distinguishable similarities. This method is performed by the United Kingdom's Serious Crime Analysis Section (Davies & Woodhams, 2019).

Woodham, Hollin, and Bull (2007) also distinguish two types of CCA, reactive and proactive. Reactive CCA uses an index crime/series of crimes to search out possible offense links from available databases. For example, after a rape has occurred, analysts will pore through crime databases searching for parallels in offender description, MO, and signature behaviors from other rape cases. Proactive CCA searches through databases for offense similarities without the use of an index crime/series of crimes. Analysts using this method try to establish a series of linked offenses before a particular offense has already been brought to their attention (Davies & Woodhams, 2019).

Offender Consistency

At first glance, crime linkage can be seen as indiscernible from criminal profiling. Both attempt to procedurally identify distinctive behaviors of offenders across multiple crimes, namely their MO and signature. One key distinction crime linkage has from criminal profiling is that it does not create offender assumptions based on the principle of homology. Homology holds that perpetrators who share similar behaviors should resemble each other in the demographic description. Homology is key in criminal profiling's assumption that analysis of an offender's criminal behavior will render a reliable composite of their background characteristics.

Case linkage is based on a two-part hypothesis: that a series of crimes perpetrated by an offender will be both consistent with each other and distinct from the crimes of another offender. The offender consistency hypothesis asserts that offenders will behave with some level of consistency across a crime spree. The offender distinction hypothesis holds that serial offenders will display traits that make their series of crimes unique from offenders who commit similar crimes.

Offender consistency is often challenged by numerous factors that disrupt the uniformity of a crime series, such as offender mood, victim behavior, intoxication, temporal proximity, and experience (Woodhams & Bennell, 2015). An example of this could be the crime spree of Altemio Sanchez. Sanchez would target lone women and girls along bike paths in and around Buffalo, New York, in which they were strangled with a ligature, beaten, and raped, often with the perpetrator expressing remorse after the attack. These MO and signature behaviors were used to link a dozen rapes and two murders to the same attacker. It took a DNA match to link his third murder victim, a sex worker he raped and asphyxiated, to the crime series. The attack was starkly inconsistent with Sanchez's MO, the woman knew him and while raping her he decided to kill her to keep her silenced. She wasn't assaulted and murdered on a bike path but was dumped near train tracks. This crime was inconsistent with the other because of differences in factors, including his relationship with the victim, the setting in which the offense occurred, and the altered circumstances of his encounter with the victim (Vaughan, Trahan & Krebs, n.d.) (Fahim & Staba, 2007).

The measure of how distinct a series of crimes are rests on how attributable the events of the offense are to the offender's personality and behavior, and how much is contextual to the environmental factors present in the event (i.e., victim behavior, setting of the offense, intoxication, time of day, etc.). The belief that behavior is the result of the interaction between a person and environmental factors is called interactionism. Mischel and Shoda's (1995) Cognitive-Affective Personality System (CAPS) formalized the concept. CAPS is a crucial concept in CLA as it applies to both consistency and distinctiveness in human behavior. It can also provide predictions on when consistency and distinctiveness are most likely to be observed. This can be empirically investigated to determine whether these predictions are applicable to criminal behavior and case linkage practices. The CAPS model proposes that the everyday situations an individual encounters contain factors of psychological importance that impact them on a cognitive and emotional level. Why and how these factors impact their behavior will depend on various aspects of their background, personality, and situational awareness (Woodhams & Bennell, 2015).

Applying the CAPS model to criminal behavior can be challenging for a number of reasons. In the case of serial offending, offenders perpetrate multiple crimes, typically against multiple victims. Because of this, each offense is considered a unique situation that provides varying challenges and contexts to the offender, as well as a variety of environmental factors that will impact their CAPS. Despite this, however, it is still possible to observe distinct and consistent behavior across this spectrum of chaotic incidents. Serial offenders often have preferential targets, and this preference allows them some exertion of control over the environmental variables they will encounter. The early stages of an offender's MO can ensure some similarity, such as when a trapper-style offender uses subterfuge or charm to entice a victim to a more vulnerable location. In the case of interpersonal offenses such as rape and murder, in which the offender is typically targeting a new victim with every offense, there are a finite number of responses victims can issue when being faced with an attack. This limits the range of unique offense demands the offender will contend with over the course of their crime series, likely rendering similar offender responses in these incidents. However, these are only mitigating factors in assessing consistency throughout a crime series. Notably, offenders have been known to shift behaviors with different victims through their offense series. For example, some rapists have been known to treat victims differently based on their perceivable differences (Woodhams & Bennell, 2015).

Offender Fantasy

Sexual fantasy is the deliberate withdrawal of an individual from the stress of the external into an imaginative and internal world defined by concentrated and erotic desires that create or intensify the individual's state of arousal. Deviant sexual fantasy is scored by paraphilic desires, ranging from sadism and violent sexual expression; illegal fetishes like pedophilia and rape; and socially taboo behaviors like voyeurism, exhibitionism, humiliation, and degradation. In the context of its commission in criminal behavior, offense-focused fantasy has been conceived to distinguish the preparatory sexual fantasies of sexual predators from deviant fantasies of non-offenders. The core sexual fantasies of an individual are theorized to be adopted from basic themes and incidents experienced early in life. A sexual fantasy script is a "collection of rules for predicting, interpreting, responding to, and controlling a set of interpersonal scenes that are meaningful to an individual." Repetition develops incongruous sexual imagery into a consolidated sexual fantasy script. These scripts are composed of a number of important facets, such as the sexual behavior occurring in the fantasy, the situation and setting in which the fantasy is occurring, how the various participants in the fantasy are related, the characteristics of those fantasized about, and the self-perception of the individual within the fantasy. The source material of the sexual fantasy can be sourced simply from the individual's own imagination, or from external factors, such as pornography, childhood abuse, previous sexual experiences, etc. (Woodhams & Bennell, 2015).

The development of offense-based sexual fantasies leads to the creation of an offense script, through which the offender will obsessively return over and over, slowly generating an attack plan for their real-world crimes. The offender's frequent withdrawals into this fantasy will allow them to zero in on aspects that they find most gratifying, slowly modifying the fantasy into the true, fully realized sexual desire they wish to act upon. Once the offender acts upon their aberrant sexual fantasy, each victim and the circumstances of their victimization become new components of the fantasy. Upon repetition with more victims, the offender will likely escalate over time to experience new and increased stimulation upon their next offense. Research has found that offense-focused sexual fantasies often influence and/or structure an offender's MO (Woodhams & Bennell, 2015).

It is theorized that sexual fantasy provides a reasonable explanation for the consistency observed between linked cases, as the situation-independent factors in which the offender can maintain control are the most likely to display a high level of consistency. Repetition of these offenses gives offenders more experience, allowing them to bend situations to their will. This means that consistent behaviors observed in familiar situations are more likely to reflect the offender's fantasy than environment-dependent factors. One particular challenge associated with case linkage is the ability to detect behavioral shifts or graduation. The evolution of an offender's sexual fantasy can lead to pattern shifts in their crime series, making it imperative for crime linkage processes to consider behavioral changes. In the early offenses in a series, the offender can find themselves struggling to manage the external factors of the event and find difficulty properly working their fantasy into the crime. This can result in frustration, leading the offender to further alter their MO to achieve their fantasy, or in the offender losing control and adopting higher risk behaviors in a desperate bid for sexual release (Woodhams & Bennell, 2015). Harbort and Mokros (2001) found in their research that significant behavioral shifts occurred most commonly between the first and second offenses, with the third offense commonly resembling the second. They also found that for some rapists, an escalation of violence between their first and second rape correlated with an increased level of sadism in their sexual fantasies.

To account for temporal shifts in an offender's sexual fantasy, a tripartite model was developed to measure and illuminate the function, content, and structural properties of offense-focused sexual fantasies across an offense series. The balance between consistency and change is often dictated by which phase of the offense chain the perpetrator is in, being background, pre-lapse, lapse, initial offense, or post-offense. This can also be impacted by whether the offender is committing their first offense, a subsequent offense, or is in a post-offense period, possibly because they have been incarcerated. In some instances, the evolution of an offender's sexual fantasy can lead to the devolution of their crime series, as an over-emphasis on an increasingly intricate and complex sexual fantasy can result in neglect of important MO factors and slippage in the offender's execution of their offense (Gee & Belofastov, 2007).

Effectiveness and Accuracy of Linkage Analysis

A literature review conducted by Davies and Woodham (2019) found that the accuracy of the case linkage process was wide-ranging in performance and was largely reliant on the types of observable behaviors that practitioners prioritized when conducting a CLA. A study conducted by Santtila, Korpela, and Häkkänen (2004) displayed that car crime experts found more reliable results when considering fewer variables, focusing on offender vehicle type, time, location, or chains of thefts. Participants who focused on the type or extent of property stolen more frequently found errors in their case linkage. Davies and Woodham note that all of the studies share major limitations, including an absence of any description as to which particular crime linkage method they used, and that the tasks given to participants in the studies were simplified from the real-life processes undertaken by case linkage analysts. While these studies may grant some insight into the efficacy of case linkage, Davis and Woodham maintain there can be no certainty that these studies accurately reflect the validity they achieve in practice, nor the factors that may impact that validity.

Use of Computers with Crime Linkage

The use of computerized databases is a crucial element of crime linkage analysis. Without the use of such databases, the ability to link two cases would be extremely strained. Through a critical review of criminal databases, Bennell, Snook, MacDonald, House, and Taylor (2012) found four key factors that impact the efficacy of crime databases. The first is the reliability of the data entered, which they posit can be tested by determining a high degree of inter-rater reliability of data coded by various analysts. The second is that the data needs to be accurate, and the third is that the data needs to be reflective of both distinction and consistency. Finally, the data needs to be conducive to analysts' ability to determine the linkage between cases. The inter-rater reliability of the Canadian database ViCLAS was tested by Martineau and Corey (2008) and replicated by Snook, Luther, House, Bennell, and Taylor (2012). Martineu and Corey found encouraging results in participants' inter-rater reliability when coding a homicide case at 79.30% and 87.70% for a sexual assault case. However, the percentage occurrence agreement (POA; the percentage of times raters agree that information is present) and percentage non-occurrence agreement (PNOA; the percentage of times raters agree information is absent) results were of much lower performance, with a total POA of 38.43% and 25.38% and a total PNOA of 54.67% and 68.80%, respectively. Snook, Luther, House, Bennell, and Taylor used real-world cases instead of fictional ones, which were given to participants to code. Measuring only POA, they found a similarly low score of 30.77 agreement overall. Finally, Davies, Imre, and Woodhams (2021) conducted another replication, using a Belgian Federal Police unit as a participant. This was to analyze the difference in international coding using ViCLAS, as Canadian coders are the officers conducting the investigation, while European countries like Belgium employ specialized crime analysts confined to a centralized unit. The results of this study were more positive, with a total POA of 55.80% and a total PNOA of 88.99%. The results of this study demonstrate that the transference of criminal behavior into quantifiable data is complex and difficult, and that the best remedy is expert analysts and experience-based familiarity with databases like ViCLAS. Davies, Imre, and Woodhams identify that these studies only analyze the first part of the coding process, with the potential reliability improvement of quality control processes still unstudied.

Conclusion

This chapter has demonstrated that the efficacy and accuracy of crime linkage can be highly variable depending on the context of available data and the quality of the analyst's expertise.

However, there is still a critical lack of replicated peer-reviewed studies to layout a concrete conclusion as to the efficacy of case linkage as it exists in real-world applications. Future research should include disclosure of the type of crime linkage process used to better compare how effective each method is. Future studies should also set up tests that more closely simulate the actual process of crime linkage over a simplified version to ensure higher validity. Finally, future research should consider the entirety of the coding process when analyzing the use of computerized databases for case linkage to better identify the error rate when logging data and linking cases.

References

Bennell, C., Snook, B., Macdonald, S., House, J. C., & Taylor, P. J. (2012). Computerized Crime Linkage Systems. *Criminal Justice and Behavior*, *39*(5), 620–634. https://doi.org/10.1177/0093854811435210

Canter, D.V., & Youngs, D. (2003). Beyond offender profiling: The need for an investigative psychology. In R. Bull & D. Carson (Eds.), *Handbook of psychology in legal contexts* (2nd ed.,) pp. 171–206). Wiley.

Davies, K., Imre, H., & Woodhams, J. (2021). The utility of the violent crime linkage analysis system for conducting comparative case analysis. *Journal of Criminological Research, Policy and Practice*, *7*(1), 77–90. https://doi.org/10.1108/jcrpp-02-2020-0019

Davies, K., & Woodhams, J. (2019). The practice of Crime Linkage: A review of the literature. *Journal of Investigative Psychology and Offender Profiling*, *16*(3), 169–200. https://doi.org/10.1002/jip.1531

Fahim, K., & Staba, D. (2007, January 18). *The suspect in 3 murders and 8 rapes blended in*. The New York Times. https://www.nytimes.com/2007/01/18/nyregion/18bike.html

Gee, D., & Belofastov, A. (2007). Profiling sexual fantasy. *Criminal Profiling*, 49–71. https://doi.org/10.1007/978-1-60327-146-2_3

Harber, E., Deslauriers-Varin, N, Beauregard, E. & Van Der Kemp, J.J. (2012). Testing the behavioural environmental consistency of serial sex offenders: A signature approach. *Journal of Investigative Psychology and Offender Profiling*, *9*, 259–273.

Harbort, S., & Mokros, A. (2001). Serial murderers in Germany from 1945 to 1995. *Homicide Studies*, *5*(4), 311–334. https://doi.org/10.1177/1088767901005004005

Hazelwood, R.R., & Warren, J.I. (2003). Linkage analysis: Modus operandi, ritual, and signature in serial sexual crime. *Aggression and Violent Behavior*, *8*, 587–598.

Koegl, C.J., & Farrington, D.P. (2022). Advancing knowledge about motivations for criminal offending. *Victims & Offenders*, *17*, 313–334.

Leclerc, B., Beauregard, E., & Proulx, J. (2008). Modus operandi and situational aspects in adolescent sexual offenses against children. *International Journal of Offender Therapy and Comparative Criminology*, *52*, 46–61.

Leonard, D. (2001). Character and motive in evidence law. *Loyola of Los Angeles Law Review*, January, 439–546.

Martineau, M. M., & Corey, S. (2008). Investigating the reliability of the Violent Crime Linkage Analysis System (viclas) crime report. *Journal of Police and Criminal Psychology*, *23*(2), 51–60. https://doi.org/10.1007/s11896-008-9028-5

Mischel, W., & Shoda, Y. (1995). A cognitive-affective system theory of personality: Reconceptualizing situations, dispositions, dynamics, and invariance in personality structure. *Psychological Review*, *102*(2), 246–268. https://doi.org/10.1037//0033-295x.102.2.246

Petherick, W.A., & Turvey, B.E. (2008). Criminal motivation. In B.E. Turvey (Eds.), *Criminal profiling: An introduction to behavioral evidence analysis* (pp. 273–307). Elsevier.

Santtila, P., Korpela, S., & Häkkänen, H. (2004). Expertise and decision-making in the linking of car crime series. *Psychology, Crime & Law*, *10*(2), 97–112. https://doi.org/10.1080/10683160210000030559

Schlesinger, L.B., Kassen, M., Mesa, V.B., & Pinizzotto, A.J. (2010). Ritual and signature in serial sexual homicide. *Journal of American Academy of Psychiatry and the Law*, *38*, 239–246.

Snook, B., Luther, K., House, J. C., Bennell, C., & Taylor, P. J. (2012). The Violent Crime Linkage Analysis System. *Criminal Justice and Behavior*, *39*(5), 607–619. https://doi.org/10.1177/0093854811435208

Turvey, B.E. (2008). Offender *modus operandi* and signature. In B.E. Turvey (Eds.), *Criminal profiling: An introduction to behavioral evidence analysis* (pp. 309–356). Elsevier.
Vaughan, B. P., Trahan, A., & Krebs, K. (n.d.). *Altemio C. Sanchez.* Maamodt. http://maamodt.asp.radford.edu/Psyc%20405/serial%20killers/Sanchez,%20Altemio.pdf
Woodhams, J., & Bennell, C. (2015). *Crime linkage: Theory, research, and Practice*. CRC Press, Taylor & Francis Group.
Woodhams, J., Hollin, C. R., & Bull, R. (2007). The psychology of linking crimes: A review of the evidence. *Legal and Criminological Psychology*, 12, 233–249. https://doi.org/10.1348/135532506x118631

4 Victimology

Nicholas Stone and Kevin Borgeson

Introduction

Discussions on offender profiling often tend to focus on the perpetrator, analyzing their crimes, their MO, and their signature behaviors. In media, profiling a series of crimes is often portrayed as a brilliant profiler getting into the mind of a serial offender, thinking like they do in order to catch them. Understanding the MO and signature of the perpetrator is an important aspect of profiling and case linkage, but victimology is an incredibly understated aspect of the process which is critical in conducting a thorough profile with a high likelihood of accuracy. There isn't an offense without a victim, and if the victim is ignored, then very little will be understood about the crime.

Definition

The simple definition of victimology is that it is the analytic study of victims. The term in its general application can refer to victims of any circumstance, including crime, accidents, or natural disasters. Victims are defined as individuals who have suffered harm, loss, injury, or death (Turvey). Victimology examines all relevant aspects of a victim; their lifestyle, behavior, and personality are all analyzed. As it relates to offender profiling, victims of crime are those that are analyzed. The definition of victimology can be expanded to focus on many particular aspects of victimization. One definition could be that victimology focuses on how victims become victimized. Examples could include examining the factors that lead to sex workers being victims of physical or sexual violence or analyzing the socio-political aspects that influence spikes in hate crimes against particular vulnerable groups. Another potential definition of victimology can pertain to examining the relationship between an offender and their victim. Regardless of the particular definition of victimology that is applied, understanding a victim—the aspects of their personality and way of life—is a critical aspect of any criminal investigation.

Theory

The study of victims is largely considered to have begun with the research of Hans von Hentig and Benjamin Mendelsohn, often referred to as the "fathers of victimology." The studies of von Hentig and Mendelsohn between the 1930s and 1950s focused on the nexus between victim characteristics and the commission of criminal acts, and the possibility that they may even precipitate it. Mendelsohn developed a typology of six different victim types to describe their role in the commission of the crime. Von Hentig would expand on this research by developing his own typology of six victims who caused the crime to occur. This research would later serve as the foundation of Victim Precipitation Theory (Ressler, Burgess, & Douglas, 1988, p. 7).

DOI: 10.4324/9781003366300-5

The work of von Hentig and Mendelsohn was later adapted by Marvin Wolfgang to develop the concept of victim-precipitated criminal homicide. Wolfgang's theory does not accuse victims of being at fault for their victimization, but holds that the circumstances of a victim-offender relationship or interaction manifest into the conditions that precipitate the victim's death (Pettler & Pettler, 2021, pp. 106–207).

Another important victim theory is Lifestyle Exposure Theory. Lifestyle Exposure Theory posits that individuals of certain demographic profiles are likelier to experience victimization because the nature of their lifestyles exposes them to dangerous situations. Particularly, it has less to do with the lifestyle itself, and more with the exposure those lifestyles generate that increases the risk of victimization. For example, sex work can be considered a high-risk lifestyle. People who engage in sex work are not at a higher risk of victimization simply because they are sex workers, but because engaging in sex work exposes them to potentially risky situations with clients who may be dangerous (Hindelang et al., 1978).

Similarly, Routine Activity Theory (RAT) also posits that exposure to a risky situation increases an individual's likelihood of being victimized. However, RAT puts forward elements different from lifestyles that precipitate the exposure. According to the theory, crime is likely to occur when three key elements of crime converge in space and time: a vulnerable or attractive target, a motivated offender, and a lack of capable guardianship (Cohen & Felson, 1979; Cohen et al., 1981). The last main victimology theory is Deviant Place Theory. Like Lifestyle Exposure Theory and RAT, Deviant Place Theory proposes that victimization is a by-product of exposure. In this instance, exposure to dangerous settings precipitates the commission of the crime. Simply being in a "bad part of town" may be enough for an individual to find themselves the victim of a crime (Seigel, 2006).

General Guidelines

There is no single template that should be used when constructing a victimology. When constructing a victimology, a profiler must analyze each evident characteristic and make note of it. These characteristics should be compared to those of other victims to test for patterns. While aspects of a victim and their life will always be relevant, like factors that determine their typical risk level, it is always a possibility that unusual traits will be important in understanding why this victim was targeted, and which other cases, if any, the case may be tied to. An example would be a series of child killings in Rochester, New York, in the early 1970s known as the Alphabet Murders. Three young girls were abducted, sexually assaulted, and strangled to death. What made the case unusual, however, was that all three girls had surnames that began with the same letter as their first name and were dumped in villages or towns outside Rochester beginning with the same letter as their names. Although there is some debate as to whether all three cases were committed by the same perpetrator, the aspect of the letters remains a perplexing and quite possibly crucial element to the murders that easily could have been discarded from a typical victimology (Kahn, 2020).

One useful template that covers many of the basics of forming a victimology of homicide victims comes from the NIJ's *National Guidelines for Death Investigation*, Section E: "Establishing and Recording Decedent Profile Information." The template can be divided into five major steps:

- Document the Discovery History: Document information covering who discovered the body, what circumstances of discovery were, where the body was discovered, when the body was discovered, and how the discovery of the body was made.

- Determine Terminal Episode History: It is important for the profiler to obtain records of the victim's pre-terminal circumstances and medical treatment to distinguish medical history from trauma. Distinguishing these two factors aids the medical examiner in determining the cause and manner of death.
- Document Decedent Medical History: Establishing a thorough medical history allows investigators to focus their investigation and helps to determine if post-mortem examination or other laboratory analysis is necessary.
- Document Decedent Mental Health History: Establishing the mental health history of the victim allows for the proper evaluation of their state of mind and contributes to the determination of the cause, manner, and circumstances of their death.
- Document Social History: Information pertaining to the victim's social history obtained from reliable sources can be helpful in determining the cause, manner, and circumstances of death. Helpful social history information includes marital, family, sexual, educational, employment, and financial information, their friends and associates, and their daily routines, habits, and activities.

(National Institute of Justice, 1999, pp. 39–43)

The following is a non-exhaustive list of basic victimological queries that a profiler should consider and attempt to rectify when constructing a victimology. Again, there is no single template a profiler should rely upon when building their victimology; the profiler must be prepared to explore each and every aspect of a victim's life and history, treating nothing as trivial and with no preconceived theories.

- Determine the hard physical characteristics of the victim. This includes but is not limited to race, weight, height, hair color, eye color, etc.
- Determine the occupation or place of work of the victim, as well as their shift schedule.
- Compile all details of the victim's criminal history.
- Compile psychosexual history. Should be gathered from friends, relatives, and acquaintances.
- Develop a list of all the daily routines, habits, and activities of the victim.
- Compile an exhaustive list of the victim's family members, friends, coworkers, peers, and any other apparent associates, along with their contact information. Each of these individuals should be interviewed.
- Compile all records of the victim's medical history.
- Compile all records of the victim's psychiatric history; all of the victim's mental health care providers should be interviewed.
- Compile a list of the victim's past and present medications. Compare this with the victim's known toxicology.
- Compile all information on the victim's financial history (credit card usage, tax returns, etc.).
- Compile the details of the victim's educational history.
- Compile the victim's residential history. This would include where they have lived, when, and with whom, etc.
- Spend time in the victim's personal environments, such as hangouts, work, school, home/bedroom, etc. Examine the personal items of the victim, such as photo albums, diaries, or journals. Learn more about the media the victim enjoyed, such as movies, TV, music, video games, and books. Examining this information tells the profiler who the

victim believed they were, who they wanted to be, how they wanted to be perceived by others, and how they may have felt about their lives.
- Compile all available information regarding the victim's activities online and on their computer. The following are specific details that should be sought after.
- The victim's ISP.
- The victim's email addresses.
- The victim's address book/contact database.
- The victim's incoming and outgoing e-mail.
- All documents on the victim's computer.
- The computer and various software applications that are last known to have been used by the victim.
- A timeline of the victim's last known activities should be constructed.
- Travel the last known route taken by the victim before they were attacked. Try to observe the surroundings both from the perspective of the victim and the perspective of the offender.
- Try to find any CCTV cameras that may have captured the victim's last known activities or the actual crime itself.

(Turvey, 2002; Holmes & Holmes, 2009)

One useful guideline that can help with the construction of a solid victimology was developed by Weston and Wells (1974, p. 97). This checklist provides preliminary questions that the profiler should focus on when searching for useful investigative information. This is all information that should be gathered as soon as possible.

- Was the victim familiar with the offender?
- Does the victim suspect anybody? If so, why?
- Does the victim have a criminal history or a history of reporting any crimes?
- Did the victim possess a weapon?
- Did the victim have an aggressive personality?
- Has the victim ever been named in any previously filed police field reports?

Timelines

One of the most critical aspects of constructing a victimology is constructing a timeline of the victim's last known whereabouts and actions. Creating a timeline allows the profiler to form a better and more concise understanding of the victim's personality, understanding their relationship toward the events and environments around them, and how they became targeted and accosted by the offender. The steps to construct a timeline are as follows:

- Assemble all accessible forensic and factual data.
- Examine and compile all crime scene photographs.
- Compile all available witness data.
- Produce a timeline of the events and locations surrounding the victim before and during their victimization.
- Produce a map of the victim's whereabouts for the 24 hours prior to the incident, in as much detail as possible. The profiler should physically walk through the whereabouts the victim occupied in the last 24 hours to gain context and insight. They should use the map and available forensic evidence and crime scene photographs to guide them.

- The profiler should document all background elements they observe along the route of the victim's last known whereabouts. This should include a list of people, vehicles, businesses, and events they witness. In addition, the profiler should try and record which of these background elements were present before and during the attack on the victim. There is a distinct possibility that the perpetrator is or could be associated with one or more of these elements. For example, if the victim was attacked near a venue where a concert was occurring, the offender could have attended the concert. Given that offenders often have a tendency to revisit crime scenes, another example could be that if a person or vehicle is witnessed at the scene both before, during, and or after the attack, that they could be the perpetrator.

A well-constructed timeline implementing these steps should prove a helpful tool in determining the following.

- At which point the offender accosted the victim.
- Which place the offender accosted the victim.
- How secluded the location of the attack was. Would the attack have been visible to people in surrounding locations?
- If the offender would have to have specific knowledge of the area to know of this specific location or how to get to it.
- If accosting the victim would require knowledge of the victim's schedule, and if so who would be familiar with their schedule.
- If the offender did have knowledge of their routine, did they stalk the victim in order to achieve that knowledge?
- If this route puts the victim at a higher risk or lower risk of victimization.
- If accosting the victim on that route or in that particular place would put the offender at higher risk or lower risk of being identified, injured, interrupted, or apprehended (Turvey, 2002).

Risk Assessment

One of the most important aspects of developing a victimology is uncovering the risk involved in the case. Risk refers to the level of possibility of suffering injury or loss. When developing a victimology, risk is divided into two major categories: victim risk and offender risk. These are differentiated by the perspective being considered. Victim risk refers to the level of possibility prescribed by a profiler that the victim would be victimized. Perpetrator risk is the level of possibility that the offender will be caught or suffer some other form of harm or loss when attempting to offend against a victim.

Victim Risk

Victim risk is categorized into three distinct classifications: *low risk, medium risk, and high risk*. A low-risk victim is an individual whose lifestyle would not put them at high likelihood of being victimized. A medium-risk victim lives a lifestyle that exposes them to possible victimization, but not to the degree of a high-risk victim. A high-risk victim would live a lifestyle that would put them at continuous risk of being victimized. (Hazelwood, 1995). An important note about these classifications is that they are not simultaneously applicable to all forms of victimization. For example, a woman living with a violent and abusive partner may be at high risk of being a victim of domestic violence, but will not necessarily be at high risk of being abducted and murdered by a stranger.

Furthermore, victim risk is not a constant state, but fluctuates over time and is influenced by context. Victim risk can be further subdivided into two distinct categories, victim lifestyle risk and victim incident risk. Victim lifestyle risk is defined as the overall risk that a victim is open to due to their personal, social, and professional environments, as well as their personality and behavior. Certain environments, professions, and life circumstances are more conducive to victimization, and certain personality traits and mental health conditions have the potential to be aggravating or mitigating factors. A victim with a low lifestyle risk will have a profession and live in environments that do not lend themselves to the potential of victimization and are unlikely to have personality or mental health issues that may make them more ideal victims. A prominent example of low-risk victims would be those who were targeted by serial killer Dennis Rader. Rader's victims were usually women, and in one case, an entire family. The victims mostly lived in the suburbs of Wichita, which were low-crime areas not typically conducive to victimization. The victims had solid living situations, with professions and lifestyles that would not typically put them into high-risk situations. None of the victims were characterized as having reckless personalities or mental health issues that would instigate their victimization or impair their ability to respond to the situation (Ott, 2021).

A victim with a high lifestyle risk will have a profession or exist in environments that will have a higher likelihood of putting them in contact with dangerous criminal elements or leave them more vulnerable in the incident of being attacked by an offender. They will also likely have personality and mental health issues that may lead them into more high-risk situations or impede their ability to react when faced with a dangerous situation. An example of high-risk lifestyle victims would be the victims of serial killer Alfred Gaynor. Gaynor targeted female drug addicts who would trade sex for drugs. The circumstances of these women's lives put them at high risk of victimization as they were frequently occupying high-crime areas of Springfield, and would exhibit behaviors that would allow Gaynor to notice and acquire them. Their drug use would also inhibit their ability to fight back or flee when Gaynor would attack them (Deseret News, 2000).

Victim incident risk refers to the risk present toward the victim in the instance in which they are accosted by the offender and is primarily influenced by the circumstances of the victim's environment and their state of mind. There are a number of factors that can determine the risk level of the incident. The first is the victim's lifestyle risk. Lifestyle risk is essential to properly contextualize the incidence of their victimization and properly assess their state of mind. The victim's state of mind before, during, and after the incident is critical information in assessing incident risk. Victims in a heightened state of distress or anxiety may be at a higher incident risk. State of mind can be analyzed by profilers from reliable witness or survivor testimony.

The time of the day the attack occurred is another important factor to consider when assessing risk, although it is highly dependent on the location itself. For example, if the offender chose to attack a victim in a park, the victim would be at higher risk if the assault occurred after dark, as there would be fewer witnesses to intervene or contact authorities, and lack of natural light, which would allow for the attack to be more easily concealed. On the other hand, if a victim was located in some sort of venue or street that is more bustling at night, then the victim would be at higher risk during the day when the location contains fewer potential witnesses. The location itself, regardless of the time of day, is one of the most important aspects of assessing incident risk. Certain locations are more conducive to illegal activity or maybe isolated enough that victims may not be able to escape or seek help.

The use of drugs or alcohol can be a serious factor in increasing the risk of victimization, even for victims who are low lifestyle risk victims. Substances that affect objectivity and performance of the mind will affect the victim's judgment and ability to respond and will likely make them more vulnerable to offenders. The final factor to consider when assessing incident risk is the number of individuals any potential victim is with. Generally speaking, the larger the group that an individual is engaging with, the lower the chance of victimization. However, this can be different if the people the individual is engaging with are not a high-risk lifestyle or high-risk incident individuals. This factor is highly dependent on context.

A working example of a series of high-incident risk victims could be the victims of Peter Sutcliffe. Some of Sutcliffe's victims were sex workers, and most were living in impoverished neighborhoods, making many of them high lifestyle risk victims. Sutcliffe typically attacked his victims at night, on vacant streets and fields, with no other witnesses. Some of Sutcliffe's victims had been under the influence of alcohol at the time of the attacks. All of these factors working in tandem make the majority of Sutcliffe's murders high-risk incidents (Netflix, 2020; Bilton, 2012). An example of low-risk incident victims would be the victims of spree killer and mass murderer Elliot Rodger. Rodger went on a killing spree, first killing three men in a house, then shooting dead two girls near a sorority house, and finally murdering a young man in a deli. Additionally, Rodger injured 14 more people during his rampage. Rodger's final three victims were all killed publicly in populated areas. There is no evidence that any of the victims were under the influence of drugs or alcohol, or that they were in any sort of agitated state of mind before being attacked. All of the victims were seemingly low lifestyle risk victims as well. The only difference with Rodger's first three victims is that they were murdered in an apartment, which isolated the victims from any witnesses and prevented them from seeking aid (Magnoli, 2015).

Offender Risk

When assessing offender risk, the profiler must consider the obstacles that the offender must have perceived in order to accost their victim while avoiding harm, injury, detection, or capture, and how the offender formulated that they would be able to overcome those obstacles. How much risk did the offender believe they were putting themselves in to acquire this particular victim or victims? Offender risk can be divided into two separate categories, *MO risk* and *offender incident risk*.

MO risk refers to the depth and essence of the methods, planning, and precautions exhibited by the offender's behavior before, during, and after the act to both avoid detection or capture and to accomplish their goals. Low MO risk is applicable to perpetrators who exhibit an apt ability to plan their criminal acts and possess the capability and precautionary attitude to accomplish their objectives without being detected by law enforcement. Low MO risk can refer to different aspects of the offender's MO. It could be applied to the offender's choice of victims, being individuals exhibiting high lifestyle risk and may not have people in their lives to miss them if they turn up missing or dead, or individuals who would be less likely to report criminal acts against them if they survived the incident. An example could be the victims of British serial killer Dennis Nilsen. Nilsen's victims were young men living in London, often homeless and gay, and resorting to sex work to make ends meet. Nilsen's murders came at an incredibly homophobic era in the United Kingdom, and many of these men and boys were in London to escape broken homes that did not accept them. Nilsen's victims were of such low MO risk that there was no knowledge of a serial killer preying on men in the area until he was caught and confessed. Nilsen had numerous victims who were able to escape, but because of the homophobic climate in the police force and the lack of support systems in their lives, they never reported the attempted murders until Nilsen went on trial. It is important to note that high-risk victims don't always translate to being low MO risk. For example, a young woman who is close with her family, leaving a bar drunk and alone in a bad neighborhood, may be at high risk, but if she were to go missing, her disappearance would immediately be noticed and investigated. Low MO risk can also be about the attack occurring in a setting that allows the perpetrator to have an elevated level of control over their victim and supplies the isolation and privacy that minimize the offender's risk of being detected. This, too, could apply to Dennis Nilsen's crimes. Although he made mistakes that allowed some victims to escape, Nilsen's apartment still allowed him a position of control over his victims that allowed enough privacy from his neighbors. Nilsen would lure his victims to his apartment with the promise of shelter, alcohol, or food, and strangle them in their sleep before dismembering them and burning their bodies in a bonfire with old tires to mask the stench of burning flesh (Netflix, 2020; D'Averc, 2018).

High MO risk applies to perpetrators who exhibit poor ability to plan their criminal acts and possess low capability and precautionary attitude to accomplish their objectives without being detected by law enforcement. Like low MO risk, high MO risk can apply to different aspects of the perpetrator's MO. High MO risk can apply to the acquiring of victims who will likely be immediately missed, or committing the act in locations where it is of a higher likelihood that the perpetrator could be noticed. It is worth noting that an offender could exhibit a high MO risk in this area, but implement a low risk in the other aspects of their MO. An example could be the serial killer Edmund Kemper. Kemper's victims were often young coeds or teenagers whom he picked up hitchhiking in somewhat public areas where he could have been potentially spotted and remembered. Kemper's victims held enough social capital that their disappearances and murders prompted investigations and social awareness that there was a predator abducting women. Despite this, however, Kemper would still be considered an organized killer, and the other aspects of his MO were low risk. Kemper would take his victims to isolated locations to kill them and would dispose of their bodies in ravines. Kemper took precautions to avoid leaving evidence and heavily studied law enforcement to get ahead of the investigation into his crimes. While Kemper's choice of victim and means of acquiring them were of a high MO risk, the other aspects of his MO were methodically planned and carried out to a degree of efficiency that they would be considered low MO risk (Douglas & Olshaker, 2017; Martingale, 1995).

High MO risk can also be applied to instances where the offender is not careful to conceal their identity during the act, such as letting the victim see their face, attacking victims who know who the perpetrator is or who could be linked to them in the instance of their death or disappearance, or letting victims survive. An example could be serial killer and rapist Altemio Sanchez. Sanchez raped dozens of women along bike paths and wooded areas and murdered three. Many aspects of Sanchez's MO were low risk, such as attacking the victims in isolated areas and making sure to take the weapons he used in the attacks with him. However, Sanchez left the majority of his victims alive and didn't wear a mask during the attacks, so most of the victims saw his face. Sanchez would ultimately become a suspect and be arrested in the case due to one of his victims recognizing him (Vaughan, Trahan & Krebs, n.d.; Edwards, 2017; Fahim & Staba, 2007).

Offender incident risk refers to the likelihood of harm or misfortune befalling the offender when acquiring their victim. This differs from MO risk for several reasons. MO risk is about the offender's perspective. Incident risk does not necessarily account for the offender's perspective but rather is an objective lens to the level of risk that the offender undertook to acquire their victim. It is important to understand what factors an offender considered before, during, and after accosting their victim, and what factors they neglected to consider despite their existence. An example of this could once again be applied to the victims of Peter Sutcliffe. Sutcliffe attacked women under the belief that they were sex workers. However, Sutcliffe attacked numerous women who had no history of sex work, erroneously believing they were sex workers who would likely not be missed. After Sutcliffe murdered a 16-year-old schoolgirl, the investigation into the murder rapidly gained steam and public attention (Netflix, 2020; Bilton, 2012). The importance of assessing offender risk is to understand the perspective of the offender, and how their viewpoint influenced their behavior. These behaviors should then be compared and contrasted with the actual incident risk present to determine the offender's level of comprehension. Not all offenders take protective measures when acquiring their victims, despite the risks being blatant. Similarly, observing the level of risk that some offenders are willing to take up to acquire a certain victim tells a profiler both what an offender's ideal victim is and what means they are willing to encumber to reach their goals.

Victim Blaming and Challenges

An important aspect of assessing victim risk that a profiler must take into account is that there is a fine line between accurately assessing the risk of violence a victim was in and blaming them for their victimization, whether it be inadvertent or on purpose. When it comes to delivering an assessment on a high lifestyle risk victim, tone and objectivity are key. It is undeniable that many assessments of high lifestyle risk victims can sound as if the profiler is blaming a victim for their victimization. The history of victimology, unfortunately, has this bias toward victims deeply ingrained into it. Mendelsohn's research and victim typology explicitly blame victims for the commission of criminal acts. This research was later adapted into Victim Precipitation Theory, which posits that crimes are precipitated by the actions of the victim (Ressler, Burgess, & Douglas, 1988, p. 7). While victimology has evolved from this point, this perspective that victims precipitate their victimization and are consequently to blame for their misfortune still persists in law enforcement, the news media, and the public at large.

Sex work and drug addiction are typically products of a victim's agency, so it can easily be viewed as saying it's their fault for being victimized because the choices they made put them at higher risk. Of course, this is untrue, as victims hold no responsibility for the actions of predators. Unfortunately, victims have routinely been blamed for their assaults and deaths throughout history, and often still are today. Many investigations into serial killers and sexual predators have often been derailed by apathy toward victims who investigators regard as either having deserved their fates or being less bad to victimize than other victims. Because of this atmosphere, many victims are reluctant to report crimes against them for fear of revictimization from a legal system and media that regard them with skepticism and intolerance. Victim blaming fails on all fronts. It denies victims and their loved ones the chance to see justice and the ability to heal from their trauma, it allows for a perpetrator to elude capture by continuing to target disenfranchised populations, and it puts future victims at risk. This must be avoided at all costs. Profilers who are unable to reel in any judgment they feel toward a victim, or who do not treat the offenses toward all victims with the appropriate amount of respect and attention, should not have any involvement in the construction of a victimology. In addition, profilers must take into account how the tone of a victimology may be read by investigators and the public. If a serial rapist is targeting sex workers addicted to heroin, those attributes of the victim's lifestyle risk must be included in the victimology. However, careful consideration must be taken to avoid sounding as though this is the fault of the victims. The point of a victimology in this case is to aid law enforcement in investigations and to serve as an alert to potential victims of what precautions they may want to take or to influence victims to come forward with information if they recognize the perpetrator's MO. An apathetic tone could bias investigators, influence potential victims to ignore law enforcement, and shun any victims with valuable information into silence. A victimology must be objective, but must also be empathetic and constructed in the interest of obtaining results.

Likewise to vilifying victims, deifying them as perfect individuals can also be detrimental to an investigation. This decision to deify a victim is often influenced by the political climate and social culture of the region or city where the crime occurred. Deifying victims can often result in allocating more time and funding to certain cases at the expense of cases involving victims who have been vilified. It also produces a biased victimology that may exclude proper context about a victim to better fit the preconceived narrative. This dishonest portrayal of a victim will prove ineffective in an investigation, as a victimology will only be effective if it is based on accurate evidence; otherwise, it is only a waste of expenses that fails all involved, especially the victim (Turvey, 2002).

Both deification and vilification of victims are products of political bias, either the bias of the profiler themselves or pressure applied to the profiler's work by authorities seeking to mitigate the negative image the victimology may generate. The investigation into Peter Sutcliffe would be an excellent example. Although it would appear that Sutcliffe targeted women he believed were sex workers, many of the women he killed had no history of sex work. Regardless, these victims were referred to as such by police anyway because they were poor and single, guiding the assumption that they must be sex workers. Furthermore, multiple women were attacked by Sutcliffe and survived, but because they were not sex workers, their attacks were not considered to be true Yorkshire ripper attacks, and the accounts of survivors who had witnessed Sutcliffe's face were discarded (Netflix, 2020; Bilton, 2012).

Another example could be that of the Atlanta Child Murders. Profiler John Douglas theorized that because the victims were all black children who were abducted from mostly black neighborhoods, the killer would likely be a black male, as he would stand out less while trolling for victims. However, public authorities weren't happy with this theory, as Atlanta was still reeling from a history of segregation and institutional racism, and worried that theorizing the killer was black would result in backlash. This was aggravated by extensive criticism of the police by the black community already for a failure to investigate the cases as being linked earlier. Douglas claims that he was met with a lot of opposition when in Atlanta, with members of law enforcement sometimes telling him the profile was wrong. When Douglas stated that if the suspect Wayne Williams was found to be guilty of the two murders for which he had been charged, he would likely be responsible for a sizable percent of the murders, he was officially censured by the Director of the FBI. Bias is always a danger to criminal investigations, and whether a victimology is squandered by an investigator operating on their own preconceived notions or by kowtowing to authorities more concerned about public appearances, it is always a dangerous form of negligence that can allow a predator to continue to operate.

The case of the Atlanta child murders exposes other major challenges to constructing an adequate victimology: competition and bureaucracy. Douglas notes that as the case was ongoing, everyone seemed to want to be the one who caught the killer, and each agency involved was competing for the credit. Douglas claims there was friction with the Atlanta PD, who didn't want anybody stealing their show. This partially also links back to the issue of political pressure, as the Atlanta PD had already been criticized by the media and community for their slow arrival to a coordinated investigation, and likely felt it was incumbent on them to solve the case and restore the faith in local law enforcement and leadership (Douglas, 2017).

Bureaucracy was also a fatal flaw that dragged out the investigation. After a public search of a road for bodies that turned up no leads, the killer proceeded to dump a body on the road after it had been searched. Douglas noted that this was a stark difference in offender incident risk and that the killer was clearly following the media and investigation, and adopting high-risk behaviors to prove his intelligence over the police. Douglas proposed to use the narcissism of the killer to their advantage by creating setups to lure in the killer, including putting up private security notices for a charity concert organized for the victim's families and setting up crosses at a public vigil near body dump sites that the killer may try to revisit. However, neither of these plans came to fruition as red tape and lengthy waits for approval squandered time until it was too late (Douglas, 2017). Another case example where bureaucratic shortcomings challenged an investigation was the case of serial killer Ted Bundy. Bundy went to far lengths to dump his victims far apart, often in different counties and killed across multiple states. The police agencies responsible for each investigation didn't communicate properly with other jurisdictions to compare the victimology and potentially link cases, which allowed Bundy to operate unnoticed (RadicalMedia, 2019; Rule, 2022).

Inductive/Deductive

Victimology methods can be divided into two key types, inductive and deductive. The deductive approach begins with general questions before narrowing down to specialized questions in regard to the specific incident. Deductive methods begin by developing a theory and then proceed toward the development of a testable hypothesis. Approaching a victimology using a deductive method can be considered a sort of "top-down" approach. A deductive victimology requires special education and training in forensic science and the reconstruction of the crime scene. The deductive approach tends to be more specific than the inductive method, with the goal being to provide aid in accomplishing the primary objectives of the investigation process. The victimology processes that have been covered in this chapter thus far have been primarily deductive in nature, with the key goal being to find specific results pertinent to the investigation. There are inductive qualities to these processes, however. Risk of victimization by its very nature is defined by the possibility of suffering harm and or loss. This process requires the examination of specific victim circumstances and comparing them to other similar victim circumstances.

Inductive victimology methods differ from deductive methods in that it is an empirically based approach where conclusions are obtained from scientific analysis. Inductive reasoning is from the specific to the general. For example, inductive profiling obtains accepted principles about the behavior of serial rapists through the empirical examination of a large number of solved cases. As opposed to the deductive method, which begins with assumptions about the observable behavior, the inductive process relies on the data gathered to be empirically analyzed and subsequently to support a theory. An important step in the inductive process is to formalize operational definitions (hypotheses) to be tested. Once completed, coding the data for statistical analysis comes next. Subsequently, the results of this statistical analysis are to be supported with theories (Turvey, 2002; Rubtcova, Pavenkov & Pavenkov, 2017).

Case Study: Boston Strangler

Now that we have laid out the tools for constructing a thorough victimology, let's apply these principles to a real case. The Boston Strangler case is a particularly puzzling one. The alleged serial killer terrorized the city of Boston between 1962 and 1964 and left a total of 13 women dead. The killer would seemingly be let into the homes of his victims willingly, before attacking them, sexually assaulting them, and, in most cases, strangling them to death. Applying victimology to this case immediately reveals the challenge of treating the murders as being committed by a single perpetrator. Serial killers may deviate from their patterns, but typically, there is some consistency in the type of victim targeted. The Boston Strangler is unusual in that there are two very distinct victim types, elderly white women, and young women of various races. The first six victims of the strangler killings were Anna Slesers, Mary Mullen, Nina Nichols, Helen Blake, Ida Irga, and Jane Sullivan. All six of these initial victims held a lot of similarities. All of the women were Caucasian and lived alone. They were all between the ages of 56 and 85. These similarities are very significant and, paired with the similarity in MO, it's a sound conclusion that these killings were committed by the same offender or offenders. However, this consistency in victim targets would become muddled as the case continued.

The next victim was Sophie Clark, a young African American woman who was only 20. Both the race and age of the victim are sharply different from the previous victims. Additionally, unlike the other victims, Clark did not live alone. The next victim was also young, Patricia Bissette, who was 23, although she was also white like the previous victims. The next reported victim was once again an elderly white woman, Mary Brown, who was 69. The next victim in the reported sequence was Beverly Samans, another young Caucasian woman at the age of 26. Killed next was Evelyn Corbin, the final older Caucasian woman murdered in the series, who was 58. The final two victims attributed to the Boston Strangler murders were Joann Graff and Mary Sullivan, both of whom were young Caucasian women; Graff was 22 and Sullivan was 19.

Now let's attempt to apply the tools of this chapter to these cases. This will be limited in scope as the only information available is public information, so many aspects of the victim's personal lives and the contextual conditions of the 1960s Boston area neighborhoods where these crimes were committed may not entirely be accessible to us for this exercise. First, let's discuss the similarities and differences between the victims. The most notable aspects of these victims are the hard physical characteristics, especially the race and age of the victims. The victims can effectively be divided into three categories. The first category would be older Caucasian women, which includes the initial six victims, Anna Slesers, Mary Mullen, Nina Nichols, Helen Blake, Ida Irga, and Jane Sullivan, as well as Mary Brown and Evelyn Corbin. All these victims were between the ages of 56 and 85. The second category was young Caucasian women, which included Patricia Bissette, Beverly Samans, Joann Graff, and Mary Sullivan. These victims are between the ages of 19 and 26. That means there was a 30-year difference between the oldest of the younger victims and the youngest of the older victims. The third category would just be occupied by Sophie Clark, as the only African American victim, and the first young victim attributed to the Boston Strangler. Most of the victims had dark hair and a slim build, and all of the victims lived in the Boston area, either in the city itself or in the surrounding cities of Lawrence, Lynn, Salem, and Cambridge.

First, rudimentary timelines must be constructed for each of the victims. Anna Slesers was seen entering her apartment alone at 5:30 PM alone, before her body was discovered by her son at 7:45 PM on June 14, 1962. Mary Mullen was discovered on June 28, 1962, though neither the time of death nor when her body was discovered was publicly disclosed. At an imprecise time during the afternoon of June 30, 1962, the brother of Nina Nichols attempts to call her, but nobody picks up. Her body was later found at 7:30 PM. Helen Blake was last seen alive at 4:30 PM by her housekeeper on June 29. Her body was discovered at 6 PM on July 2. Her death was believed to have occurred on June 30. Ida Irga was murdered at some point on August 19 and was found at 7:47 PM on August 21. Jane Sullivan was murdered on August 21, 1962, and found ten days later. Sophie Clark was found dead by a roommate at 5:30 PM on December 5, 1962. Patricia Bissette didn't show up to be picked up for work at 8 AM on December 31, and after multiple missed calls, her boss discovered her body after a welfare check later that day. Mary Brown was discovered dead at 8:15 PM on March 3, 1963. Beverly Samans was found dead at 7 PM on May 8, 1963. Evelyn Corbin was last seen alive at 10:30 AM after having breakfast with her neighbor and was discovered dead at 1:00 PM on September 8, 1963. The body of Joann Graff was found at noon on November 24, but she had been murdered the previous day. The body of Mary Sullivan was reported at 6:20 PM on January 4, 1964. She had moved into the apartment four days prior (Kelly, 2013; Thomas, 2013).

For most of the victims, there unfortunately isn't substantial information on their whereabouts 24 hours before the attack. Most of the victims whose times of death could be well approximated were murdered in the late afternoon. The detail of every victim's timeline that remains consistent is that each of the victims was found dead in their residences, either in their bedrooms or living rooms. Because of this, it is likely that the perpetrator accosted them in their residences. Generally speaking, these residences would afford the perpetrator a fair deal of seclusion. The degree of this would depend on a case-by-case basis, depending on factors such as how far noise travels outside of the apartments and proximity to neighbors. However, given there were never any witnesses to the killings themselves purporting to have seen or heard the crime in progress, it would seem the locations gave the killer a great deal of seclusion. It also doesn't suggest that the killer would have to possess a thorough knowledge of the area to commit the crimes. The killer would simply have to locate an apartment building and knock on doors until a woman answered. It would be beneficial for the killer to have knowledge of these areas, as it could give them insight into the potential of security, and witnesses, or would better indicate to them if any victims they would consider ideal resided in those apartments, but these insights are not necessary for the killer to have committed the acts.

Knowledge of the victim's schedules would only be required of the killer if they had particular victims in mind. If, for example, the killer had knowledge of Anna Slesers' schedule and had preselected her as a victim, they would know that her brother was coming to pick her up at 7:45 PM and would have to kill her before then. However, if the killer was knocking on doors until a victim he found suitable answered, specific knowledge of their routine would not have been inherently required for them to commit the crime. If the killer did possess knowledge of his victim's schedules ahead of time, he would likely have had to stalk them, as the victims had no known connections to each other and lived spread out over the city and other nearby cities. This would seem especially unlikely in the early murders, however, as the killer would have had to have stalked four different women all around the same time. Given that all of the victims were found in their apartments and that some of them had absent roommates, it seems most likely that the killer did not possess knowledge of their schedules or stalk them ahead of time, but simply knocked on their doors and attacked when they realized they were alone. The locations, being the homes of the victims, would certainly have been low risk. There's no information to suggest that the residences of any of the victims were in especially high-crime neighborhoods that would have made the victims any likelier to be exposed to dangerous criminal elements. Accosting the victims in these locations would have also been of a relatively lower risk for the perpetrator as well. As stated before, the perpetrator would have had a good degree of seclusion by killing the victims in their apartments. The main risk of being caught would be if a guest or other resident, the perpetrator was unaware of, were to enter. In some instances, this would have served as a considerable risk as some of the victims had roommates or guests that very same day. The risk of being seen and reported otherwise could have been mitigated by seemingly having a valid reason to be in the building, such as posing as a maintenance man or food delivery service. The locations range from low to medium risk of being detected.

The next step is to assess the victim and offender risks. All of the victims, considering the information available to the public, would be considered low risk in all regards. None of the victims were known to have mental health issues, professions, or life circumstances, or existed in environments that would have increased their likelihood of victimization. The only trait the victims may have had that could have made them more ideal victims to the perpetrator is perhaps naivety. This is less based on any known tendencies of the victims to be too trusting, but on the observation that there was no evidence of forced entry in any of the murders, so it is most likely that the victims willingly let their killer inside. However, in all other regards, based on public information, the victims were of low lifestyle risk. Additionally, all of the victims were in low-risk incidents at the time of their sexual assaults and deaths. The setting of the murders was their own homes, which would not pose any significant chance of being victimized. Additionally, there is no evidence that the victims were inebriated or in a compromised state of mind at the time of their deaths.

The MO risk of the strangler could probably be considered high. On one hand, the killer chose victims who would decidedly have a difficult time defending themselves, as they were either exceptionally young or exceptionally old, and would be likely to be easily overpowered by their killer. The killer targeted victims who would be missed and whose deaths would prompt thorough investigations. This is especially notable given that the killer left evidence at many of the crime scenes, most notably semen. If the killer targeted low-risk victims but went to considerable lengths to avoid leaving evidence, their MO would likely be considered of lower risk, but targeting such victims and leaving evidence would make the killer especially careless. The killer would also seemingly exhibit poor planning in how he would attack the victims after entering their homes. In most cases, the victims were strangled with their own clothes fashioned into ligatures, but on one occasion strangled the victim manually, and on two occasions stabbed the victims. The violence seems impulsive, as the killer would attack the victim with whatever they could use at the scene, as opposed to bringing a weapon and taking it with them. As stated before, while no witnesses ever saw the killer, it was certainly possible that the killer could have been interrupted or seen by witnesses before, during, or after the attacks. While the possibility that the offender used a disguise could have mitigated some of these risks, it certainly was a significant risk for the offender during each murder. The incident risk varies by case. Some of the murders had a considerably low incident risk, as the victims were found days later, one victim as late as ten. In other incidents, the victims were found only a couple of hours later, in some cases by the victim's own roommates, who were able to immediately enter the residence. These incidents would have been of a higher risk, especially if the killer truly didn't have any preexisting knowledge about the victims and their schedules and were going in blind without any knowledge of who else may potentially arrive at the apartment (Kelly, 2013; Thomas, 2013).

Conclusion

Serial killers have become an iconic aspect of Western pop culture. Movies, TV series, books, and podcasts all scramble to analyze the lives, minds, and actions of cruel and banal killers and rapists in an attempt to explain and explore how they became murderers. It is often reduced to the old debate of nature versus nurture, whether a serial offender was born that way, or whether their surroundings and influences during their upbringing molded them into murderers. We ask this question as we hope the answer will prevent an individual from devolving into a serial killer. However, if we hope to achieve this goal, perhaps a better question would be to ask how we can prevent individuals from becoming vulnerable to victimization.

Serial offenders most often target individuals who are disenfranchised from society and frequently exposed to dangerous situations. Offenders don't hunt for victims, assault them, and kill them in a vacuum. An argument can be made that if an individual can rape and kill over and over, the offender's intelligence and skill have little to do with it. Rather, it is the biases and incompetency of societal institutions that enable predators and offer them vulnerable victims. In short, serial offenders are not made by society, they are allowed by it. The study of victims not only can be a tool to apprehend offenders but also has the potential to prevent certain individuals from being as susceptible to victimization in the first place.

References

Bilton, M. (2012). *Wicked beyond belief: The hunt for the yorkshire ripper*. Harper Press.

Cohen, L. E., & Felson, M. (1979). Social change and crime rate trends: A routine activity approach. *American Sociological Review*, *44*(4), 588. https://doi.org/10.2307/2094589

Cohen, L. E., Kluegel, J. R., & Land, K. C. (1981). Social inequality and predatory criminal victimization: An exposition and test of a formal theory. *American Sociological Review*, *46*(5), 505. https://doi.org/10.2307/2094935

D'Averc, R. (2018). *Boy under water*. Rhiannon D'Averc.

Deseret News. (2000, May 20). *4 life terms and no parole for handyman in sex killings*. Deseret News. Retrieved September 13, 2021, from https://www.deseret.com/2000/5/20/19507633/4-life-terms-and-no-parole-for-handyman-in-sex-killings

Douglas, J. E., & Olshaker, M. (2017). *Mindhunter: Inside the FBI's Elite Serial Crime Unit*. Pocket Books.

Edwards, N. (2017). Altemio Sanchez. *Born to Kill? Class of evil*. episode, ID Discovery.

Fahim, K., & Staba, D. (2007, January 18). The suspect in 3 murders and 8 RAPES blended in. *The New York Times*. https://www.nytimes.com/2007/01/18/nyregion/18bike.html

Hazelwood, R. (1995). Analyzing the Rape and Profiling the Offender. In A. Burgess, & R. Hazelwood (Eds.), *Practical aspects of rape investigation: A Multidisciplinary approach* (2nd ed.) CRC Press.

Hindelang, M. J., Gottfredson, M. R., Garofalo, J. (1978). *Victims of personal crime: An empirical foundation for a theory of personal victimization*. Ballinger Pub. Co.

Holmes, R. M., & Holmes, S. T. (2009). *Profiling violent crimes: An investigative tool*. Sage Publications.

Kahn, R. (2020, February 6). *Will the double initial murders of upstate New York ever be solved?* A&E. Retrieved September 25, 2021, from https://www.aetv.com/real-crime/double-initial-murders-alphabet-unsolved-child-murders

Kelly, S. (2013). *The Boston stranglers*. Pinnacle Books.

Magnoli, G. (2015, February 19). *Timeline of Isla VISTA Massacre reconstructs a MURDEROUS SEQUENCE*. Noozhawk.com Santa Barbara & Goleta Local News. Retrieved September 13, 2021, from https://www.noozhawk.com/article/timeline_of_isla_vista_massacre_investigation_report

Martingale, M. (1995). *Cannibal killers: The history of impossible murderers*. St. Martin's Press.

National Institute of Justice. (1999). *Death investigation: A guide for the scene investigator*. U.S. Department of Justice, Office of Justice Programs, National Institute of Justice.

Netflix. (2020, December 16). *The Ripper*. Whole, USA. Retrieved September 13, 2021, from https://www.netflix.com/search?q=the%20rip&jbv=81006684

Ott, T. (2021, August 13). BTK killer: A timeline of His MURDERS, reappearance and capture. *Biography.com*. Retrieved September 13, 2021, from https://www.biography.com/news/btk-killer-dennis-rader-timeline

Pettler, L. G., & Pettler, L. G. (2021). Victimology. In *Crime scene staging dynamics in homicide cases* (pp. 105–131). essay, CRC Press.

RadicalMedia. (2019). *Conversations with a Killer: The Ted Bundy Tapes* . Netflix. https://www.netflix.com/search?q=ted&jbv=80226612

Ressler, R. K., Burgess, A. W., & Douglas, J. E. (1988). *Sexual homicide: Patterns and motives*. Lexington Books/D. C. Heath and Com.

Rubtcova, M., Pavenkov, O., & Pavenkov, V. (February 2017). Deductive and Inductive Methods of Crime Scene Investigation. In *Proceedings of the Applied Research in Crime and Justice Conference, Dockside Function Centre, Darling Harbour*, Sydney, 15–16 February 2017, Available at SSRN: https://ssrn.com/abstract=2920823

Rule, A. (2022). *The stranger beside me*. W.W. Norton & Company.

Seigel, L. J. (2006). *Criminology*, 10th Edition. University of Massachusetts, Lowell. Thomson Wadsworth.

Thomas, J. (2013, July 11). *Victims of the boston strangler - the boston globe*. BostonGlobe.com. https://www.bostonglobe.com/metro/2013/07/11/victims-boston-strangler/CwbsZlSNcfwmhSetpqNlhL/story.html

Turvey, B. E. (2002). *Criminal profiling: An introduction to behavioral evidence analysis* (2nd ed.). Academic Press.

Vaughan, B. P., Trahan, A., & Krebs, K. (n.d.). Altemio C. Sanchez. *Maamodt*. http://maamodt.asp.radford.edu/Psyc%20405/serial%20killers/Sanchez,%20Altemio.pdf

Weston, P., & Wells, K. (1974). *Criminal Investigation: Basic Perspectives* (2nd ed.) Prentice-Hall.

5 Organized/Disorganized Offenders

Stephanie Cappadona

Introduction

Violent criminal behavior is a perpetual social concern due to its grave and enduring consequences for individuals and society. Law enforcement at the town, city, state, tribal, and federal levels faces pressure from their communities to control criminal behavior and to apprehend offenders quickly, especially in cases of serial violent crimes. Historically, medical doctors, psychologists, and psychiatrists have been consulted by law enforcement to guide the investigation of a particularly heinous or puzzling murder or series of murders. Beginning in the mid-19th century, alienists—physicians of the time who studied the criminal mind and precursors to psychiatrists and psychologists—were considered expert witnesses and testified in court. Scholars have attempted to uncover the answer to why serial offenders—homicides and other violent crimes—repeatedly commit their crimes. The notion was that if behavioral patterns among like crimes could be determined, serial offenders could be classified into a "type." It was anticipated that if serial criminals could be studied to determine the causes of their behaviors, effective prevention and intervention programs could be developed.

Serial homicides are only a tiny fraction, less than 1%, of total homicides committed in America (Morton et al., 2014). Homicide itself is not in the top three of reported violent crimes. In 2019, the FBI recorded 1,203,808 violent crimes and 6,925,677 property crimes (US Department of Justice, FBI Crime Data Explorer, n.d.). The three most committed violent crimes were aggravated assault, robbery, and rape. The overwhelming majority of property crimes were larceny/theft and burglary. The FBI reported a violent crime rate of 366.7 and a property crime rate of 2,109.9 incidents per 100,000 people. In 2022, the FBI recorded a slight increase in violent crime with a rate of 380.7 and a decrease in property crime with a rate of 1,954.

Any singular act of criminal violence is dreadful and affects those close to the targeted individual, in addition to the neighborhood in which it occurs. A series of criminally violent events had an even broader impact due to the multiplicity of victims. Serial crimes, by their nature, are difficult to quantify. Fox and Zawitz (2007) analyzed FBI crime statistics in their study of trends in homicide in the United States. They concluded that homicides with multiple offenders are a small fraction of the overall homicides committed in the United States. They state it is even rarer still for homicides to include multiple victims. Results showed that there was a steady increase in multiple-victim homicides from 3% to 4.5% of all homicides committed between 1976 and 2004. However, Fox et al. also found that in 2004, when looking at all homicides, 4% involved two victims, but less than 1% for homicides with more than three victims. More recently, Cooper and Smith (2011) analyzed homicide data from 1980 to 2008 and found that those with two victims rose slightly from 2.7% to 3.7%. While still at less than

DOI: 10.4324/9781003366300-6

1%, the authors found that homicides with three or more victims also increased. It is difficult to pinpoint which of these multiple-victim homicides is serial in nature or the result of a mass murder. Was the homicide a single event with several victims or numerous events with one or two victims? Despite the difficulty in determining the true scope of the problem, serial crimes remain a serious social issue.

To learn the motive for serial homicides, convicted serial killers needed to be studied to determine life histories and similarities in behavioral patterns. Combined with psycho-sociobiological theories of aggressive behavior, profiles containing certain traits of the offender can be constructed to assist in serial murder and other serial violent criminal investigations (Sears, 1991).

Brief History of Profiling

Crime scene, personality, and GP have existed in some more rudimentary forms for centuries. Humans have long sought to understand what motivates criminally violent offenders, particularly serial offenders. Most of society cannot fathom the violation of another human through sexual assault, decimating another through torture and sexually sadist murders, inflicting severe pain on another human, or what appear to be senseless acts of repeatedly setting fires. But, at the same time that these heinous behaviors repulse society, it cannot help being enthralled by those who commit serial crimes.

The latter half of the 20th century is referred to as the "golden age" of serial murders in the United States (Vronsky, 2021). According to the Radford University-Florida Gulf Coast University Serial Killer Database, the number of serial killers first increased from double to triple digits (251) in the 1960s. The number of serial murderers continued to rise until a high of 823 serial killers in the 1980s (Aamodt et al., 2023). During this time, many Americans began their morbid fascination with serial killers. Public captivation with violent crime, especially sexually sadist serial murderers, has flourished to this day. However, it was during the "golden age" of serial homicides that the FBI focused its attention on developing a classification system of serial offenders to assist law enforcement in serial crime cases, especially sexual assault and murder cases.

Prior to the death of FBI Director J. Edgar Hoover in 1972, strict limitations on the use of psychology in an official capacity at the FBI existed (Bartol & Bartol, 2013). During the 1970s, a new academy was created at the FBI to train agents and law enforcement with investigative techniques and processes. The BSU was established to study criminal behavior from a criminological, sociological, and psychological perspective. The unit was intended to provide resources and investigative assistance to state and local law enforcement. Crime was increasing, and serial crimes, especially serial murders, were garnering more public attention. Ramsland (2011) states that during the early 1970s, law enforcement recognized the need for enhanced investigative techniques due to the rise in serial murder and stranger criminal incidents. She further explains the process by which Howard Teten contributed to the development of criminal profiling at the FBI. In the early 960s, Teten joined the FBI. Around this same time, he synthesized his psychological education with his experience in police investigations. In an interview with Ramsland, Teten recalls, "I had developed a hypothesis that in certain types of homicides, **you'd be able to determine the kind of person you were looking for by what you could see at the crime scene**" (emphasis in original, Ramsland, 2011, p. 24). Teten, in collaboration with another FBI special agent, Patrick Mullaly, taught other agents an Applied Criminology course that soon morphed into a Psychological Profiling course. After his retirement in 1986, the newly created BAU at the FBI continued to research and advance the profiling process. Special Agents Douglas and Ressler are credited with further developing the FBI criminal profiling process. Douglas and Burgess (1986) define the profiling process as "an investigative technique by which to identify the major personality and behavioral characteristics of the offender based upon analysis crime(s) he or she has committed" (p. 1). An essential component of this criminal profiling is a systemic classification procedure.

Theoretical Framework

To understand how classification systems function, it is necessary to recognize the fundamental theoretical framework involved in the process. Megargee and Bohn (1979) posit that personality and behavior patterns are two core elements of classification systems. Personality is commonly referred to in the social sciences as "the enduring … characteristics and behavior that comprises an individual's unique adjustment to life, including major traits, interests, drives, values, self-concept, abilities, and emotional patterns … [and] helps determine behavior" (American Psychological Association, 2018, para 1). The relative stability of personality across the life course has been repeatedly evidenced in the literature (Harris et al., 2016).

Human behavior is very complex and relies on a reciprocal relationship with other individuals, institutions, and the environment (Reiss et al., 2000). In what is termed reciprocal determinism, Bandura (1978) proffered that personality and cognitive elements influence human behavior and beliefs, which in turn affect an individual's social environment. In criminological literature, personality traits are a robust predictor of criminal behavior (Tharshini et al., 2021). It has been documented that serial crimes, especially serial sexual crimes, are conducive to profiling due to the similarities in personality and, therefore, behavior among offenders (Douglas & Burgess, 1986; Ainsworth, 2001).

Kocsis and Irwin (1998) propose that identifying the unique psychological systems innate in serial murderers may uncover a pattern of serial crime, regardless of the serial crime committed. The authors assert that several behavioral traits associated with psychopathy are demonstrated in serial criminal offenders. Psychopathy is a personality disorder characterized by glibness, impulsivity, antisocial behavior, lack of concern and empathy for others, callousness, and repeated violations of the rights of others (Hare, 1998). As Kocsis and Irwin (1998) explain further,

> psychopathy frees the offender from the injunctions of society against narcissistic and sadistic behaviour; narcissism defines the primacy of self-gratification in the offender's lifestyle and fuels the sense of superiority by which the offender self-justifies sadistic and psychopathic behaviour; and sadism serves to give form to the antisocial self-gratification and pursuit of superiority and dominance.
>
> (204)

Therefore, personality can be predictive of behavior, especially criminal behavior. That is the first element of the theoretical basis for a criminal profile. In a psychological profile of serial murderers, Sears (1991) explained how all features of the crime scene are meticulously studied to gain an understanding of the serial offender's personality. It is expected that certain traits will be revealed at the crime scene, whether left behind intentionally or unintentionally. A trained profiler endeavors to ascertain these identifying characteristics through investigation of these elements. Investigators can utilize the information to focus their investigation on the most likely offender and to include or exclude particular suspects.

The second critical element to criminal personality offender profiling is a combination of at least two suppositions. Chifflet (2015) identified two essential components underlying the criminal profiling process with respect to serial criminal offenders. The first is termed behavioral consistency, the theory that serial offenders typically exhibit reliably similar behavior as they commit crimes. Underlying this is the notion that personality drives their behavior, which is displayed in the evidence and characteristics of the crime scene. Second is the behavioral homology assumption. The theory is that those who display comparable behaviors retain the same personal characteristics. Within the serial criminal profiling literature, Petherick and Ferguson (2014) express that behavioral consistency and the homology assumption are not well supported.

Both components, behavioral consistency and the homology assumption, correspond to the stability of personality traits and how they influence stability in behavior. Crabbe et al. (2008) reviewed numerous studies in the field to determine if empirical support exists for either assumption, and the results were mixed. Some research indicated moderate support for both behavioral consistency and behavioral homology assumptions. However, results from other studies that the authors reviewed indicated no support for the hypothesis.

Bartol and Bartol (2013) explain that expert profilers consider psychopathological serial violent offenders to be most amenable to criminal profiling. The belief is that these offenders "demonstrate greater consistency in behavior from situation to situation than persons not so disordered" (p. 36). However, they also claim that no clear empirical evidence has consistently supported this hypothesis. These inconsistencies in the research findings may be more a function of the variations in crimes than the inadequacy of the consistency and homology assumptions. It is possible that they are only expressed in certain criminal behaviors, and the suppositions are not generalizable across all criminal behaviors.

Development of the Typology

While the systematic research on behavioral consistency and homology provides mixed results, various typologies of criminal behavior based on these theories have been proposed. Douglas, Burgess, Burgess, and Ressler (1992) identify the process of classification as a method of "data collection and analysis in which data are grouped according to previously determined characteristics" (ix). The development of formal and informal taxonomic structures is fundamental to human nature. To effectively manage massive amounts of information, humans typically activate their ability to recognize patterns by identifying and assessing observable information and proposing categories to more logically process the evidence with which they are presented (Knight & Prentky, 1990). In this way, humans more effectively manage the vast quantity of information they take in and make sense of their world.

Taxonomies have been developed for centuries to classify plants, animals, and humans and their behavior. Crimes may be classified according to numerous factors (Douglas et al., 1992). This is typically done according to either type of crime, number of victims, or the style in which the crimes are committed.

The most widely recognized classification of serial criminal behavior is that developed by the FBI to categorize sexual homicide offenders. Douglas and Burgess (1986) maintain that sexual homicides are typically able to provide investigators with considerable knowledge regarding perpetrator cognitions and motives. Knight and Prentky (1990) concur that classification systems have been a mainstay of research in sexual offending literature. They assert that classification systems are essential in the empirical research on atypical criminal behaviors. An assortment of typologies has been advanced in an endeavor to classify individual serial offenders based on their behavioral traits, with varying levels of success (Godwin, 2002; Homant & Kennedy, 1998). For example, in the realm of sexually aggressive criminal behavior, a variety of studies over the decades have accepted the validity of typologies to categorize such offenders. Further evidence to support the use of classification in sexual offending is provided by Ainsworth (2001) who proffers three reasons profiling has been used most frequently in serial sexual homicides and rapes. First, as the statistics indicate, these crimes, while rare, tend to get the most media attention since serial crimes represent the heinous nature of human behavior. Second, such crimes are usually the most challenging for law enforcement to solve due to frequent stranger relationships between the perpetrator and target. Third, by the nature of their serial occurrence, investigators and profilers can obtain the greatest amount of evidence regarding the perpetrator's motive and personality characteristics.

Organized/Disorganized and Mixed Offender Typologies

The original construction of the organized and disorganized classification of serial sexual murderers was developed by special agents at the FBI's BSU. The unit received numerous requests from local and state law enforcement in the early 1970s to provide criminal profiles for complicated and unsolved homicide cases (Ressler et al., 1985a). The profiles were created using the perpetrator's behavior at the crime scene, derived from evidence found there, to determine if any common characteristics among them could be used to advance a criminal profile. Special agents from the FBI focused on the state of the crime scene as a crucial component in crime classification (Douglas et al., 1992). They suggest three important conclusions that can be drawn from the appearance of the crime scene. First, the condition can provide information about the level of expertise of the perpetrator. Next, the order and disorder left at the crime scene can determine if the incident was well-planned or a spontaneous occurrence. Lastly, it will confirm whether the offender was able to control the victim or if the crime was committed in a frenzied, uncontrollable manner.

Morton et al. (2014) describe the dichotomy as "reflective of an offender's personality, development, criminal history, and social interactions" (p. 4). The two original categories of sexual murderers were designated as organized and disorganized (Douglas et al., 1992). In the most basic terms, the authors distinguish between the two categories in that the organized offender commits premeditated murders in an orderly manner with the ability to maintain control. The disorganized offender is impulsive and opportunistic, often leaving behind a chaotic crime scene.

Following the formation of the organized and disorganized types, the special agents sought to provide empirical support for their new classifications. Ressler et al. (1985b) assert that their study was the first conducted by law enforcement, not academics or medical professionals, that employed the use of crime scene characteristics to analyze criminal sexual homicides. The authors note that they provide only general information about the perpetrators, with not every characteristic true of all the perpetrators. The study included 36 convicted sexual murderers with 118 victims between them. Of the 36 offenders examined, 25 were serial sexual murderers, and 11 were sexual murderers who were single, multiple, or spree. The analysis resulted in 24 organized offenders with 97 victims, and the disorganized offenders accounted for 12 offenders with 24 victims (Ressler et al., 1985c). Through their examination of their typologies, the authors state that they indeed found important discrepancies in the crime scene and perpetrator backgrounds.

Concerning the 24 organized offenders and their profile characteristics, Ressler et al. (1985c) described them as very bright, usually with higher-than-average intelligence. The offenders held occupations beneath their capabilities, preferred more skillful positions, and maintained an erratic employment history. They were found to be competent in their social and sexual capabilities and traditionally lived with a partner. Organized offenders were mobile, usually possessed a decently running vehicle, took a keen interest in media reports of their crimes, and commonly collected news articles about the crimes. Authors found financial, relationship, and occupational issues were possible contributors to situational stress that manifested prior to the criminal behavior. When the authors looked at crime scene indicators, they determined the organized offender sustained control over the scene throughout the crime, which was frequently made apparent in the offender's use of restraints during the crime. The organized offenders reported being either angry or depressed, possibly drinking alcohol preceding the crime, and claimed to be calm and deliberate during the commission of the sexual murders. They learned that the offender meticulously planned the crimes, pursued stranger targets, and at all stages of the crime carefully dictated the conversation and commanded subservience from their victims. These serial offenders perpetrated their crimes out of a psychopathic tendency and with a compulsion to control the target of the crime (Ressler et al., 1992). The organized offenders brought a weapon to the scene, took it with them when they left, and conscientiously removed evidence to avoid identification.

Ressler et al. (1985c) concluded that 12 of the disorganized offenders had lower-than-average intelligence, were socially and sexually inept, and lived alone or with parents. When they did hold a job, it was unskilled, and they were not as mobile as the organized offenders and often lived or worked near the crime scene. The actual crime was committed swiftly, usually a blitz-style attack, and may contain evidence of overkill. The disorganized offender was associated with psychosis, their crimes driven by passion, acting on their urges out of frustration (Ressler et.al., 1992). The crimes were spontaneous, with little to no planning, and the perpetrators admitted to being edgy during the attack and did not appear to have a specific situational stressor. While these perpetrators said they didn't use alcohol or drugs just prior to or during the crime, they did have behavioral changes after the crime in the form of increased or fanatical religiosity, substance use, or other similar behaviors. There was little, if any, conversation during the impulsive attack, wherein the victim was immediately subjected to violence, and sexual acts occurred after the death of the victim. Disorganized offenders did not usually bring weapons to the scene but used what was available, leaving it behind, along with other evidence. The crime scene itself was disheveled and haphazard in appearance.

Following the initial study by the special agents at the FBI, Douglas et al. (1992) concluded that conceivably, some sexual murderers could be classified as either organized or disorganized. They created a third category for those offenders who did not fit neatly into one or the other of the original types and termed them mixed-category offenders. The authors provide several examples of why perpetrators, especially serial offenders, may not be well-suited for the organized or disorganized types. The crime may be committed by a team of offenders and not a single individual. It is also possible that the offender was young or under the influence of drugs or alcohol when committing the crime. Another reason offenders may not fit into one of the primary discrete types is if an unexpected event occurred during the crime. The offender might need to change the course of action, thrown off from the original plans.

Criticism

Many weaknesses of the organized and disorganized dichotomy have been proposed. First, the developers of the typology themselves state that investigators should not expect every serial criminal case to be amenable to criminal profiling (Douglas & Burgess, 1986). Due to the complexity of human behavior, it should not be expected that every serial offender would fit neatly into one of the categories. They note that the typologies should be viewed on a continuum, not as strict categories.

Kapardis (2017) commented on the small sample size used to develop the original classification system and the lack of inter-rater reliability. Another issue with the categories is the creation of a mixed offender group, which seemed to be introduced only after a small number of sexual offenders wouldn't fit neatly into either of the other two. Kapardis's final assessment criticized the classification of offenders based on only the crime scene, suggesting that this could likely lead to an incorrect assessment and thus lead the investigator on an incorrect path. For example, the offender may try to confuse law enforcement by staging a crime scene (though a seasoned investigator will often be able to determine if that is the case).

Canter et al. (2004) challenge the typology of sexual murderers set forth by the FBI special agents from the BSU. They suggest the need for a mixed type of serial offender, which necessarily calls into question the utility of the original dichotomy. If the original classification system requires a category for serial criminal cases that won't precisely fit into one of the other two, then it is likely that the dichotomy will not pass a methodological examination. As an example, Canter et al. analyzed the organized and disorganized systems with serial murderers. Their results indicated that the majority of serial offenders were classified as organized offenders. A much smaller number of offenders could be labeled as disorganized. The authors argued that if the organized serial murderer was the conventional classification, there is likely no need for two or even three distinct categories.

Despite the Bartol and Bartol (2013) report of mixed results as to the reliability and validity of constructing profiles to assist in law enforcement, the authors state that continued research is necessary before drawing a definitive conclusion.

Conclusion

Societies persistently seek means to decrease antisocial and criminal behavior. Law enforcement needs continually evolving tools to assist with crime-solving and seeking justice for individuals and communities affected by crime, especially serial violent crimes. As such, a classification system that could assist in categorizing serial offenders can be useful in managing copious amounts of information and evidence from a crime scene.

Two hypothetical foundations for criminal offender typologies underlie a system of classification. One is the stability of personality traits over the life course and the influence of personality on behavior. The second derives from the first, which leads to the theories of behavioral consistency and homology. Studies have attempted to determine the legitimacy of these theories, but the results have been contradictory. Additional research is necessary in order to resolve the issue.

DEs, completed by a psychiatrist or psychologist, are used to determine psychopathologies and behavioral patterns from a crime. As Kapardis (2017) described, the FBI expanded on this to develop a criminal offender profile using crime scene data to surmise the following:

> The primary motive and the personality of the person likely to have committed one or more crimes from a detailed examination of the crime scene and all the information available about the victim, the crime(s), the forensic evidence and autopsy reports
>
> (p. 742).

Results from the FBI analysis initially produced two types of sexual offenders—the organized and the disorganized. A third category was added later, the mixed-type offender. Douglas et.al. (1992) determined that the organized sexual murder offender had the cognitive ability to target a specific victim and maintain dominance throughout the crime from beginning to end. This type of offender demonstrated more criminal experience and sophistication than the disorganized type. In direct contrast to the organized offender, the disorganized serial murderer, the authors posited, may leave a disordered crime scene that indicates a youthful offender, a lack of proficiency in criminal behavior, or whether the offender had substance use issues or a mental condition. It was further noted that a disorganized scene is not likely to include staging because the offender is either inexperienced or disordered. The additional, mixed-type offender was developed to include a smaller number of cases that were not clearly identified as organized or disorganized.

While details about what factors profilers use to determine whether a case can be profiled are not revealed by Douglas et al. (1992), even if a complete profile is not possible, the authors affirm that the FBI can still be of assistance in the investigation. By relying on the tenets that personality is stable throughout one's life and that those traits influence behavior, expert profilers can still use the classification system in a number of ways, which may include "providing interview/interrogation techniques, investigative suggestions or techniques, establish probable cause for search warrants … assist prosecutors relative to prosecutive strategies" (13). By understanding how personality shapes behavior, experts can offer the most effective techniques for interacting with a suspect. They can inform the investigation by suggesting questions, vocal tones, or themes to extract information about the crime from the disorganized or organized offender.

Researchers are currently exploring effectual means to incorporate the latest computer technology for use with classifications of serial criminal offenders. For example, computer software to identify crime series patterns can provide support with crime scene linkage and detection of criminal patterns (Isafiade & Bagula, 2020). Another study used space, time, and text data to enhance case linkage in serial crimes (Shixiang & Yao, 2022). In departments lacking access to trained experts in the field, crime scenes that might not otherwise have been linked could be recognized and included in the investigation. In so doing, it may provide law enforcement with additional evidence to elucidate the classification of serial criminal offenders.

References

Aamodt, M. G., Leary, T., & Girimurugan, S. (2023). *Radford/FGCU Annual Report on Serial Killer Statistics: 2023* Radford, VA: Radford University. https://doi.org/10.13140/RG.2.2.14080.20489

Ainsworth, P. (2001). *Offender Profiling and Crime Analysis*, Taylor and Francis.

American Psychological Association (APA), (2018). APA Dictionary of Psychology https://dictionary.apa.org/personality

Bandura, A. (1978). The self system in reciprocal determinism, *American Psychologist*, 33(4), pp. 344–358.

Bartol, C.R. & Bartol, A.M. (2013). *Criminal and Behavioral Profiling: Theory, research, and practice*, Sage Publications.

Canter, D.V., Alison, A.J., Alison, E., & Wentink, N. (2004). The organized/disorganized typology of serial murder: myth or model? *Psychology, Public Policy, and Law*, 10(3), pp. 293–320.

Chifflet, P. (2015). Questioning the validity of criminal profiling: an evidence-based approach. *Australian & New Zealand Journal of Criminology*, 48(2), pp. 238–255 https://doi.org/10.1177/0004865814530732

Cooper, A.D. & Smith, E.L. (2011). *Homicides in the United States 1980-2008*. NCJ Number 236018, United States Department of Justice, Bureau of Justice Statistics.

Crabbe, A., Decoene, S., &Vertommen, H. (2008). Profiling homicide offenders: A review of assumptions and theories, *Aggression and Violent Behavior* 13, pp. 88–106.

Douglas, J. E. & Burgess, A.G. (1986). Criminal Profiling: A viable investigative tool against violent crime. *FBI Law Enforcement Bulletin*. December, pp. 1–5 https://vault.fbi.gov/Criminal%20Profiling/Criminal%20Profiling%20Part%201%20of%207/view

Douglas, J. E., Burgess, A. W., Burgess, A. G., & Ressler, R. K., (1992). *Crime Classification Manual*. Lexington Books/Macmillan.

Fox, J.A. & Zawitz, M.W. (2007). *Homicide Trends in the United States*. United States Department of Justice, Bureau of Justice Statistics.

Godwin, M. (2002). Reliability, validity, and utility of criminal profiling typologies, *Journal of Police and Criminal Psychology*, 17(1), pp. 1–18.

Hare, R.D. (1998). Psychopathy, affect, and behavior. In: Cooke, D.J., Forth, A.E., & Hare, R.D. (eds) *Psychopathy: Theory, Research and Implications for Society*. NATO ASI Series, 88. Dordrecht Springer, https://doi.org/10.1007/978-94-011-3965-6_6

Harris, M.A., Brett, C.E., Johnson, W. & Deary, I.J. (2016). Personality stability from age 14 to age 77 years, *Psychology and Aging*, 31(8), pp. 862–874.

Homant, R.J. & Kennedy, D.B. (1998). Psychological aspects of crime scene profiling, *Criminal Justice and Behavior*, 25(3), pp. 319–343.

Isafiade, O.E. & Bagula, A.B. (2020). Series Mining for Public Safety Advancement in Emerging Smart Cities. *Future Generation Computer Systems*, July, 108, pp. 777–802.

Kapardis, A. (2017). Offender-profiling today: An overview, Essays in Honour of Nester Kourakis. *Crime in Crisis (upload) Ant*. N. Sakkoulas Publications L.P. http://crime-in-crisis.com/en/wp-content/uploads/2017/06/41-KAPARDIS-KOURAKIS-FS_Final_Draft_26.4.17.pdf

Knight, R.A., & Prentky, R.A. (1990). Classifying sexual offenders. In: *Handbook of Sexual Assault*, Marshall, W.L., Laws, D.R. & Barbaree, H.E. (eds), pp. 23–52, Springer.

Kocsis, R. N., & Irwin, H. J. (1998). The psychological profile of serial offenders and a redefinition of the misnomer of serial crime. *Psychiatry, Psychology and Law*, *5*(2), 197–213. https://doi.org/10.1080/13218719809524934

Megargee, E.I. & Bohn, M.J. (1979). *Classifying Criminal Offenders: A New System Based on the MMPI*, Sage Publications.

Morton, R.J., Tillman, J. M. & Gaines, S.J. (2014). *Serial Murder Pathways for Investigations*. United States Department of Justice, Federal Bureau of Investigation.

Petherick, W., & Ferguson, C. (2014). Behavioral consistency, the homology assumption, and the problem of induction. In: *Profiling and Serial Crime: Theoretical and Practical Issues* (3rd edition) Wayne Petherick (ed.), pp. 37–61. Elsevier.

Ramsland, K. (2011). Howard Teten: An FBI visionary. *Forensic Examiner*, 20(2), pp. 22–27.

Reiss, H.T., Collins, W. A., & Berscheid, E. (2000). The relationship context of human behavior and development, *Psychological Bulletin*, 126(6), pp. 844–872.

Ressler, R.K. & Burgess, A.W. (1985a). The men who murdered, *FBI Law Enforcement Bulletin*, 54(8), pp. 2–6.

Ressler, R.K. & Burgess, A.W. (1985b). Classifying sexual homicide scenes: Interrater Reliability, *FBI Law Enforcement Bulletin*, 54(8), pp. 13–17.

Ressler, R.K. & Burgess, A.W. (1985c). Crime scene and profile characteristics of organized and disorganized murders, *FBI Law Enforcement Bulletin*, 54(8), pp. 18–25.

Ressler, R. K., Burgess, A.W., & Douglas, J.E. (1992). *Sexual Homicide: Patterns and Motives*, Simon and Schuster.

Sears, D.J. (1991). *To Kill Again: The Motivation and Development of Serial Murder*, Rowman & Littlefield.

Shixiang, Z. & Yao, X. (2022). Spatiotemporal-textual point processes for crime linkage detection, *The Annals of Applied Statistics*, 16(2), pp. 1151–1170.

Tharshini, N.K., Ibrahim, F., Kamaluddin, M.R., Rathakrishnan, B., & Mohd Nasir, N.C. (2021). *The Link between Individual Personality Traits and Criminality: A Systematic Review*. United States Department of Justice, Federal Bureau of Investigation, Crime Data Explorer. https://cde.ucr.cjis.gov/LATEST/webapp/#/pages/home

Vronsky, P. (2021). *American Serial Killers: The Epidemic Years 1950-2000*. Berkley.

6 Geographic Profiling

Kevin Borgeson and Nicholas Stone

Introduction

Although most people believe that GP is a relatively new instrument used in criminal investigation, it got it's start roughly around the same time as the creation of profiling by the FBI. GP origins began in the 1980s when Kim Rossmo used it to help solve a case for the Canadian Police, and he would go on to develop one of the first GP software systems to help assist law enforcement with the location of both violent and non-violent serial offenders.

At the same time of its origins in Canada, a British Psychologist, David Canter, used GP to solve a series of rapes which had taken place near railways surrounding the city of London, England. From 1975 to 1986, 23 women, ranging from late teens to mid-twenties, had been raped by a man in a mask. Canter, along with two London police officers, took four years' worth of data on the crimes and began to lay out the sites on a map, which allowed them to see similarities between the cases. After an extended analysis, Canter believed that the perpetrator would live in the Kilburn/Crickelwood area. After finding the area, Canter did a geographical analysis of the police suspect pool, which consisted of over 2,000 people. After the profile, the suspect pool was reduced to two, and they were close to finding their perpetrator.

Canter's profile went beyond just the possibility of where a perpetrator may reside—he also gave demographic characteristics which the offender would possess. Canter predicted that the perpetrator would be married, have no children, have marital issues, loner, be small in stature, martial artist, have a need to have power over women, and have a vivid fantasy life. When the police finally found their man, John Duffy, Canter's profile was amazingly accurate. When the police began to delve into Duffy's background, they found that he was married, had no children, separated, a short, martial artist, violence against his spouse, and tied her up before having sex with her.

Duffy was convicted of the crimes, and Canter showed the world of law enforcement that GP was a valuable tool that could be used in many ways—especially in constructing and reducing suspect pools.

While Rossmo gets credit for inventing this investigative tool, it was Canter who saw the potential for such an investigative tool and advanced the knowledge in this area dramatically over the last 40 years. Canter did this in several ways: one way was by launching an academic journal, *The Journal of Investigative Psychology*, creating a platform where social scientists have a venue to advance the knowledge of understanding criminal behavior—which helps the law enforcement community develop policies on combating crime. Another way Canter has advanced the field of profiling was by creating a graduate degree program, at the University

DOI: 10.4324/9781003366300-7

of Liverpool, for the advancement of study in the areas of GP and IP. According to Canter, there are three main ways that the field of GP, as it's positioned in the field as a tool within IP, has contributed to the field of criminal justice, and specifically in profiling, they are:

- Conducting studies of criminal spatial behavior
- Development of decision support tools that incorporate research findings
- Exploration of how such tools may help police investigations and the effectiveness of these applications.

(Canter & Youngs, 2008)

Thanks to Rossmo and Canter, the field of GP has become the most successful profiling tool to law enforcement. In the section below, we will delve into the accuracy of GP—especially as it applies to different violent and non-violent serial crimes.

The Role of Environmental Criminology

While GP is famous for its abilities to find geographic areas where a serial violent offender may be, it got its beginnings in less violent crimes such as burglary and robbery. Since Canter was an environmental psychologist, it was an easy transition to apply earlier theories dealing with space and surroundings to that of detecting the possible location of where an individual's home base may be. Its application is helpful in serial crimes—whether they are violent or not—since it is based on theories that describe non-crime patterns in general. All crime has a component of time and place—even those that are virtual. All crimes have patterns and a logic that can be gathered from theories of both legal and non-legal behavior. GP taps into those patterns and tells us about the inner workings of almost any event. As Canter points out (Canter & Youngs, 2008):

> there is no a priori need to assume that the findings and approach will only be of relevance to serious crime or series of offenses. The great majority of criminal investigations can be enhanced by considering the geographical aspects of criminality. Indeed, much general, non-criminal human activity is open to and informed by spatial analysis. If routine activity holds sway then it can be assumed that criminal journeys will not be that different from other forms of legal journey.
>
> (Canter & Youngs, 2008: 6)

The theories geographic profilers used were based on earlier environmental psychologists and criminologists, who had no hint that their findings would start the most successful field of criminal profiling. For example, some of these theories go way back to the mid-late 1800s. Mayhew (1861) wrote about how criminals who lived a half mile away from the homes they would rob. According to Canter (2008), these rookeries lived near this area because it was an affluent area, and they saw it as an opportunity to commit their crimes in a time-efficient manner and profit, while putting in minimal effort. Most serial crimes involve a short distance that these offenders will travel. Just like the average worker, time is precious, and even criminals want to find the road of least resistance and make shortcuts to get their result.

It was the 1920s, in the United States, research was being done on juvenile delinquency in Chicago, Illinois. Robert Park and Ernest Burgess used a social ecology model to look at how structures and organization of one's community affected an environment. Park and Burgess adopted a social pathology model where they looked at social environment like a disease was affecting it. They looked at the city like it had body parts and that each "limb" could be effected differently. Park and Burgess divided the city into a series of five zones, which were based on its relationship to the central business district. The five zones were: central business district, zone of transition, zone of workingmen's homes, zone of better residences, and the commuter zone. The farther that one got from the central business district, the less deviance and crime one had in the community. What the researchers found was that the growth of the city of Chicago was not random; it was part of a pattern that repeats itself regardless of who lives there. If one immigrant community moved out, another immigrant community moved in—although the group population would change, the problems (deviance and crime) remained the same regardless of who was in residence in the community.

After analyzing the data and interviewing residents who lived in these zones—especially those in the zone of transition—they found that immigrants lived there because it was relatively cheap and had public transportation that would allow them to get to their factory jobs in the central business zone. Shaw and McKay's work would go on to influence two paradigms of research in sociology, criminology, and psychology: one was called social disorganization theory, and the other environmental criminology.

Environmental criminology emphasizes what Canter refers to as "the significance of time and place," and these social scientists are interested in the relationship of geographic features and their architectural surroundings, and the amount of victimization that takes place within these areas. Hot spots in crime areas are analyzed to see what type of resources should go into combating crime in these high-crime zones. Through this research, social scientists became aware that there are a range of different mechanisms that are involved in committing a crime, and the environment can be a reliable predictor or detractor. Environmental criminologists learned from earlier theorists like Park and Burgess, and Shaw and McKay, that surroundings of an area can enhance, or decrease, the chances of one becoming the victim of a crime. By addressing the community surroundings, one can remove criminal opportunity and reduce the chance of victimization.

Concepts and Theories

There are many theories that influenced GP. Several concepts and theories on which GP is based allow the investigator to infer the area an offender may be working from.

Profiling can be difficult. When social scientists are looking at a social problem, they develop hypothesis, collect data, analyze it, and come up with findings. In profiling, the opposite equation is used. A scene is found, collect evidence, and surmise why the event happened. Canter and Youngs (2003) came up with what they call the A => C equation to explain the GP process:

> A represents the Actions in a crime, more generally what is known to detectives when the crime is being investigated and before the offender is apprehended, which includes where and when the crime happened and to what or whom. The C describes the characteristics of the offender that the police can use to find him/her; most crucially of course, where to look for the offender. The => is the science of investigative psychology. This arrow is a shorthand for the process of inference that allows investigators to draw conclusions about offenders from information about the crime.
>
> (Canter & Youngs 2008:4)

The above equation of GP is based on several theories in criminology. Below is an explanation of eight concepts that are the most important in understanding the makeup of this investigative tool.

Routine Activity Theory

RAT has become one of the most used theories in criminology to describe the occurrence of crime. In order for crime to take place, there has to be an interaction of time, place, offender, victim, and authority. According to most theorists, there are three elements that must be in place in order for a crime to occur: motivated offender, suitable targets, the absence of capable guardian. For a crime to take place, a criminal has to be motivated at the time of the event. There is no such thing as a motiveless crime—all crimes have a reason why they did it. The motive may not make sense to you, but it makes sense to them and becomes a motivating factor for them to go through with the crime. Targets must be perceived as suitable in order for the event to take place. For a criminal, they are committing the crime for some psychological need. When they determine crime is the way to get that desire, they choose targets that fit their criteria. Targets will always have some function to them. For instance, when Ted Bundy chose his victims, they had to have a resemblance to his ex-fiancé and have to have a certain body type and hairstyle.

The last component of this theory is the absence of a capable guardian. What is meant by "guardian" here is the lack of a person in authority being around. For routine activity theorists, this can include parent, teachers, police, security, or other citizens in the area.

RAT can be summarized as an equation of:

$$\text{crime} = (\text{offender} + \text{target} - \text{guardian})(\text{place} + \text{time}).$$

Felson (1988) added a very important piece to this theory—especially as it is applied to GP—and that is the VIVA model. VIVA stands for:

- Value or desirability of the target
- The inertia of the target
- The visibility of the target
- Access and escape from their target

As one can see, Felson felt the target one chose was important, and not enough research went into how criminals looked at the choosing. Felson came up with what he referred to as rhythms. Rhythms are what make up an area and how people manage their daily lives through an area. Things that Felson felt were important were time of day, traffic, weather, and how busy an area was.

Crime Pattern Theory

Crime pattern theory suggests that criminal acts are more likely to occur in areas where the awareness space of the offender intersects with perceived suitable targets … this idea suggest that most offenders do not chose their crime sites randomly. While any given victim may be selected by chance, the process of such random selection is spatially structured whether the offender realizes it or not (Rossmo, 2000: p. 116).

> Crime pattern theory combines rational choice, routine activity theory, and environmental principles to explain the distribution of crimes. Target choice is affected by the interaction of offenders with their physical and social environments. Potential victims are not considered in isolation from their surrounding environment; the entire target situation must be seen as acceptable by the offender before a crime will occur.
>
> (Rossmo, 2000: p. 117)

Mental Maps and Social Construction Theory

> Cognitive images of familiar areas such as neighborhood or cities, formed from a distillation of the particular transactions a person has with his or her surroundings. Unlike hummingbirds and other animals that retain detailed images of their spatial experiences, humans generalize this knowledge within their memories. Mental maps have an influence on crime site selection because a target cannot be victimized unless an offender is first aware of it.
>
> (Rossmo, 2000: 89)

According to Lynch (1960), there are five components which contribute to the images one uses when making up their mental maps:

1 Paths: places of travel which place a heavy importance on a person's image of a city
2 Edges: physical boundaries that help create one's cognitive map
3 Districts: fuzzy areas that contribute to establishing cognitive borders
4 Nodes: major areas with intense activity
5 Landmarks: symbolic areas

Journey to Crime

Journey to crime is a way of looking at an offender's actions in a systematic fashion. Just like everyday citizens, criminals have a systematic routine that is carried out in a calculated manner—in other words, criminal behavior is not random and has direction and motive that means something to that person. According to Canter (2000), criminals are influenced by three factors:

- Geographic region operating in
- The offender's history with an area
- The desire to minimize effort and maximize rewards

Journey to crime originated from research in criminal psychology and forensic geography (Wortley, 2008), which used theories stating that offenders will travel to commit crimes in areas they are familiar with and will follow patterns of travel they know—especially roads and regions they have traveled to before. Since familiarity is a variable making up their decision to commit crime, offenders must have a starting point. Rossmo (2000: 91) refers to this as an anchor point.

> anchor points are the bases which are the most important places in one's special life. The main anchor points for the vast majority of people are their residence.

In other words, an anchor point is the base which a perpetrator works from to commit their crimes. Several things could qualify as an anchor—work, home, school, parents' home, or some other area of comfort. Humans are creatures of habit in both their legal and non-legal activities. Just like a person chooses a mechanic because they are conveniently located near their home, criminals pick areas to commit crimes that are near them as well. There are three main reasons why people do this: time, convenience, and avoiding getting caught.

Based on the above theories, a geographic profiler attempts to map the patterns and behaviors of an offender by focusing on the areas where the crimes were committed. This analysis is done through what profilers refer to as criminal spatial distribution (Rossmo, 2000). This simply means that the profiler tries to determine the location of the offender over time by looking at radiuses of behavior from their anchor points. Since we know that offenders work in a consistent manner, we can determine these locations by inputting the geographic data gleaned from the crime scene into computers using geographic information system (GIS) software.

> Geographic Information Systems (GIS) represent a cornerstone in the technological advancements of geographic profiling. GIS technology enables the collection, analysis, and visualization of spatial data, providing investigators with a powerful tool to map crime patterns, identify hotspots, and create comprehensive geographic profiles. The integration of GIS with geographic profiling methodologies enhances the accuracy of predictions and aids law enforcement in making informed decisions during criminal investigations.
>
> (Geographic Profiling Techniques, n.d.)

Research done by Canter (2000) has shown that as criminals gain experience in committing their crimes, they become bold and begin to travel farther distances from their original anchor point, which will create a larger area to investigate the offender's location.

GP can be a useful tool to law enforcement and is especially helpful in attaining a suspect pool, as well as narrowing the pool down over time based on their locality to the scene(s). Unlike other forms of criminal profiling, GP has the capacity to be used in both serial and one-off crimes. GP has been used in the following crimes to aid the criminal justice community:

- BTK Killer
- D.C. Sniper
- Green River Killer
- Grim Sleeper

Practical Usages of GP

Palermo and Kocsis (2005) identify five main uses for GP: suspect prioritization, database trawling, bloodings, patrol saturation, and peak of tension polygraphy. Suspect prioritization is used to predict the likely area where the offender is residing. Predicting this area can be used as a vetting tool to prioritize the investigation into viable suspects that reside in or near that area. Database trawling is when the predicted area of the offender's residence is cross-referenced with information located in other databases in order to identify or prioritize potential suspects to be investigated. Bloodings are DNA collection operations focused on the predicted area of the offender's residence. This is achieved by conducting large-scale DNA surveys in a given area and cross-referencing them with DNA samples secured from crime scenes. Patrol saturation relates to the focus of police presence in areas predicted to contain the offender's residence or their hunting ground. An influx of police presence in these areas can increase the likelihood of the offender being caught in the act or being dissuaded from carrying out an attack. Peak of tension polygraphy refers to the use of GP when conducting interrogations of suspects using polygraph testing. This involves focusing questions around geographic areas considered relevant to the offender, whether that be the area of their residence or the area of their hunting ground. The reactions and answers of the suspect can potentially be used to focus the investigation and reveal relevant information (Palermo and Kocsis, 2005, p. 232).

Offender Typology

Serial offenders don't all engage in the same geographic behaviors, and thus classification is necessary to differentiate the different types. Rossmo has developed numerous offender typologies over his career to assign classification to numerous types of offenders. Rossmo's serial killer hunting pattern typology is based conceptually around the idea that crimes are committed in multiple stages, and that perpetrators can shift locations from one phase of the offense to the other. While the whole scope of the criminal event and its locations may not always be observable to investigators, two phases typically will be: (1) encounter with the victim/beginning of the crime event and (2) release of the victim/end of crime event. The MO of the offender will likely influence the sites of these two phases, with their victim encounter site being influenced by victim search method and their victim release site influencing their attack method (Rossmo, 2000).

Rossmo's offender typology is a two-fold combination of victim search method (hunter, poacher, troller, and trapper) and attack method (stalker, raptor and ambusher). The *hunter* commits crimes around his home, he will seek out victims without leaving his territory (Rossmo, 2000). An example would be Peter Sutcliffe, who would leave his home in Yorkshire, England, looking for women, patrolling the streets with weapons like a hammer, knife, and sharpened screwdriver to murder them (Newton, 2019). The *poacher* will travel out of their home territory to find victims, sometimes operating out of an activity node away from their home (Rossmo, 2000). An example would be Israel Keyes, who would bury kill kits in remote areas across the United States, before traveling back to those locations to use the kits on victims he had selected (FBI, 2013). *Trollers* won't actively seek out victims, but will instead happen upon them while engaged in routine activities. He will act opportunistically and strike, but may have already been prepared for the potential encounter ahead of time. While trollers can encounter victims anywhere, it is more common to occur in public places or outside (Rossmo, 2000). An example would be Jerry Brudos, who opportunistically encountered his victims in public areas or by knocking at his front door before abducting and murdering them in his home (Hickey, 2015). *Trappers* will use deception or their occupation to lure unsuspecting victims back to their home or place where they can maintain control. These offenders will employ a range of methods to lure in victims (want-ads; housing offers; job offers; offers of drug, alcohol, or sex work; or establishing trusting relationships with victims) (Rossmo, 2000). An example would be John Wayne Gacy, who would ply his teenage victims with drugs and alcohol, or leverage trust he had established with them before leading them to his home, and talk them into a "hand-cuff trick" where he deceives them into binding themselves before raping, torturing, and murdering them (Hickey, 2015).

In regard to attack methods, the *stalker* will shadow and observe the victim, waiting for an opportunity to strike. As a result, the attack, murder, and release sites have a strong correlation with the victim's activity range (Rossmo, 2000). An example would be David Carpenter, who would stalk victims he encountered on hiking trails until he felt the area was secluded enough to rape and murder them (Ramsland, n.d.). The *raptor*, on the other hand, attacks the victim upon encountering them (Rossmo, 2000). An example would be David Berkowitz, who would encounter the victim or victims on the streets of New York, typically sitting in their car, and would shoot them at the scene (Hickey, 2015). Finally, the *ambusher* will attack their victims in locations where they can maintain greater control, such as their private property or workplace (Rossmo, 2000). An example would be Jeffrey Dahmer, who would lure men and boys back to his apartment before drugging, sexually assaulting, and murdering them (Hickey, 2015). Cantor's offender typology is divided into two distinct types, *marauder* and *commuter*. Marauders treat their home as a centralized anchor point, from which they move out and around to commit crimes before returning. Commuters travel from their base of residence to commit crimes in another area and are not constrained to their home base for the opportunity to offend (Kocsis & Palermo, 2005).

GP and Technology

To expand the efficiency of GP, Rossmo developed a computerized GP algorithm (CGT) to assess the spatial characteristics and variables of criminal events. CGT logs the coordinates of the sites of the crime (encounter, attack, murder, release, etc.). The algorithm analyzes these coordinates and develops a color map, which denotes probabilities at various points to determine the most likely location of the perpetrator's anchor point. Using a GIS, the coordinates or addresses of crime scenes are entered as system inputs. The output is depicted as a jeopardy surface or color geoprofile, depicting the most likely locations of the perpetrator's home base or hunting ground. CGT is a patented algorithm employed by a specialized GP software called Rigel. Rigel was developed by Environmental Criminology Research Inc., a company cofounded by Rossmo (Rich and Shively, 2004).

Human Interpretation and Localized Information

While GP is largely reliant on algorithm-based computer systems analyzing data to make calculated predictions on the probability of an offender's home base or victim searching area, it still requires human interpretation to contextualize the data and properly steer the investigation. While plenty of contextual data can be inputted into the system to better enhance the quality and accuracy of the output, there will always be information that software will ignore that humans will recognize. Environments where crime occurs are complex and nuanced, with many practical features that can be ignored by computers. Say, for example, a series of murders targeting homeless people occurs in a particular neighborhood of the city. The neighborhood's crime rate isn't exceptional compared to many others in the city, but it has a worse reputation in the city because its location and high homeless population are more visible to commuters. A GIS system can input the neighborhood's crime rate as a variable, but would be unable to measure public perception of the neighborhood as a factor that may have determined why the perpetrator chose that area to encounter victims (Rossmo, 2022).

Technology evolves every day, however, and with it GIS software becomes capable of considering more variables in its analysis. Early prediction models were more accurately described as geometric profiling, as they focused on offenders traveling out of their anchor point to commit crimes, and determining offender residence by calculating distance decay probabilities. Modern GP makes more advanced predictions through a Bayesian approach of considering more localized information. This Bayesian approach establishes geographically particular data sets and derives patterns from this data to more efficiently make predictions (Kocsis & Palermo, 2005).

Model Accuracy

The accuracy of these models is entirely dependent on two precise factors: the quality of the GIS software used to generate the model, and the quality and quantity of data inputted into the system to predict offender home base and victim searching area. The quality of the software is easy to determine; there are numerous GIS software products developed for the sole purpose of determining likely areas of offender anchor points, including Rigel, Crimestat, and Geocrime. That said, the accuracy of the systems is hotly debated. One study found that the accuracy of the systems to be only marginal in comparison to simple spatial distribution strategies. Another more recent study found higher degrees of accuracy when the system analyzed a larger number of crimes (Hanayama, Haginoya & Kuraishi, 2024; Paulsen, 2006).

More prescient to the accuracy of a system's outputs is the reliability of the data inputted. There can be numerous challenges in inputting valuable and accurate data into a system. The first is human error, in which valuable data can either be omitted or entered inaccurately. If a system is presented with erroneous or missing inputs, the reliability of the output can be completely jeopardized. If two crime sites were located on John St. and Adams Rd., the results of the model can't be received as valuable or accurate if Adams Rd. is missing as an input and John St. is misinputted as James St. (located in a different neighborhood). Human error can only be avoided if system operators are competent and their inputs are adequately scrutinized for mistakes. The other common issue is if valuable data is unknown to investigators. GP models can only make predictions of the information known to investigators. In the event of a crime, not all geographic data will be evident to police. If a victim is abducted and not recovered, with the site of their abduction unclear, investigators would only be able to input the victim's last known location into the system, which, while still potentially beneficial to the investigation, cannot be reasonably expected to offer as much insight as it would if the sites of the abduction, murder, and dumping were all logged (Kocsis & Palermo, 2005; Borgeson, Valeri & Vogel, 2024; Rossmo, 2022).

Conclusion

Like other styles of profiling, GP has its limitations. This final section of the chapter will discuss the drawbacks of GP.

Another consideration in using GP centers around the legal and ethical use of it:

> The legal implications of using geographic profiling in criminal investigations involve adherence to constitutional principles and the Fourth Amendment protection against unreasonable searches and seizures. Ensuring that the collection and use of geographic data comply with legal standards is essential to prevent unwarranted intrusions into individuals' privacy. As geographic profiling becomes more prevalent in investigations, legal frameworks must adapt to address the evolving landscape of forensic techniques and their implications for civil liberties.
>
> (https://criminal-justice.iresearchnet.com/criminal-justice-process/criminal-profiling-and-behavioral-analysis/geographic-profiling-techniques/)

Bibliography

Borgeson, K., Valeri, R. M., & Vogel, S. (2024). *Serial crime: A criminological and psychological analysis.* Carolina Academic Press, LLC.

Canter, D. & Youngs, D. (2003). Beyond geographical offender profiling: The need for investigative psychology. In R. Bulland, & D. Carson (Eds.). *Handbook of psychology and legal contexts* (pp. 171–205). John Wiley and Sons, Inc.

Canter, D. & Youngs, D. (2008). *Principles of geographical offender profiling*. Ashgate.

FBI. (2013, August 13). *New information released in Serial killer case.* FBI. https://www.fbi.gov/news/stories/new-information-released-in-serial-killer-case

Geographic Profiling Techniques. (n.d.), iresearchnet. https://criminal-justice.iresearchnet.com/criminal-justice-process/criminal-profiling-and-behavioral-analysis/geographic-profiling-techniques/ Retrieved 2/11/2025.

Hanayama, A., Haginoya, S., & Kuraishi, H. (2024). Testing the accuracy of geographical profiling considering the effect of the number of crimes. *Journal of Investigative Psychology and Offender Profiling*, *21*(2). https://doi.org/10.1002/jip.1625

Hickey, E. W. (2015). *Serial murderers and their victims* (6th ed.). Cengage Learning.

Lynch, K (1960). *The image of the city*. MIT Press.

Newton, G. (2019, March 26). *The yorkshire ripper files: Why chapeltown in Leeds was the "hunting ground" of Peter Sutcliffe*. Yorkshire Post. https://www.yorkshirepost.co.uk/news/crime/the-yorkshire-ripper-files-why-chapeltown-in-leeds-was-the-hunting-ground-of-peter-sutcliffe-1757731

Palermo, G. B., & Kocsis, R. N. (2005). *Offender profiling: An introduction to the sociopsychological analysis of violent crime*. (R. Slovenko, Ed.). Charles C Thomas Publisher, Ltd.

Paulsen, D. J. (2006). Connecting the dots: Assessing the accuracy of geographic profiling software. *Policing: An International Journal of Police Strategies & Management*, *29*(2), 306–334. https://doi.org/10.1108/13639510610667682

Ramsland, K. (n.d.). *The Trailside Killer of San Francisco*. Capture - David Carpenter, the Trailside Killer of San Francisco - Crime Library. https://www.crimelibrary.org/serial_killers/predators/david_carpenter/5.html

Rich, T., & Shively, M. (2004). A Methodology for Evaluating Geographic Profiling Software. Retrieved 2025, from https://www.ojp.gov/pdffiles1/nij/grants/208993.pdf

Rossmo, D. K. (2000). *Geographic Profiling*. CRC Press.

Rossmo, D. K. (2022). Bayesian geographic profiling: A fundamental limitation. *The Professional Geographer*, *74*(4), 772–780. https://doi.org/10.1080/00330124.2022.2075408

7 Investigative Psychology

Rebecca C. Kendall

Introduction

Much of the public's perceptions about criminal profiling come from fictional accounts. Thomas Harris's 1988 book and the subsequent movie *The Silence of the Lambs* were some of the earliest fictionalized accounts of profiling to gain widespread public attention and popularize the term "offender profiling." Most of these fictional accounts portray the FBI's methods of profiling, which are heavily based on clinical judgment and the lived experience of the investigators themselves.

One criticism of offender profiling broadly is that it is not grounded in scientific knowledge and too reliant on subjective experience of the investigator. For instance, in a systematic review of the literature, Dowden et al. (2007) found that prior to 1995, less than half the studies on offender profiling were published in peer-reviewed journals. However, the number of studies on offender profiling published in peer-reviewed journals has markedly increased, with the majority of articles now being peer reviewed. In addition, Dowden et al. (2007) found that while early research on offender profiling was not generally statistically sophisticated, the proportion of articles including statistical analysis has recently increased. Over the last few decades, the number of research articles being published on offender profiling has grown significantly, and the emergence of the *Journal of Investigative Psychology and Offender Profiling* has lent more legitimacy to profiling as a field of academic study.

IP emerged in the late 1980s out of the need for a more structured, systematic approach to applying psychological concepts to crime investigation (Canter & Alison, 1999). As Canter and Youngs (2009) note, while IP was in part developed to help investigators create offender profiles, it should not be mistaken as a synonym for "offender profiling" because it has many other applications to all areas of law enforcement. In addition, "profiling" in the traditional sense is just a small piece of IP. In fact, the graduate IP program at the Investigative Psychology Unit at Liverpool University includes minimal focus on profiling. Instead, the curriculum focuses on applying psychological concepts to police enquires (Canter & Alison, 1999). Because IP is more scientifically grounded, it can be applied beyond the scope of what has traditionally been labeled "offender profiling" (Youngs & Canter, 2006). IP encompasses other ways psychologists, and the field of psychological research broadly, contribute to the prevention, management, and investigation or crime. In addition, while profilers traditionally applied their skills to investigations of more bizarre and rare crimes such as serial killing and serial rape, IP is being applied to a wider range of crimes than traditional offender profiling (Youngs & Canter, 2006).

This chapter provides an overview of IP, including its distinction within the field of psychology as well as from other types of offender profiling. The chapter begins with the history

DOI: 10.4324/9781003366300-8

and development of the field of IP, followed by discussion of how IP differs from other approaches to criminal profiling. The latter half of the chapter provides an explanation of the core concepts in IP as well as examples of the application of IP within the research and in practice internationally. Finally, the chapter will end with a brief discussion of the primary criticisms of IP.

History and Development of IP

The field of IP was developed by David Canter, psychologist and emeritus professor at the University of Liverpool. Canter's academic background is in environmental psychology, which examines the relationship between people and their physical environments as well as the ways in which the environment can shape behavior (Ainsworth, 2001). Canter's work in the area of offender profiling began in the late 1980s when he first applied his professional background to criminal investigation. Between 1982 and 1986 a series of rapes and murders in London prompted the police to approach Canter for help with their investigation, given his prior work studying human behavior (Canter & Youngs, 2009). Rather than drawing on his own personal experience like a clinician might do, he applied knowledge from relevant studies on the topic. Because his assistance with the investigation was considered useful to investigators, he was asked to contribute to further investigations. Canter saw this as an opportunity to conduct research, develop theories, and build a new scientific discipline of applied psychology. He was then provided with access to police records, from which he could collect information needed to test his hypotheses and refine his theories. This led him to develop the field of IP in 1992 (Canter & Youngs, 2009).

Canter developed his approach to offender profiling based on his background as a psychologist and thus grounded it in the scientific method of investigation (Ainsworth, 2001). IP is not an entirely new discipline; rather, it applies existing psychological research and theory to the investigative process (Canter & Alison, 1999). As a discipline, IP is concerned with three general areas: criminal behavior, information and evidence, and investigative decision making (Canter & Alison, 1997). Although there are some similarities, IP is distinct from the field of forensic psychology. Forensic psychology is broader in scope than IP and generally focuses on the treatment and management of offenders once they have been apprehended by law enforcement (Canter, 2004). IP, on the other hand, is more specifically concerned with how psychological science can aid in the detection of offenders and assist in the defense or prosecution of suspects. IP applies a wide range of psychological topics to many areas of the civil and criminal investigative process, such as confessions, police interviews, hostage negotiation, and the psychology of weapon use (Canter, 2004). Psychological topics relevant to IP include child psychology, cognitive psychology, clinical psychology, criminal psychology, social psychology, organizational psychology, environmental psychology, and forensic psychology (Canter & Youngs, 2009).

One impetus for the development of IP was the fact that a lot can be learned about all areas of criminal investigations from the behavioral sciences. For instance, a criminal investigation can be viewed as a series of decisions and thus psychological research on effective and ineffective decision making can be applied to the process (Canter & Youngs, 2009). Specifically, IP conceptualizes investigative decision making as having three distinct parts, all of which can be improved by psychological research. The first area of the investigative cycle is effective information. IP approaches the collection of information during a police investigation like it does for other areas of information collection (e.g., surveys, interviews). Information collected during investigations needs to be reliable and valid. However, there are many areas where the reliability and validity of information can be weakened. For instance, it is well known that eyewitness accounts can be faulty for a number of reasons. Thus, research within the field of IP can help develop improved information collection measures (e.g., the cognitive interview technique; Canter & Youngs, 2009).

The second distinct part of investigative decision making is appropriate inference (Canter & Youngs, 2009). Once investigators have enough information, they must determine what inferences can be made from the information. One example is making inferences about the characteristics of an unknown offender based on information gathered from the crime scene. Another example relates to weapons used in violent crimes—for instance, where did the offender get the weapon they used, and what did the offender do with the weapon afterward? Inferences can also be made that link crimes with similar characteristics in a series. Canter's (1995a) A ➔ C equation is relevant here (discussed in more detail below). *A* represents all the actions that occur during a crime that are known to police, and *C* represents the things investigators want to know about an unknown suspect that can lead to their identification and conviction. Effective inferences that link *A* to *C* should be based on empirical research rather than speculation about an offender's possible motive. The third phase of investigative decision making is focused on decisions based on all the information gathered from earlier stages (Canter & Youngs, 2009).

Distinguishing IP from Other Types of Profiling

There are two broad approaches to studying crime and criminals: the idiographic approach and the nomothetic approach (Petherick & Turvey, 2008). Idiographic (deductive) study focuses on specific cases and examines unique individuals. The main goal of idiographic criminal profiling is to understand the unique characteristics of a specific offender. Nomothetic (inductive) study, on the other hand, concentrates on groups and is concerned with universal laws. The primary goal of nomothetic criminal profiling is to generate an understanding of the characteristics of groups of offenders. These types of profiles are abstract in that they can only provide characteristics that are theoretically possible or probable, rather than the characteristics of an actual offender. IP is considered a nomothetic method of criminal profiling because, while it is grounded in empirical research, it is still entirely abstract and theoretical.

According to Bartol and Bartol (2013), one way of viewing the distinction between IP and other criminal profiling approaches used primarily in the United States is the distinction between clinical versus actuarial profiling. The clinical approach to criminal profiling is primarily based on experts' experience, training, and intuition. It is therefore considered subjective and open to cognitive bias and inaccuracies. This approach is used by most "offender" profilers, including the FBI (Canter & Alison, 1999). The actuarial approach is a research-based orientation that uses data from prior instances to estimate the probability of an outcome. Actuarial profiling relies on base rates, or "the statistical prevalence of a particular behavior in a given group over a set period of time, usually one year" (Bartol & Bartol, 2013, p. 43). IP is considered an actuarial approach because it is research-based.

As such, IP is more than just an investigator's intuition. Because human thinking is subject to distortion and biases (e.g., availability heuristic, hindsight bias), any inferences made based solely on experience and opinion will also be subject to these limitations (Canter & Alison, 1999). In fact, Canter and Alison (1999) compare traditional profilers to psychics who provide advice to investigators, because both emphasize "gut feelings" or intuition over standard procedures and systemic observation. Further, they describe the traditional profiling approach as "at best, subjective opinion, common sense or ignorance or at worst, deliberate deception" (p. 6).

One of the dangers of relying on the perceived expertise of an individual profiler is that the information they provide may be weighted too heavily by investigators because of their experience. This is in line with research on the persuasive power of authority figures (e.g., Milgram, 1963). Canter and Alison (1999) argue that accounts of traditional profilers' success stories are typically in the form of autobiographies and should be viewed as anecdotal. These accounts do not include a scientific framework such as systematic procedures, theoretical models of behavior, or common psychological principles.

IP has been more widely established in the United Kingdom than in the United States. One reason for this is the dominance of the FBI's profiling techniques in the United States (Labuschagne & Borgeson, 2010). While IP shares some similarities with the FBI's method of profiling, it differs in several important ways (Ainsworth, 2001). Specifically, IP relies more heavily on statistical analysis and places a greater emphasis on publishing relevant methods so other researchers can replicate or refute the work. One of the main criticisms of the FBI's approach to profiling is their lack of transparency, including that they have not published their work for the academic community to scrutinize (Ainsworth, 2001).

Canter has been one of the most vocal critics of the FBI's approach to criminal profiling and the American profiling movement broadly. For instance, Canter suggests that the American approach to profiling relies on making inferences based on little evidence and criticizes the lack of scientific rigor involved in the FBI's methods specifically (Ainsworth, 2001; Webber, 2010). As Webber (2010) points out, the American approach to criminal profiling is viewed more as an art than a science. This is in contrast to the British approach, which applies quantitative research to understanding criminal behavior.

Proponents of IP argue that the misrepresentation of psychology in accounts from traditional "offender" profilers should be an ethical concern for professional psychologists (Canter & Youngs, 2009; Canter & Alison, 1999). Canter and Youngs (2009) suggest that there is room for some amount of clinical judgment in offender profiling if investigators are trained on empirically based principles that then inform their professional opinions. However, there is no evidence that psychologists or experienced detectives do a better job at creating offender profiles. In other areas of investigation, such as ability to detect deception, research suggests that clinical and detective experience is not associated with better performance, and length of job experience may actually be negatively correlated with performance (Ekman, 1991; Kohnken, 1987). Therefore, amount of investigative or "profiling" experience should not be automatically assumed to increase accuracy. While seasoned investigators bring a wealth of experience to the investigative process, their opinions are not infallible just because of their experience. Opinions during investigations should always be checked and treated with caution in order to avoid bias, regardless of the experience or expertise of those involved (Canter & Alison, 1999).

One procedural difference between IP and other models of profiling relates to the working relationship between psychologists (or profilers) and investigators (Canter & Youngs, 2009). In traditional profiling, an "expert" is brought in to confer with detectives on a crime. However, given the limitations of this approach, IP promotes a more productive model in which empirical research generates policies and procedures that are then integrated into investigative practices. This approach implies that the "expert" may not be needed once these effective procedures are fully integrated (Canter & Youngs, 2009).

Another important distinction between traditional "offender" profiling and IP has to do with the scope of the discipline. IP goes further than just helping to solve crimes. As Canter and Young (2009) note, "IP deals with psychological input to the full gamut of issues that relate to the management, investigation, prosecution of crime and defense of suspects" (p. 6). In addition, by calling his work "investigative psychology" rather than "criminal profiling,"

Canter emphasizes how psychology can be used to understand how offenders interact with victims (Ainsworth, 2001). While traditional profiling methods were typically applied to egregious or bizarre crimes like serial rape or murder, IP is concerned with all manner of crimes including, for instance, arson, rape, and burglary (Canter & Youngs, 2009). IP research can also provide guidance to the courts on topics including jury decision making, eyewitness accounts and human memory limitations, criminal action patterns, and indications of human deceit (Youngs, 2009).

Central Concepts in IP

Operational Questions

As the discipline of IP progresses, investigative psychologists are increasingly able to assist investigators on a number of important classes of operational questions (Youngs & Canter, 2006). These questions include:

- Salience—what aspects of a crime are most salient and should be paid the most attention? There is a lot that can happen during a crime and the shear amount of information available at a crime scene can be overwhelming to investigators. IP can help investigators understand the most salient aspects of the crime, which can help them eventually find a suspect.
- Suspect elicitation—which records and other sources should investigators search to identify the offender? IP can help investigators narrow down a pool of suspects and determine the dominant features of likely offenders. This information can inform decisions about what searches should be made (e.g., potentially relevant databases) and what information gathered (e.g., soliciting information from the public) to find the offender.
- Suspect prioritization—which suspect from those identified by investigators is most likely to have committed the crime? Investigative psychologists can help investigators determine the likelihood of certain personal characteristics or criminal history the suspect may have from studying the crime. This information can aid investigators in narrowing down their list of suspects.
- Offender location—where is the offender most likely to be living or using as a home base? Research in IP can provide clues about the geographic patterns of criminals. Using this data, investigators may be able to focus the investigation and resources to a certain location.
- Linking crimes—are there other crimes that can be linked as committed by the same perpetrator? Research in IP has examined the salient features of different types of crimes (e.g., arson). This research can be applied to specific crimes by helping investigators determine what is consistent from one crime to the next that can point to a single offender. This can be viewed as similar to the idea of an offender "signatures."
- Prediction—where and when will the offender commit their next offense and how severe will it be? The likelihood that an offender will commit a subsequent offense, the severity of that offense, and the potential for escalating violence are significant operational concerns to investigators.
- Investigative decision making—how can the investigative process be improved? IP can provide guidance to improve how investigations are organized and how decisions are made.
- Information retrieval—can the collection of information during the investigation be made more effective? Information about the cognitive and social processes involved in collecting

information during investigations can help improve processes such as interviews of suspect, witnesses, and victims.

- Evaluation of information—can psychometric tools be used to assess information gathered during the investigation? For instance, IP can provide guidance on the use of relevant tools to detection of deception.
- Preparing a case—how can psychological models of human behavior be used to structure the legal case to be presented in court? Research from IP can inform prosecutors and defense attorneys on human behavior and human decision making to improve their legal arguments.

The Five-Factor Model

The IP method of profiling focuses on five major components of the offender's past and present, commonly referred to as the five-factor model (Petherick & Turvey, 2008). *Interpersonal coherence* refers to how a person interacts with others. Canter (1995b) proposes that offenders interact with victims similarly to how they interact with other people in their daily lives. That is to say that the interaction between an offender and a victim is a direct extension of other transactions in the offender's life. In addition, it is suggested that victims may possess similar characteristics to people who are important to the offender. *Significance of time and place* suggests that offenders specifically select the time and place for offending, so these factors of a crime can provide insight into the offender's mentality. For instance, an offender might select a location they have a high degree of familiarity with it because they feel more comfortable and in control there. *Criminal characteristics* provide insight into the nature of the crime and how it was committed. This component is similar to the FBI's organized/disorganized typology. *Criminal career* refers to the idea that the offender's behavior can provide insight into their experience. For instance, an offender's MO may change over time based on experience from previous offenses. This component reflects an offender's learning and experience. And finally, *forensic awareness* refers to the offender's understanding about the criminal investigation process. Their behavior may change over time as they become more sophisticated and learn additional techniques to evade detection (Petherick & Turvey, 2008).

The A → C Equation

One of the central concepts in IP are the A → C equations, which represent the relationship between two sets of variables vital to the investigation of a crime—the characteristics of an offender and the actions of the crime (Canter & Youngs, 2009). These equations are similar to "if … then" statements. In the equation, *A* stands for those variables that represent the actions the offender took during the crime (e.g., where, when, and how the crime was committed). *C* stands for those variables that represent the characteristics of the offender that are relevant to the investigation. The → at the center of the equations signifies that inferences are being made between predictor variables (i.e., the actions) and criterion variables (i.e., the characteristics). Inferences are made from all the information available about a crime (Canter, 2011). This includes statements from witnesses and any surviving victims, as well as details of the crime scene itself. For instance, the crime location can provide information on how the offender entered or accessed the location, whether anything was taken or left behind by the offender, and the actual location of the crime scene. One of the most important parts of this inference model is identifying what is unique about a particular crime; put another way, what are this crime's salient features? It is therefore important for IP research to examine what features of crimes are common and what distinctions can be made across any type of crime (Canter, 2011).

The A ➔ C equations are not actual mathematical equations used in criminal profiling, but rather conceptual frameworks for understanding how inferences are made during investigations. While the A ➔ C equation may appear simple, its application in the real world is quite complex. One primary reason for this complexity is that the same action may indicate multiple characteristics, and the same characteristic can be inferred from multiple actions. In addition, a change in one predictor variable can change the relationships between other sets of predictor and criterion variables. Similarly, if important variables are excluded or inaccurate variables are included in the equations, this can distort the entire outcome. The equations can also be represented as A ➔A, where investigators try to determine if the actions of one crime are related to the actions of another crime, and thus both crimes are committed by the same offender. There will be variation in the precision of inferences made during investigations.

When making inferences about offenders' behavior, it is important to consider the ways in which offenders change over time and that the way they engage in criminal behavior may reflect those changes from crime to crime. Understanding how offenders change over time can enhance the inference process. Offenders go through changes in:

- Responsiveness—criminals may change how they respond to circumstances from one occasion to another.
- Maturation—the physical maturation criminals experience over time can impact the kinds of behaviors they are capable of, so it is important to understand how factors like physical agility and sexual vitality can impact offending.
- Cognitive development—this aspect refers to the evolution of an offender's knowledge. Gaining knowledge over time can cause an offender to evolve their strategies. Evidence of some level of criminal expertise in the crime behavior can provide investigators with insight about the relative age or experience of the offender.
- Learning—criminals will typically learn from their prior actions and may adapt future behavior.
- Careers—this aspect of change refers to how offenders change their position within criminal subgroups and cultures.
- Cultural shifts—some changes in offenders' behavior can be the result of societal developments (e.g., the changing security features in automobiles).

Smallest Space Analysis

Some IP research uses a type of multidimensional scaling (MDS) called smallest space analysis (SSA; Canter & Youngs, 2009). MDS is a mathematical approach similar to factor analysis and cluster analysis, with more focus on visual representation of the relationship between variables. In MDS, the stronger the relationship between variables, the closer together they will be in the visual representation. SSA is a non-metric MDS procedure in which the correlations between variables being studied are visually represented in geometric space, where the distance between variables in geometric space represents the rank order of co-occurrence between variables. In SSA, the null hypothesis is that there is no relationship between the variables being examined. While MDS relies on the absolute values of the relevant variables, SSA relies on the rank order of the correlations between variables. Essentially, a number of variables are analyzed to produce statistical correlation coefficients, which are then ranked and used to form a visual representation. In the SSA model, the more highly correlated two variables are, the closer they will be together in space.

SSA can be used to examine patterns of relationships between variables. In one application of SSA, Canter and Fritzon (1998) used measures of behavioral indicators derived from arson investigation case files to classify arsonists. The authors found four distinct themes to arson based on whether the acts involved were expressive or instrumental. In addition, the authors were able to link the four arson themes identified with the characteristics of people who typically commit each type.

In another application of SSA, Salfati (2000) used SSA to analyze 247 British single offender-single victim solved homicides in order to differentiate homicide crime scenes in terms of the expressive or instrumental role the victim had to the offender. Findings showed that 38% of the homicide crime scenes were considered expressive, while 24% were classified as instrumental, and 38% were either a hybrid or non-classifiable. One of the most significant findings from the study was the establishment of an empirically based classification system for homicide crime scenes and homicide offenders that can aid offender profilers (Canter & Youngs, 2009).

Youngs (2004) used SSA to study 207 male offenders between the ages of 14 and 28, 90% of whom had at least one criminal conviction. Measures included a self-report delinquency scale, a questionnaire measuring interpersonal tendencies, and subjects' demographic and criminal backgrounds. Results showed that criminal behavior targeting other people in a direct way (often violent) was related to a greater interpersonal need for power, control, and dominance over others. This was particularly true in situations where a weapon was used as part of the offending. In addition, offenders involved in property crimes reported a higher level of control by others; thus, the author suggests that acts against property may be a reaction against this feeling of being controlled by others. There were also differences between those who targeted people and those who targeted property in terms of their interpersonal personality. Offenders who targeted persons rather than property reported receiving a higher level of emotional closeness from others. Youngs suggests this could indicate that people who typically elicit intimacy from others in the broader context are also those who will target others in the criminal context. Taken together, Youngs (2004) suggests that these findings elucidate the connection between offender personality and criminal behavior.

Criminal Narratives

The narrative model in IP is a framework that draws on archetypal themes from literature to understand how offenders make sense of their own behavior (Canter & Youngs, 2009). This framework is based on narrative theory in psychology, which Canter (1995b) first applied to criminal behavior in his book *Criminal Shadows*. Canter's assumption is that you can only truly understand criminal behavior by conducting an in-depth analysis of the offender's personal narrative. The narrative model can help provide insight into offenders' actions by analyzing what role the criminal plays in their own life story—essentially, how does the offender view the world, and what role do their criminal actions play in their overall storyline? This approach can also provide insight into how the offender justifies their offending, and Canter and Youngs (2009) argue that understanding offenders' personal narratives can help investigators. For instance, if investigators have insight into how an offender views themselves, they can incorporate that into their interview strategy. The narrative framework can also help form the basis for inferences about the characteristics of an offender based on the narratives suggested in their actions.

It is proposed that offenders' personal narratives will focus on one of four themes: irony, adventure, tragedy, or quest (Canter & Youngs, 2009). The irony narrative is one in which the person believes nothing in life makes sense and nothing matters. Here the offender views themself as a helpless or powerless victim in a world without rules. In the adventure narrative, the offender views the world as a challenge that they must attempt to master to gain satisfaction and pleasure. This offender views themself as a professional, using their expertise to "get the job done." They may express excitement when discussing their offending. In the tragedy narrative, the offender believes they must avenge a wrong done to them. Here, the offender is focused on revenge and views themself as the victim of wrongdoing. The offender believes their actions are justified. In the quest narrative, the offender views themself on a righteous mission. For instance, the offender might be defending their honor or looking for respect or recognition. This offender often displays bravado and casualness about the offending.

The narrative model also assumes that offenders assign roles for the victims (Canter & Youngs, 2009). The role the offender assigns to the victim will depend on their own distorted way of achieving power and intimacy. The authors identify three primary roles: victim as object, victim as vehicle, and victim as person. In some offending narratives, such as the adventure narrative, the offender views the victim as simply an object for achieving their own objectives and having no feelings or significance of their own. In the irony narrative, the offender is seeking intimacy. The victim is viewed as a person with significance to help the offender achieve that intimacy. There are several ways the victim can be viewed as a vehicle in the quest and tragedy narratives. The tragic offender may view the victim as a target to exact revenge and the offender on a quest will view the victim as part of a larger heroic mission. Unlike the victim as object, the victim here is seen as having humanity that can be exploited to serve the offender's needs.

The victim as object, vehicle, or person can be applied to cases of rape (Canter & Youngs, 2009). When the victim is viewed as an "object," the offender is expected to be self-focused in the sexual acts they use to attain pleasure. For instance, the offender might be preoccupied with the victim's physical characteristics. It is expected that there will be minimal social interaction between the victim and offender. Because the offender lacks empathy for the victim, they will use direct means of gaining the victim's control, including extreme violence, if necessary, but avoid excessive or frenzied violence. When the victim is assigned the role of "vehicle," the rape will have symbolic meaning to the offender and include anger and vindictiveness as part of the social contact between victim and offender. The offending may include excessive physical violence, verbal abuse, and cruelty. Here, the expression of power is a feature of the offending. When the victim is viewed as a "person," the offender will attempt to attain intimacy through the rape. In these cases, the offender recognizes the victim's humanity but has a distorted view of how to engage in interpersonal relationships. The social interaction in these rapes is important, as the offender may try to relate to the victim.

Canter and Youngs (2009) suggest that the narrative model can also be used to understand murder. The authors argue that serial murder is fundamentally about the offender seeking a distorted form of interpersonal interaction, and thus, the interaction between the victim and the offender is key to understanding the psychology of serial murders. The offender's behavior during serial murder scenes can provide insight into their general style of interaction with the victim. Findings from Canter et al.'s (2004) SSA of serial murder can be applied to the victim as object, vehicle, or person roles. The "victim as object" offending style is consistent with offending behaviors such as mutilation and dismemberment. Here, the offender lacks empathy for the victim and sees them merely as an object. The manner of killing would be expected to be manual strangulation, throat cutting, or the use of a firearm. When the victim is perceived as a "vehicle," the victim has symbolic significance, and the offender uses them to express anger or other desires. In these encounters, the offender does recognize and respond to the victim's reactions, which in turn propel the offender's emotional expression. Behaviors expected at the crime scene include ones demonstrating a frenzied, emotional approach, such as ransacking and scattering. Because of the heightened emotions involved, the offender is also expected to engage in extreme forms of violence beyond that necessary to control the victim. Because the victim's emotional reactions and suffering are paramount to this offender, this offending pattern is consistent with the use of torture, blindfolds, props, and specialized offending kits. When the victim is perceived as a "person," there will be evidence that the offender engaged in a distorted form of intimacy with the victim. Behaviors consistent with this offending style in the context of serial murder would be bite marks, redressing the victim, or covering the victim's body.

Applications of IP

IP is gaining more recognition and application outside the United States. The South African Police Service is one of the only agencies that offers investigative psychological services within its organization (Hickey, 2016). The South African Police Investigative Psychology Unit (IPU) was created in 1997 with the initial task of assisting in serial murder investigations but has since that time expanded its focus to other types of offenses (Canter & Youngs, 2009). While it was initially only offered in the national office, in 2013, the IPU opened additional units in each of the nine provinces. The IPU can also assist in cases throughout the country and has provided support to neighboring countries, Swaziland and Namibia. In addition, the IPU has assisted Scotland Yard and the Central Bureau of Investigation in New Delhi, India, with investigations (Labuschagne & Borgeson, 2010).

All South African law enforcement officers who will be involved in serial murder investigations are required to attend the three-week Investigative Psychology Section (IPU). As of 2016, more than 400 investigators have participated in the course, handling over 100 murder series. The IPU is composed of four full-time members with a mix of psychological and investigative experience (Labuschagne & Borgeson, 2010). The unit is run by the Colonel, who is a clinical psychologist. The Lt. Colonel is the second in command and has an investigative background. Finally, the unit has two Captains, one with a psychology background and the other with an investigative background. The IPU also has a Provisional Coordinator for Psychologically Motivated Crimes in each of the country's nine provinces.

The IPU is responsible for handling all psychologically motivated crimes in South Africa, including serial murder, spree and mass murders, domestic murders, infant rapes, extortion cases, child murders, abductions, threat assessments, murder with unusual circumstances, ritual murders, and serial rape investigations (Hickey, 2016). According to Labuschagne and Borgeson (2010), the IPU has investigated some of the most well-known cases in South Africa, including

> the Wemmerpan Serial Murderer; Moses Sithole South Africa's most notorious serial murderer to date; the rape of 9 month old baby Tshepang in Upington; Torso murder in the Thames river, London; Quarry serial murderer Richard Nyauza; the Capital Park serial murderer Samuel Sydino; the Phoenix serial murderer Sipho Twala, and the Highwayman serial murderer Elais Chauke.
>
> (p. 178)

The IPU has a number of important roles, including investigative support, training, and research (Canter & Youngs, 2009). For investigative support, any investigator in South Africa can request assistance from the IPU, who will then act in an advisory capacity during the investigation. Services can include offender profiling, investigative guidance, risk assessments, interviewing witnesses and suspects, crime scene analysis, CLA, and courtroom testimony. Because members of the unit are functional police officers, they are provided access that would otherwise not be afforded to civilian personnel (Labuschagne, 2003). They are therefore involved in investigations from start to finish. The IPU also provides training on psychologically motivated crimes to investigators in a three-week course called the "Psychologically Motive Crimes Course" (Labuschagne, 2003). This course provides training on topics related to serial murder, serial rape, child molestation, sadism, sexual murder, and paraphilia. The course also includes training for crime-scene photographers and prosecutors. The unit also provides training to officers from other police departments internationally. Finally, with regard to research, the IPU maintains a thorough database of solved and unsolved serial murders, including suspect details that can be used in subsequent offender profiles. The unit maintains affiliations with universities worldwide to assist in this research (Labuschagne, 2003).

In another practical potential application of IP, O'Meara et al. (2018) make the argument that IP research can be used in Ireland for cases of incidents of suspicious approaches to children. Suspicious approaches of children are defined by the Irish criminal justice system as a potential offender approaching someone under the age of 18 with suspicious or sinister intent. The author opines that research from IP about the empirical link between suspicious approaches to children and the possession of child sexual abuse (CSA) images can help investigators meet the reasonable suspicion standard of proof needed to obtain a warrant of suspects for such explicit material. Ultimately, the expertise of investigative psychologists can help establish that individuals who make suspicious approaches to children pose real threats to juveniles and may be reasonably assumed to possess CSA images (O'Meara et al., 2018).

Criticism of IP

One criticism of IP is that the empirical study of crimes is only as good as the data it is based on (Ainsworth, 2001). The data used to draw conclusions must be accurate, or else the conclusions drawn will be flawed. For instance, it is not always possible to determine whether a series of crimes has been committed by the same person, especially if one or more crimes go undetected or unreported. A potential challenge for IP is the variance between profilers in identifying details of a crime and applying relevant research (Petherick & Brooks, 2021). Another drawback to a research-based profiling approach is the low frequency of more extreme types of violence. Crimes that are rarer (e.g., serial murder) may not have adequate research on which to base a profile. Finally, it is still unclear whether IP represents an individual method of profiling or is a tool that can be used in the formation of an offender profile.

Conclusion

Developed in the 1980s by David Canter, IP was conceived as a more scientifically grounded approach to investigating crimes. The development of the field of IP also mirrored an increasing body of scholarly literature on offender profiling that has lent more legitimacy to profiling as a field of academic study. As Canter and Youngs (2009) note, while IP was in part developed to help investigators create offender profiles, it should not be mistaken as a synonym for "offender profiling" because it has many other applications to all areas of law enforcement. "Profiling" in the traditional sense is just a small piece of IP, and because IP is more scientifically grounded, it can be applied beyond the scope of what has traditionally been labeled "offender profiling" (Youngs & Canter, 2006). While other models of offender profiling still dominate in the United States, IP continues to grow as a field and is now used extensively within some law enforcement agencies worldwide (e.g., the United Kingdom; South Africa).

References

Ainsworth, P.B. (2001). *Offender profiling and crime analysis*. Routledge.
Bartol, C. R., & Bartol, A. M. (2013). *Criminal and behavioral profiling*. Sage.
Canter, D. (1995a). Psychology of offender profiling. In R. Bull & D. Carson (Eds.), *Handbook of psychology in legal contexts* (pp. 343–356). John Wiley & Sons.
Canter, D. (1995b). *Criminal shadows: Inside the mind of the serial killer*. HarperCollins.
Canter, D. (2004). Offender profiling and investigative psychology. *Journal of Investigative Psychology and Offender Profiling*, *1*, 1–15.
Canter, D. (2011). Resolving the offender "profiling equations" and the emergence of an investigative psychology. *Current Directs in Psychological Science*, *20*(1), 5–10.
Canter, D.V., & Alison, L.J. (1997). *Criminal detection and the psychology of crime*. Dartmouth.
Canter, D., & Alison, L. (1999). *Profiling in policy and practice*. Taylor & Francis Group.
Canter, D., & Fritzon, K. (1998). Differentiating arsonists: A model of firesetting actions and characteristics. *Legal and Criminological Psychology*, *3*, 73–96.
Canter, D., & Youngs, D. (2009). *Investigative psychology: Offender profiling and the analysis of criminal action*. John Wiley & Sons.
Dowden, C., Bennell, C., & Bloomfield, S. (2007). Advances in offender profiling: A systematic review of the profiling literature published over the past three decades. *Journal of Police and Criminal Psychology*, *22*, 44–56.
Ekman, P. (1991). Who can catch a liar? *American Psychologist*, *46*(9), 913–920.
Hickey, E. W. (2016). *Serial murderers and their victims* (7th ed.). Cengage Learning.
Kohnken, G. (1987). Training police officers to detect deceptive eyewitness statements: Does it work? *Social Behaviour*, *2*, 1–17.
Labuschagne, G.N. (2003). Offender profiling in South Africa: Its definition and context. *Acta Criminologica: Southern African Journal of Criminology*, *16*(3), 67–74.
Labuschagne, G., & Borgeson, K. (2010). Criminal profiling. In K. Borgeson & K. Kuehnle (Eds.), *Serial offenders: Theory and practice*. Jones & Bartlett Learning.
Milgram, S. (1963). Behavioral study of obedience. *Journal of Abnormal and Social Psychology*, *67*, 371–378.
O'Meara, P, Coyne, A., & Brassil, M. (2018). An appraisal of investigative psychology and the applications to suspicious approaches to children in the Irish criminal justice system. *Journal of Investigative Psychology and Offender Profiling*, *16*, 213–221.
Petherick, W., & Brooks, N. (2021). Reframing criminal profiling: A guide for integrated practice. *Psychiatry, Psychology & Law*, *28*(5), 694–710.
Petherick, W.A., & Turvey, B.E. (2008). Nomothetic methods of criminal profiling. In B.E. Turvey (Ed.), *Criminal profiling: An introduction to behavioral evidence analysis* (pp. 75–112). Elsevier.
Salfati, C. G. (2000). The nature of expressiveness and instrumentality in homicide: Implications for offender profiling. *Homicide Studies*, *4*(3), 265–293.
Webber, C. (2010). *Psychology & crime: Key approaches to criminology*. Sage.
Youngs, D. (2004). Personality correlates of offense style. *Journal of Investigative Psychology and Offender Profiling*, *1*, 99–119.
Youngs, D. (2009). Investigative psychology in the courtroom: Beyond the offender profile. *Journal of Investigative Psychology and Offender Profiling*, *6*, 1–9.
Youngs, D. E. & Canter, D. V. (2006). Introducing investigative psychology. In *Psychology and Law* (pp. 321–342). Juta & Co ltd. ISBN 9780702166624

8 Paraphilia

Rebecca C. Kendall

Introduction

Paraphilia is a psychological term that can be most simply defined as sexual preferences that are different from what is considered normal or socially acceptable. The aberrant sexual attraction can include animate or inanimate objects. While not all paraphilic behaviors are dangerous or illegal, sometimes these sexual interests include behaviors that can be harmful or extreme. In fact, deviant sexual interests can play a role in some of the most heinous crimes, including sexual abuse of children, rape, and serial murder. It is thus important for investigators to understand the wide range of deviant sexual preferences that exist and may motivate certain types of offending.

This chapter begins by presenting an overview of paraphilia, including definitions of paraphilia broadly and diagnostic criteria for specific types of paraphilic disorders. Next, it will consider etiological theories and development of paraphilic sexual interests over the life course. The remainder of the chapter will present research on the relationship between paraphilia and criminal behavior.

Defining and Diagnosing Paraphilia

The term paraphilia comes from the Greek words *para*, meaning beyond, amiss, or altered, and *philia*, meaning love (Money, 1990). So, paraphilia literally means love beyond the usual or abnormal love or sexuality. A more clinical definition of paraphilia would be sexual arousal to deviant or bizarre stimuli (images or activities). Despite the rather simple definition, conceptualization of paraphilia is difficult, given the "fuzzy border between so-called 'normal' or acceptable sexual behavior and abnormal sexual behavior" (Balon, 2016a, p. 2). Thus, it is challenging to make a distinction between acceptable and unacceptable behavior.

The recognition of paraphilic interests and behaviors is not new. For instance, according to Aggrawal (2009), the Bible is one of the oldest texts with reference to behavior we now call paraphilic (e.g., voyeurism, bestiality, exhibitionism, necrophilia). However, the term *paraphilia* was introduced by Friedrich Salomon Krauss in 1903 and was more broadly applied by Wilhelm Stekel several years later (Balon, 2016b). Since then, there have been many attempts to define and diagnose paraphilic interests as well as to understand the etiology of deviant sexual preferences.

The true prevalence of paraphilia/paraphilic disorders is unknown, primarily due to people's reluctance to disclose deviant sexual interests—either due to stigma or the fact that some of the behavior is considered illegal (Balon, 2016b). However, research from forensic and non-forensic populations provides some estimates. For instance, Bartova et al. (2020)

DOI: 10.4324/9781003366300-9

found that 31.3% of men and 13.6% of women admitted to at least one paraphilic interest, while Joyal and Carpenter (2017) found that almost 50% of non-offending adults reported sexual interest in at least one paraphilia.

There is a wide range of sexual interests that can be considered paraphilic. Scholars believe paraphilia exist on a continuum, with relatively harmless interests on one end (e.g., fetishes) and more extreme and damaging behavior on the other end (e.g., erotophonophilia; Healey, 2006). It is also possible for people to have occasional paraphilic fantasies (e.g., fantasies involving children, rape) without being diagnosed with a paraphilic disorder if the fantasies are not their only focus of sexual stimulation and they do not act on the deviant fantasy (Nolen-Hoeksema, 2004).

The American Psychiatric Association's DSM-V is used by most mental health practitioners in the United States and provides detailed diagnostic criteria for a class of paraphilic disorders (American Psychiatric Association, 2013). It should be noted that the DSM-5 criteria for diagnosing paraphilic disorders are not without critics. For instance, it has been argued by some that the diagnostic criteria are not specific enough (Lussier et al., 2021). The DSM-V describes paraphilic disorders as:

> Lasting over a period of at least six months where a person experiences recurrent, intense, sexually arousing urges, fantasies, and/or behaviors involving situations and/or objects occurring outside usual sexual norms. This may include nonhuman objects, non-genital body parts, suffering/humiliation of oneself or one's partner or persons who cannot give consent such as children and persons disabled. These urges and fantasies and/or behaviors create impairment and/or significant distress for the subject.

An important distinction is made in the DSM-5 between having a paraphilia and a paraphilic disorder. The latter refers to a paraphilia that is accompanied by significant distress to either oneself (e.g., guilt or shame) or another person if acted upon (e.g., a non-consenting person) or impairment in functioning. Therefore, a paraphilia is necessary but not sufficient to be diagnosed with a paraphilic disorder (Craig & Bartels, 2021). Previous versions of the DSM essentially viewed the presence of a paraphilia as a disorder. As Balon (2016a) notes, this change in more recent versions of the DSM is a step toward de-pathologizing paraphilia by emphasizing the impact the sexual interest has on the person's overall functioning.

The DSM classifies paraphilic disorders into two groups: anomalous activity preference and anomalous target preference (Balon, 2016a). The former includes courtship disorders and algolagnic disorders. Courtship disorders are considered those in which the focus of the paraphilic interest is on elements of normal human courtship behavior. Examples include voyeuristic disorder, exhibitionistic disorder, and frotteuristic disorder. Algolagnic disorders include pain and suffering as primary features of the sexual interest. Examples include sexual masochism disorder and sexual sadism disorder. Among those with an anomalous target preference, the paraphilia can be directed at humans (e.g., pedophilic disorder) or elsewhere (e.g., fetishistic disorder or transvestic disorder).

Some scholars have provided their own classification system for paraphilia, including those not specifically included in the DSM-V and those with small populations. For instance, Shaffer and Penn (2006) outline five categories of paraphilias on the basis of whether physical or non-physical behavior is included as well as the presence of violence. Physical paraphilias are considered those carried out in the presence or general vicinity of another person, while non-physical paraphilias are those in which the person gets sexual gratification without any physical contact or within view of another person. The categories include non-violent, physical paraphilias (e.g., swinging, exhibitionism, voyeurism); non-violent, non-physical paraphilias (e.g., telephone scatologia, technophilia); sadistic paraphilias (e.g., sadism, pyromania); masochistic paraphilias; and sadomasochistic paraphilias (e.g., sadomasochism, apotemnophilia; see Shaffer & Penn [2006] for a comprehensive list of known paraphilias based on their classification system).

It is common for one person to have multiple paraphilias, although one is typically dominant (Hickey, 2016). In their study of 561 non-incarcerated paraphiliacs, Abel et al. (1987) found that each subject was diagnosed with 2.02 paraphilias on average, with some subjects having as many as ten distinct paraphilic diagnoses (based on DSM-III diagnostic criteria). Researchers also examined the number of paraphilic acts committed by the subjects. Results showed great range in the number of completed paraphilic acts, with an average of 7.2 rapes to an average of 1,139.2 masochistic acts. The highest frequency of paraphilic acts involved masochism, frottage, transvestism, exhibitionism, and voyeurism. Among pedophiles, the highest number of sexual crimes against children was committed by paraphiliacs targeting young boys outside the home. The authors conclude that those with paraphilias that have been traditionally considered more harmless (e.g., exhibitionism, voyeurism) may also engage in more aggressive and harmful paraphilic acts (Abel et al., 1988).

Research suggests there is a high degree of comorbidity with paraphilic disorders (Balon, 2016a). For instance, courtship disorders (e.g., voyeurism, exhibitionism, frotteurism) often co-occur. Paraphilic disorders also frequently co-occur with other non-paraphilic disorders, such as hypersexuality, personality disorders, mood disorders, anxiety disorders, attention-deficit hyperactivity disorder, and conduct disorder.

There are many lesser-known paraphilias, including both legal and illegal behavior (a more complete list can be found elsewhere, e.g., Federoff, 2020). The following section provides a description of the paraphilic disorders listed in the DSM-V.

Voyeuristic Disorder

The term *voyeur* comes from the French word *voir*, meaning "to see" (Kaylor & Jeglic, 2021). A voyeur is often portrayed as someone looking into the window of a stranger's home, thus being colloquially called a "Peeping Tom." Voyeuristic disorder is characterized by intense and recurrent arousal from watching an unsuspecting person(s) while they are disrobing, naked, or engaged in sexual activity (American Psychiatric Association, 2013). According to Federoff (2020), voyeuristic disorder is one of the most misdiagnosed disorders in the DSM-V as it includes behaviors that often present in prosocial courtship behavior. Federoff emphasizes that a diagnosis of voyeuristic disorder requires that the person experience arousal, not just from observation, but from the belief that the observation is occurring without the person's knowledge or consent. The prevalence of voyeuristic disorder is unknown, as many people who engage in the behavior are able to avoid detection (Kaylor & Jeglic, 2021). Based on non-clinical samples, the highest lifetime prevalence of voyeuristic disorder is 12% for males and 4% for females (American Psychiatric Association, 2013). While voyeuristic disorder appears to be primarily diagnosed in men, this may be in part because women are less likely to be prosecuted for such behavior (Kaylor & Jeglic, 2021).

Exhibitionistic Disorder

Exhibitionism was first described clinically by French physician Ernest-Charles Lasegue in 1877, but it was the work of German psychiatrist Richard von Krafft-Ebing that brought it wider acknowledgment (Kaylor & Jeglic, 2021). The exhibitionist is often portrayed in pop culture as a "flasher"—a male who opens his long trench coat to reveal his genitalia underneath. Exhibitionistic disorder was first introduced to the DSM in the third edition. According to the DSM-V, exhibitionistic disorder refers to recurrent and intense sexual arousal from exposing one's genitals to a non-consenting person(s) (American Psychiatric Association, 2013). For some individuals, their sexual arousal revolves around the act or fantasy of exposing oneself, while for others, their arousal focuses on engaging in sex acts such as masturbation in public without the wish to be seen (Federoff, 2020). While research suggests that roughly twice as many men engage in exhibitionism than women, the large majority of individuals who are arrested for such behavior are men (Kaylor & Jeglic, 2021). Therefore, it may be more likely that women face fewer repercussions for this behavior. Like voyeurism, the true extent of exhibitionism is unknown. However, according to the DSM-V, the highest possible prevalence for exhibitionistic disorder is between 2% and 4% (American Psychiatric Association, 2013).

Frotteuristic Disorder

The term *frottage* comes from the French word *frotter*, meaning to rub or put pressure on someone (Balon, 2016c). Frotteurism was first described by French psychiatrist Valentin Magnan, but it was popularized and incorporated into a sexual context by Richard von Kraft-Ebbing (Balon, 2016). Frotteuristic disorder is defined in the DSM-V as the presence of recurrent and intense sexual arousal from rubbing against or touching a non-consenting person(s). Research suggests that frotteuristic behavior begins during adolescence, typically occurs between the ages of 15 and 25, and declines with age (Abel & Rouleau, 1990). Although the DSM-V estimates that frotteuristic acts may be committed by up to 30% of the population (American Psychiatric Association, 2013), accurate prevalence rates are difficult to attain. Frotteurism is not well understood, and there is a dearth of research on the disorder. Because frotteurism often occurs in public places, such as subways or elevators, the offender has the opportunity to disappear, and many victims may not be fully aware of the act. Thus, frotteurism is often unreported, and when it is reported, the offender can easily claim the act was accidental (Balon, 2016c).

Sexual Masochism Disorder

The term *masochism* was coined by Richard von Kraft-Ebbing after Austrian writer Leopold von Sacher-Masoch whose book *Venus in Furs* centers on a man who signs a contract with a woman to treat him as her slave (Federoff, 2020). Sexual masochism refers to recurrent and intense sexual arousal to being humiliated, beaten, bound, or made to suffer (American Psychiatric Association, 2013). While the true prevalence of sexual masochism is unknown, the DSM-V cites the prevalence of masochistic behaviors at 2.2% of males and 1.3% of females. However, other studies have found the presence of masochistic fantasies to be substantially higher. For example, in a study of 1,516 individuals in Quebec, 30–60% of the women sampled endorsed sexual fantasies of being tied up, dominated, spanked, whipped, or forced to have sex (Joyal et al., 2015). Given the potential that masochistic fantasies are relatively common, some scholars argue that masochism should be considered along a spectrum of sexual normality (Wylie & Wylie, 2016).

Not everyone who engages in masochistic behaviors/practices meets the criteria for masochistic disorder; an important element of the diagnostic criteria is that the condition causes significant distress or impairment in functioning. In addition, there are many people who engage in consensual masochistic behaviors/practices. Members of communities that engage in bondage-discipline, dominance-submission, sadism, and masochism (BDSM) emphasize the importance of consent (Federoff, 2020).

Sexual Sadism Disorder

The term *sadism* is derived from French author Donatien Alphonse François, Marquis de Sade, whose writings included themes of sexual violence. According to the DSM-V, sexual sadism disorder includes recurrent and intense sexual arousal from the physical or psychological suffering of another (American Psychiatric Association, 2013). It is unclear whether the sexual sadist's arousal comes from the violent or humiliating actions themselves, the victim's response to the violence or humiliation, or the feeling of power and control obtained from inflicting these actions on a victim (Hamilton & Rosen, 2016). Most estimates of the prevalence of sexual sadism disorder come from forensic samples, thus the true extent of sexual sadism in the general public is unknown. While the DSM-V estimates the prevalence of sexual sadism at 2–3% (American Psychiatric Association, 2013), one study of Austrian incarcerated sexual offenders found that 6% met the DSM-V criteria for sexual sadism (Eher et al., 2010).

Studies of paraphilic content in sexual fantasies from Germany and Canada suggest that while less common than fantasies of voyeurism and fetishism, fantasies involving masochistic or sadistic content were endorsed by a substantial portion of the samples (16–19% in Ahlers et al., 2011; 9–22% in Joyal & Carpenter, 2017). This suggests that fantasies with sadistic themes should not be considered rare and not all sexual sadists engage in harmful practices (Higgs et al. 2021). As with sexual masochists, some individuals with sadistic sexual fantasies may participate in consensual BDSM interactions. A fundamental rule in these interactions is that consent must be explicitly given, even when there is a dominant and submissive partner (Higgs et al. 2021).

Pedophilic Disorder

As defined in the DSM-V, pedophilic disorder refers to intense and recurrent sexually arousing fantasy or behavior involving prepubescent children (typically 13 years or younger; American Psychiatric Association, 2013). In addition, to meet diagnostic criteria, individuals must have either acted on the sexual urges or the sexual urges must cause them significant distress or impairment. Finally, for a diagnosis of pedophilic disorder, the individual must be older than 15 years and at least 5 years older than the child or children to whom they are attracted. While it is generally illegal to engage in sexual behavior with individuals under the age of 18 (depending on the specific legal jurisdiction), the sexual attraction to pubescent children is not considered an indication of pedophilia. In fact, a persistent and intense sexual attraction to pubescent children (typically between the ages of 11 and 14) has been labeled *hebephilia*. While pedophilia gets a lot of attention among the sexual deviant behaviors, it is estimated that the prevalence of the disorder in the male population is between 3% and 5%, and significantly lower in females (American Psychiatric Association, 2013).

It is important to distinguish between fantasy and actions. Although pedophilic preference is one of the strongest risk factors for sexually offending against children (Seto, 2008), the sexual interest (i.e., pedophilia) and behavior (i.e., sexually offending against children) are distinct phenomena. Thus, the mere presence of pedophilic disorder does not necessitate that one has ever acted on fantasies involving sexual behavior with a child. In addition, as will be discussed later in the chapter, not all individuals who sexually offend against children meet the criteria for pedophilic disorder (Box 8.1).

Box 8.1 Case Study: Pedophilic Sexual Offender*

Donald is a White male with a diagnosis of pedophilic disorder. Donald's sexual offending history involved three prepubescent females under the age of 13. During treatment, Donald discussed the development of his sexual interests. He described an incident when he was ten years old in which he and a male neighborhood friend played "strip poker" with his older sister. He explained that he attempted to touch his sister, but she would not let him. Donald indicated that he later initiated several games of "strip poker" with his younger sister when he was 15 and she was eight years old. He explained that these games resulted in two incidents of oral rape and one incident of vaginal rape against his sister. Donald explained that at the time of his sexual offending against his sister, he was unable to have a relationship with someone his own age and that he "felt like an outcast." He stated that he had tried previously to initiate relationships with female peers, but that "nobody would go out with [him]." He reported that he was therefore motivated to engage in sexual behavior with his sister because he had easy access to her and could gain control over her. Donald reported that he exposed himself in public at the age of 15 when he ran outside his house naked to see what it would feel like. Donald also indicated that he looked into windows on several occasions as an adolescent to see his sisters and their friends getting dressed. Donald indicated that he was "obsessed" with receiving oral sex between the ages of 15 and 30 and that as an adult he "begged" his ex-wife for oral sex every day.

Donald stated that he believes he was preoccupied with sex, particularly oral sex, and that he typically thought about sex on a daily basis. He indicated that he thought about sex a lot in adolescence when he was unable to have sex with anyone and that he believes his excessive thoughts of sex contributed to his sexual offense against his sister. Donald also explained that he fantasized about oral sex whenever he saw his wife or infant daughter sucking on anything (e.g., pacifier or, lollipop). Donald stated that he is attracted to children with small buttocks, of a small stature, with thin lips, and a small mouth.

* *The Case of Donald (as provided by the author)*

Fetishistic Disorder

According to the DSM-V, fetishistic disorder refers to recurrent and intense sexual arousal to non-living objects or specific non-genital body parts (American Psychiatric Association, 2013). Federoff (2020) notes that the broad definition of fetishism causes diagnostic confusion because any paraphilia could be called a fetish. Fetishistic disorder is less likely than other paraphilia to involve illegal behavior or victimization (Martin, 2016). Despite the probable high prevalence of fetishistic interests, individuals are unlikely to seek help for fetishistic disorder, even when accompanied by significant distress, because they either view the condition as unworthy of clinical care or feel embarrassed to discuss it in treatment (Martin, 2016).

The DSM-V does not provide prevalence rates for fetishistic disorder (American Psychiatric Association, 2013). Because fetishism is unlikely to involve illegal behavior for which individuals are prosecuted and clients often do not present with the condition in treatment, it is difficult to estimate the true prevalence of the disorder. In a study of 381 internet discussion groups with a total of 150,000 members, Scorolli et al. (2007) found that the primary sexual preferences were non-genital body parts and features (33%) and objects associated with the body (30%). Body parts of interest included feet or toes, body fluids such as blood or urine, and body features, including obesity or height, hair, muscles, and body modification (e.g., tattoos or piercings). Objects associated with the body included items such as stockings, skirts, footwear, and costumes. While information provided from internet discussion boards may not generalize to the wider population, this is the largest study of fetishistic interests and provides an interesting reflection into atypical sexual interests.

Transvestic Disorder

Although the term *transvestism* was introduced by Magnus Hirschfeld in the early 20th century, there have been references to transvestic behavior in earlier works, including the Bible (Balon, 2016d). According to the DSM-V, transvestic disorder refers to recurrent and intense sexual arousal from wearing clothes of the opposite gender (American Psychiatric Association, 2013). While transvestism refers to cross-dressing for the purpose of sexual arousal, there are individuals who engage in cross-dressing for other, non-sexual purposes (e.g., drag queens). There is also a wide range of clothing that is not gender specific. The prevalence rate for transvestic disorder is believed to be less than 3% among males (American Psychiatric Association, 2013) and considered extremely rare among females (Balon, 2016d). However, as Federoff (2020) points out, acts of transvestism (or sexual arousal from wearing women's clothing, particularly lingerie) appear to be relatively common, and thus it may be harmful to label these individuals as having a psychiatric disorder.

Other Specified Paraphilic Disorder and Unspecified Paraphilic Disorder

The DSM-V includes a category of disorders called *Other Specific Paraphilic Disorders* that refers to specific paraphilia that do not meet the full criteria for any of the other paraphilic disorders. These include, but are not limited to, telephone scatoalogia (obscene phone calls), necrophilia (corpses), zoophilia (animals), coprophilia (feces), klismaphilia (enemas), and urophilia (urine). Rare paraphilia (e.g., vampirism) with small known populations would be included in this category (Briken et al. 2016). The DSM-V also includes a "catch-all" category of disorders called *Unspecific Paraphilic Disorders*, which includes any disorder with characteristics of a paraphilic disorder that does not meet the criteria for any other paraphilic disorder (American Psychiatric Association, 2013).

Etiology and Development over the Life Course

While theoretical explanations have developed over the past century, the true etiology of paraphilias is unknown. In addition, there are likely to be different etiological processes at play depending on the specific paraphilic interest (e.g., pedophilia vs. fetishism) as well as multiple developmental pathways to paraphilic interests. The following is an overview of developmental and etiological models of general sexual interests, broadly, and paraphilias, specifically.

One prominent theory of human sexuality and the development of paraphilic interests is Money's (1984) concept of "lovemaps." Money proposed that human sexual interests develop during critical periods in a similar way to how children acquire language during critical periods. Money proposed that lovemaps develop shortly after birth and are fully developed by puberty. He also posited that one's lovemap could be influenced by relevant experience. In the case of paraphilias, Money suggested that these deviant sexual interests develop when the lovemap is "vandalized" by experiences such as sexual abuse. Money proposed that a paraphilic lovemap will most often be fully developed by puberty, and that once a lovemap is established, it is likely to remain stable throughout one's life.

The onset of puberty appears to be an important milestone in the development of sexual interests, including deviant sexual preferences. The average age of puberty is 13 and that is typically when masturbation begins among adolescents (Healey, 2006). It is believed that one important way sexual interests are developed is through the conditioning process by pairing sexual arousal via masturbation with sexual fantasy (Laws & Marhsall, 1990; McGuire et al., 1964; Storms, 1981). Bartels et al.'s (2021) Dual-Process Model of Sexual Thinking describes how fleeting sexual thoughts can become prolonged sexual fantasies through masturbation. In the model, initially, a person will experience a spontaneous sexual thought. Next, the person will appraise the thought and either validate it or reject it. If the thought is validated, it may be elaborated upon. If it is rejected, the person will try to suppress or forget it. When thoughts are elaborated upon, the person will engage in prolonged mental imagery, such as retrieving related memories to reconstruct a previous experience or envisioning a future sexual scenario. Frequent sexual fantasizing will strengthen the imagery and facilitate generation of new imagery. Sexual fantasizing that accompanies masturbation will tend to have a longer duration because it will last until the person reaches climax.

Several factors have been linked to the development and/or maintenance of deviant sexual arousal in juveniles, including prior maltreatment, exposure to pornography, substance abuse, and exposure to aggressive and violent models (either older youth or adults; Hunter & Becker, 1994). In one study of 97 offenders (including paraphilic sex offenders and non-sex, non-violent, non-drug-related property offenders) in Australia, Lee et al. (2002) found that the odds of receiving a paraphilic diagnosis were significantly and positively associated with scores for childhood emotional abuse and family dysfunction, childhood behavior problems, and childhood sexual abuse. Further, findings showed that experiencing childhood sexual abuse, childhood emotional abuse and family dysfunction, and childhood behavior problems were predictive of pedophilia. Childhood emotional abuse and family dysfunction were predictive of rape. Interestingly, childhood sexual abuse had a negative relationship with exhibitionism, meaning the odds of receiving a diagnosis of exhibitionism were lower for those who experienced childhood sexual abuse.

Scholars suggest that paraphilias exist on a continuum, with more harmless interests on one end (e.g., fetishes) and more extreme and damaging behavior on the other end (e.g., erotophonophilia). Healey (2006) proposes a dichotomous etiological model of paraphilias to explain the development of these two broad groups of paraphilias. The first group of paraphilias includes those resulting from the introduction of deviant stimuli to one's developing sexuality. The more harmless paraphilias are believed to be explained by this developmental pathway. Essentially, a particular stimulus is introduced while one is developing their sexuality, and that stimulus is conditioned through masturbation and fantasy. Healey posits that the tendency to become sensitized to the stimulus may explain why people develop other closely related paraphilia. For instance, a lingerie fetish may progress to become a cross-dressing paraphilia. The second group of paraphilias are those resulting from psychological or physical trauma experienced during the development of one's sexuality. Healey suggests this group includes more harmful paraphilias that derive from trauma, as the person learns to associate feelings of shame, inadequacy, guilt, fear, aggression, or hatred with sex. The traumatic experience will occur during the child's sexual development, or if it occurs prior, it will leave a long-lasting impression. During puberty, the adolescent's negative emotions will become linked with their incoming sexual feelings. Healey suggests that paraphilias such as exhibitionism and frotteurism are linked to feelings of inadequacy by a caregiver during their developing sexuality. Sadism, erotophonophilia, and biastophilia may be caused by an abused child or adolescent attempting to regain some form of control by victimizing others.

For decades, researchers have sought out biological explanations for paraphilic sexual interests. Results from this body of research have been mixed and limited by methodological issues, so any conclusions should be viewed with caution (Balon, 2016). In addition, while biological factors may play a significant role, it is likely that the development of deviant sexual preferences involves an interaction of genes, hormones, and environmental factors (Alanko et al., 2016).

Quite a few studies have examined the neurobiological processes involved in the development of pedophilic preference. For instance, Cantor et al. (2005) found that pedophilic child sexual offenders not only had lower IQ scores, but that the lower the IQ, the younger the victim. Cohen et al. (2002) also found lower IQ scores in incarcerated pedophilic men compared to controls. Cantor et al. (2004, 2005) have also linked pedophilia to left-handedness and other potential cognitive deficits. While studies have shown that pedophilic child sexual offenders may have distinct neurocognitive deficits, the methodological limitations inherent in these studies (e.g., potential uncontrolled variables) prevent definitive evidence of a neurodevelopmental cause of pedophilia.

There is some evidence for pedophilia-specific functional brain correlates. For instance, Fonteille et al. (2019) found that activation in the right inferior temporal gyrus is positively correlated with arousal to visual sexual stimuli of children. In addition, Ponseti et al. (2012) were able to differentiate between men with sexual preference for children versus preference for adults based on differences in blood oxygen level-dependent response to sexual stimuli. Walter et al. (2007) found differences in brain activity, specifically in the hypothalamus and dorsolateral prefrontal cortex, during processing of sexual stimuli between pedophilic child sexual offenders and controls. Although the research is preliminary, there is some emerging evidence to suggest heritability and androgenic factors in the development of pedophilia. For example, Kruger et al. (2019) found that child sexual offenders showed increased prenatal androgen exposure.

Interestingly, research suggests that the etiology of paraphilias may depend on the origin of the specific disorder. For instance, paraphilic behaviors have been noted in patients with some diseases and medical conditions, such as Parkinson's disease, Tourette's syndrome, stroke, dementia, traumatic brain injury, and epilepsy. Scarpazza et al. (2021) distinguish between idiopathic and acquired pedophilia, suggesting that they may be two different disorders involving distinct neural networks. Acquired pedophilia is considered the development of pedophilic urges and/or behavior in individuals after focal brain lesions. In this case, pedophilic interests are considered a symptom of an underlying neurological insult. Conversely, idiopathic pedophilia has an unknown etiology, is considered a psychiatric disorder, typically develops in adolescence, and remains stable across the life course. In their meta-analysis of studies on the neural underpinnings of pedophilic behavior, Scarpazza et al. (2021) found evidence for a shared neurobiological substrate in acquired pedophilia, involving the orbitofrontal cortex areas, the posterior midline structures, the right inferior temporal gyrus, and the left fusiform gyrus. On the contrary, idiopathic pedophilia did not appear associated with consistent brain alterations that could be detected by structural or functional neuroimaging. The authors conclude that these findings have implications for further studies on the neural basis of pedophilic behavior, as it may be necessary to investigate these two groups separately.

One recent study examined sex differences in paraphilic interests between men and women in a non-clinical Canadian sample (Dawson et al., 2016). Findings indicated that men reported less repulsion to most paraphilic interests and more arousal to a variety of paraphilic acts.

Results also showed that sex drive (i.e., hypersexuality and sexual compulsivity) fully mediated the relationship between sex differences in paraphilics interests. The authors propose that a high sex drive prompts the development of atypical sexual activities.

Paraphilia and Criminal Offending

As noted at the outset of this chapter, it is important to distinguish between paraphilia and criminal behavior. Not all individuals who commit sex crimes have paraphilic interests, and not all those with atypical sexual interests sexually offend. In fact, Eher et al. (2019) found that only 43% of persons with convictions for sexual offending had a diagnosed paraphilic disorder. In addition, research suggests that paraphilic sexual interests are relatively common in people who do not engage in sexual offending. However, it is evident that paraphilia *can* motivate some individuals to engage in criminal offending. Thus, the remainder of this chapter will discuss the role of paraphilia in several types of criminal behavior, including sexual offending and murder.

Sexual Offending

Although not everyone with paraphilic interests engages in illegal or harmful behavior, it is also not uncommon for people convicted of sexual offenses to have multiple paraphilia or paraphilic diagnoses (Abel et al., 1988; Eher et al., 2019). Thus, although paraphilia and sexual offending are not synonymous, there can be significant overlap between these phenomena. So, what prevents some individuals with paraphilia from engaging in sex crimes? Some researchers suggest that self-regulation is important because those with low self-control are unable to control their sexual urges, which may lead them to seek immediate gratification without consideration of the consequences (Craig & Bartels, 2021). Some paraphilia also appear to be more closely linked to criminal behavior than others. For instance, in a study of 95 civilly committed male sex offenders, Stinson et al. (2008) found that the most common paraphilia (both behavior and DSM-IV-TR diagnosis) was pedophilia, followed by paraphilia NOS and rape. Further, 50% of the sample met the criteria for more than one paraphilia.

Ward and Beech (2008) note that there are multiple trajectories to sexual offending, and paraphilia may play a role in some types of sexual victimization. Hickey (2016) distinguishes between *sex offenders* and *sexual predators*. Hickey describes sex offenders as those offenders who have one victim (often a family member), are "non-progressive" in their deviant sexual behavior, are non-psychopathic, are non-paraphilic, and pose a lower risk to the general public (p. 160). Hickey considers sexual predators to be those individuals who commit multiple sex offenses (including family and/or stranger victims), are progressively more sexually exploitive, have psychopathic traits, often have one or more paraphilias, and pose a more significant risk to the general public. Therefore, while paraphilic interests can be helpful in explaining some sexual offending behavior, they are less relevant in other types of sexual victimization.

It is estimated that between 2% and 5% of sexual offenders are sadistic (Langevin, 1990). Salter (2003) notes that some sadistic sexual offenders receive a generalized high from the pain and suffering of others, that she likens to being high on drugs. She also notes that the way sadistic sex offenders discuss the high they get from violent behavior is similar to drug addiction in that they require more and more to get the same effect. Salter attributes the escalation of violent behavior of sadists to this need to chase the high. While sadistic sexual offenders are certainly callous, Salter (2003) suggests they do not lack empathy in the traditional sense. Rather, they seem to be in tune with the victim's emotions and actually thrive off the pain and suffering they cause. Salter refers to this as a type of "reverse empathy" (p. 108).

While pedophilia and CSA often co-occur, not all offenders who sexually abuse children have a deviant arousal pattern for children. For some sex offenders, such as psychopathic offenders, the child may be the only available victim to fulfill their sexual needs. Other offenders sexually abuse children because they seek intimacy with others and do not have the social skills to attain it from other adults (Salter, 2003). In addition, sexual offenders of children describe other motivations for their offending, such as seeking affirmation or deriving a sense of power and control from sexual contact with children (Sullivan & Sheehan, 2016).

Although most individuals who sexually abuse children are male, there is a small group of child sexual offenders that are female. Research suggests there are three basic groups of female offenders who molest children (Salter, 2003). The first group is the largest and is known to sexually abuse younger victims (under the age of six) and typically their own children. The second group primarily offends against adolescents and is known as the "teacher/lover" group. Finally, there is a group of female sex offenders who are at least initially coerced into having sex with children by a male partner.

Murder

Although sexual murders constitute only a small minority of all violent crimes, they engender a significant amount of fear in the public. These are also crimes that receive wide press coverage when they occur. It is a widely held belief that most serial murders are sexual in nature (Lunde, 1976; Ressler, 1985, 1988; Revitch, 1965). In some serial murders, there may appear to be no overt sexual motive; however, the sexual element of the crimes may be hidden by more overt motives such as financial gain (Hickey, 2016). Therefore, it is important to examine the role of deviant sexual interests in homicidal behavior.

There appears to be some discrepancy in definitions of sexual murder. According to the FBI (Ressler et al., 1988), there are six characteristics that can be used to define sexual homicide (SH), including the victim's attire or lack of attire; exposure of sexual parts of the victim's body; sexual positioning of the body; insertion of foreign objects into the victim's cavities; evidence of sexual intercourse (oral, anal, or vaginal); and evidence of substitute sexual activity, interest, or sadistic fantasy. It is also not entirely clear how SH is distinct from non-sexual homicide (NSH) and non-lethal, violent sexual assault (VSA). In a recent study, Chopin and Beauregard (2019) examined 1,736 French cases of NSH, SH, and VSA to determine distinguishing characteristics between these groups. Results showed significant differences between the groups, suggesting that sexual murderers are a unique class of offender. There were significant differences between SH and both NSH and VSA related to both MO and offender characteristics. Specifically, SH offenders were more likely than VSA and NSH offenders to show evidence of paraphilia, sexual collections, and sexual dysfunction. The authors conclude that sexual murderers should be considered a distinct type of offender that is distinguished from NSH offenders and non-lethal sexual offenders.

Researchers have also examined the differences between serial sexual murderers (SSM; i.e., three or more victims) and non-serial sexual murderers (NSM; i.e., one or two victims). James and Proulx (2014) suggest that SSM are characterized by psychosexual problems (e.g., compulsive masturbation, paraphilia, and sadistic sexual fantasies) and the early development of coercive sexual behavior, while NSM are more characterized by their antisocial traits such as impulsivity and hostility. In addition, in their systematic review of the characteristics and MO of SSM and NSM, James and Proulx (2016) found thematic differences in the behavior between the two groups. The most common themes during the commission of the offending among the SSM were control, domination, rage, and vengeance. The most common themes for the NSM were agitation, anger, and excitement by killing. SSM were more likely to torture the victim, keep the victim confined for more than 24 hours, and record the murder. SSM were more likely to perform necrophilic acts than the NSM. The authors conclude that these findings suggest there are two distinct profiles for sexual murderers: one for SSM and one for NSM.

An understanding of paraphilia can help in the development of SH typologies. In their study of 342 males convicted for violent sexual offenses resulting in either physical injury or death of the victim, Healey et al. (2016) found four distinct groups of violent offenders based on their crime scene behaviors. The first group, labeled the *Angry—low/moderate lethality* sex offenders, represented 44% of the sample. This group primarily offended against a known victim, did not use a weapon, did not use restraints, and did not spend a lot of time with the victim. These offenders were largely non-homicidal, as there was no evidence they were sadistically or sexually motivated to murder the victim. The second most common group was labeled the *Situational Precipitated—moderate/high lethality* sex offenders and represented 29% of the sample. This group was similar to the *Angry* group, with the primary difference being the use of a weapon during the offending in the *Situational Precipitated* group. The majority of these offenders are considered homicidal sexual offenders. When these offenders did kill the victim, there was little evidence of sexual sadism. The authors suggest that the primary motivation of these offenders is to sexually assault the victim, but as they become increasingly angry during the offending coupled with the presence of a weapon, they may end up killing the victim. The presence of other situational factors, such as the offender being intoxicated, can also increase the likelihood of the outcome being lethal.

The third group, labeled the *Sadistic—low lethality* sex offenders, represented 18% of the sample and was characterized by high levels of humiliation, use of a weapon during the offending, and the use of physical restraints of the victims (Healey et al., 2016). These offenders appear to be primarily sexually motivated. The majority of the offenders in this group were considered non-homicidal sex offenders. Finally, the *Predatory—high lethality* group represented the smallest portion of the sample. They almost exclusively targeted strangers, had high levels of weapon use during the offending, were unlikely to use restraints, were very likely to spend more than 30 minutes with the victim, and were unlikely to humiliate the victim or engage in a variety of sexual behaviors with the victim. The authors conclude that the profile of the *Predatory* group is most consistent with that of the sexual murderers. This offender likely plans the sexual assault, sets out to kill the victim, and picks strangers to avoid detection. Findings from this study support the distinction between homicidal and non-homicidal sexual offenders. In addition, the authors suggest that homicidal sexual offenders are not a homogeneous group, and that distinction should be made based on the degree of lethality between at least two groups of sexual murderers.

One subtype of sexual murder is erotophonophilia, also known as lust murder (Arrigo & Purcell, 2001). Erotophonophilia includes a component of sadism, and the offender receives sexual satisfaction from torturing the victim. With erotophonophiliacs, their fantasies will become increasingly violent and deadly over time, and this will manifest in their killings. Arrigo and Purcell (2001) combine elements of Burgess et al.'s (1986) motivational model and Hickey's (1997) trauma-control model to develop an integrated model for explaining paraphilia and the role of sadistic sexual acts as motivation for SH. According to the authors, paraphilic behaviors are proposed to originate during their formative development (i.e., childhood and early adolescence). Offenders may possess certain factors that predispose them to deviant behavior, including psychological (e.g., personality disorder), sociological (e.g., dysfunctional family dynamics), or biological factors (e.g., extra Y chromosome). Trauma can also impact one's psychosocial adjustment, and this model suggests paraphilia are at least in part the result of unresolved trauma during the offender's formative development. As a consequence of traumatic events during the offender's formative years, they are likely to develop feelings of personal failure, self-doubt, anger, and rejection from society. This will then interfere with the adolescent's ability to form attachments with others. The offender will then rely on fantasy and daydreaming in the place of these missing attachments. The offender's anger and hostility toward society will combine with their social isolation to form the basis of their violent fantasies. The offender will develop fetishes that have some important symbolic link to their traumatic experiences. The offenders' paraphilic development will then be sustained through compulsive masturbation, fantasy, and facilitating factors (e.g., alcohol, drugs, pornography). Reliance on facilitators will escalate over time until the offender is desensitized and may eventually act out their violent fantasies in SH. The offender may experience stressors (e.g., rejection, isolation, ridicule) that trigger them to lose control and act out (in some cases engaging in erotophonophilia). And finally, the offender will experience increasingly violent fantasies over time.

Examination of the role of paraphilia in serial homicide can help with crime scene investigations. Several studies have been conducted looking at sexualized crime scene behavior of serial murderers. For instance, Hickey (2006) found that roughly half of serial killers engaged in sexual activity with the victims, but this did not include those who sexualized the victims without leaving evidence. Some crime scenes may show evidence of sexual sadism, including whips, chains, animal mutilation, hair cutting, mutilation of the corpse, or cannibalism. Engaging in signature behavior can help offenders fulfill their fantasies. Such signature behavior could include specific language, necrophilia, use of foreign objects, bondage, or mutilations. Some behaviors can be both the mode of the victim's death and the offender's sexualized signature. Not all serial murders will show signs of signature, in some cases because the offender is still in the process of developing their fantasies. Hickey (2006) suggests that when signatures are present in serial murders, they will likely be later in the series due to the progression of sexual fantasies over time, as many offenders experiment with acting out parts of their fantasies before fully embracing them. This can be helpful to investigators who may look for the level of progression or sophistication of the offender over time.

In their study of ritual and signature in 38 serial SH offenders, Schlesinger et al. (2010) found that 97.4% engaged in ritualistic behavior with at least two victims in their series of homicides. The most common ritual behaviors were penis penetration (39.2%), binding (31.6%), overkill (25.3%), beating (21.5%), posing (17.7%), and mutilation (13.3%). The authors identified four themes from the offenders' ritual behavior, including power, control, and domination (e.g., making victim engage in specific acts); rage and revenge (e.g., overkill); degradation and humiliation (e.g., forced bestiality); and sexual fixation (e.g., collecting specific items from victims such as underwear). The authors conclude that findings did not support the idea that serial SH offenders leave unique signatures at every crime scene; rather, while they engaged in some ritualistic behavior, they typically did not engage in the exact same behavior at every offense. Although most of the rituals were not the exact same, they were thematically and behaviorally similar and consistent.

Conclusion

Studies of non-clinical, non-forensic samples suggest that paraphilic sexual interests may be more common than initially believed. It is important to consider, however, that paraphilia exist on a continuum with more harmless interests on one end and more harmful or dangerous interests on the other end. So, while paraphilic interests, broadly, may be relatively common, it is only a subset of individuals who have more extreme deviant sexual preferences. While sexual offending is not necessary or sufficient for a diagnosis of paraphilic disorder, there is certainly some overlap between these phenomena. There also appear to be some paraphilia, such as pedophilia or sadism, that are more closely tied with criminal offending, particularly more extreme and lethal violence. Although burgeoning research is beginning to shed light on the etiology and development of paraphilic interests, there is still much that we do not know about how and why people develop deviant or unusual sexual preferences and the role these interests play in violent offending.

References

Abel, G. G., Becker, J. V., Mittelman, M., Cunningham-Rathner, J., Rouleau, J. K., & Murphy, W. D. (1987). Self-reported sex crimes of nonincarcerated paraphiliacs. *Journal of Interpersonal Violence*, *2*, 3–25.

Abel, G. G., Becker, J. V., Cunningham-Rathner, J., Mittelman, M., & Rouleau, J. K. (1988). Multiple paraphilic diagnoses among sex offenders. *The Bulletin of the American Academy of Psychiatry and the Law*, *16*, 153–168.

Abel, G., & Rouleau, J. (1990). The nature and extent of sexual assault. In W. L. Marshall, D. R. Laws, H. E. Barbaree (Ed.), H*andbook of sexual assault: Issues, theories and treatment of the offender* (pp. 9–12). Plenum.

Aggrawal, A. (2009). References to the paraphilias and sexual crimes in the Bible. *Journal of Forensic and Legal Medicine*, *16*, 109–114.

Ahlers, C. J., Schaefer, G. A., Mundt, I. A., Roll, S., Englert, H., Willich, S. N., & Beier, K. M. (2011). How unusual are the contents of paraphilias? Paraphilia-associated sexual arousal patterns in a community-based sample of men. *Journal of Sexual Medicine*, *8*(5), 1362–1370.

Alanko, K., Gunst, A., Mokros, A., & Santtila, P. (2016). Paraphilias: Genetic variants associated with male pedophilic sexual interest. *The Journal of Sexual Medicine*, *13*, 835–842.

American Psychiatric Association. (2013). *Diagnostic and statistical manual of mental disorders* (5th ed.).

Arrigo, B. A., & Purcell, C. E. (2001). Explaining paraphilias and lust murder: Toward an integrated model. *International Journal of Offender Therapy and Comparative Criminology*, *45*, 6–31.

Balon, R. (2016a). Introduction to the realm of paraphilias. In R. Balon (Ed.), *Practical guide to paraphilia and paraphilic disorders* (pp. 1–14). Springer.

Balon, R. (2016b). General information: History, etiology and theory (e.g., courtship), diagnosis, comorbidity and prevalence. In R. Balon (Ed.), *Practical guide to paraphilia and paraphilic disorders* (pp. 15–30). Springer.

Balon, R. (2016c). Frotteuristic disorder. In R. Balon (Ed.), *Practical guide to paraphila and paraphilic disorders* (pp. 93–106). Springer.

Balon, R. (2016d). Transvestic disorder. In R. Balon (Ed.), *Practical guide to paraphilia and paraphilic disorders* (pp. 171–186). Springer.

Bartels, R. M., Beech, A. R., & Harkins, L. (2021). Understanding sexual thoughts and sexual fantasizing: The dual-process model of sexual thinking. In L. A. Craig, & R. M. Bartels (Ed.), *Sexual deviance: Understanding and managing deviant sexual interests and paraphilic disorders* (pp. 53–66). John Wiley & Sons, Ltd.

Bartova, K., Androvicova, R., Krejcova, L., Weiss, P., & Klapilova, K. (2020). The prevalence of paraphilic interests in the Czech population: Preference, arousal, the use of pornography, fantasy, and behavior. *Journal of Sex Research*, *58*(1), 86–96.

Briken, P., Klein, V., & von Franque, F. (2016). Other specified paraphilic disorders. In R. Balon (Ed.), *Practical guide to paraphilia and paraphilic disorders* (pp. 187–196). Springer.

Burgess, A. W., Hartman, C. R., Ressler, R. K., Douglas, J. E., & McCormack, A. (1986). Sexual homicide: A motivational model. *Journal of Interpersonal Violence*, *13*, 251–272.

Cantor, J.M., Blanchard, R., Christensen, B.K., Dickey, R., Klassen, P.E., Beckstead, A.L., Blak, T., & Kuban, M.E. (2004). Intelligence, memory, and handedness in pedophilia. *Neuropsychology*, *18*, 3–14.

Cantor, J.M., Blanchard, R., Robichaud, L.K., & Christensen, B.K. (2005). Quantitative reanalysis of aggregate data on IQ in sexual offenders. *Psychological Bulletin*, *131*, 555–568.

Chopin, J., & Beauregard, E. (2019). The sexual murderer is a distinct type of offender. *International Journal of Offender Therapy and Comparative Criminology*, *63*, 1597–1620.

Cohen, L.J., Nikiforov, K., Gans, S., Poznansky, O., McGeoch, P., Weaver, C., King, E.G., Cullen, K., & Galynker, I. (2002). Heterosexual male perpetrators of childhood sexual abuse: A preliminary neuropsychiatric model. *Psychiatric Quarterly*, *73*, 313–336.

Craig, L.A., & Bartels, R.M. (2021). An overview of sexual deviance and paraphilic disorders. In L. A. Craig, & R. M. Bartels (Ed.), *Sexual deviance: Understanding and managing deviant sexual interests and paraphilic disorders* (pp. 3–22). John Wiley & Sons, Ltd.

Dawson, S. J., Bannerman, B. A., Lalumiere, M. L. (2016). Paraphilic interests: An examination of sex differences in a nonclinical sample. *Sexual Abuse: A Journal of Research and Treatment*, *28*, 20–45.

Eher, R., Rettenberger, M., Turner, D. (2019). The prevalence of mental disorders in incarcerated contact sexual offenders. *Acta Psychiatrica Scandinavica*, *139*, 572–581.

Eher, R., Rettenberger, M., & Schilling, F. (2010). Psychiatrische Diagnosen von Sexualstraftätern: Eine empirische Untersuchung von 807 inhaftierten Kindesmissbrauchstätern und Vergewaltigern [Psychiatric diagnoses of sexual offenders. An empirical investigation of 807 delinquents imprisoned for child abuse and rape]. *Zeitschrift für Sexualforschung*, *23*(1), 23–35.

Federoff, J.P. (2020). *The paraphilias: Changing suits in the evolution of sexual interest paradigms*. Oxford University Press.

Fonteille, V., Redoute, J., Lamothe, P., Straub, D., Lavenne, F., Le Bars, D., Moulier, V., Marchand, J.J., Vittoz, A., Leriche, C., & Stoleru, S. (2019).

Hamilton, D.V., & Rosen, J. (2016). Sexual sadism disorder. In R. Balon (Ed.), *Practical guide to paraphilia and paraphilic disorders* (pp. 123–140). Springer.

Healey, J., Beauregard, E., Beech, A., & Vettor, S. (2016). Is the sexual murderer a unique type of offender? A typology of violent sexual offenders using crime scene behaviors. *Sexual Abuse: A Journal of Research and Treatment*, *28*, 512–533.

Healey, J. (2006). The etiology of paraphilia: A dichotomous model. In E. W. Hickey (Ed.), *Sex crimes and paraphilia* (pp. 57–68). Prentice Hall.

Hickey, E. W. (2006). *Sex crimes and paraphilia*. Pearson.

Hickey, E. W. (1997). *Serial murderers and their victims* (2nd ed.). Wadsworth.

Hickey, E. W. (2016). *Serial murderers and their victims* (7th ed.). Cengage Learning.

Higgs, T., Proulx, J., Gauthier, A., Garant, E., & James, J. (2021). Sexual sadism and offending. In L. A. Craig, & R. M. Bartels (Ed.), *Sexual deviance: Understanding and managing deviant sexual interests and paraphilic disorders* (pp. 189–206). John Wiley & Sons, Ltd.

Hunter, J. A., & Becker, J. V. (1994). The role of deviant sexual arousal in juvenile sexual offending. *Criminal Justice and Behavior*, *21*, 132–149.

James, J., & Proulx, J. (2014). A psychological and developmental profile of sexual murderers: A systematic review. *Aggression and Violent Behavior*, *19*, 592–607.

James, J., & Proulx, J. (2016). The modus operandi of serial and nonserial sexual murderers: A systematic review. *Aggression and Violent Behavior*, *31*, 200–218.

Joyal, C.C., & Carpenter, J. (2017). The prevalence of paraphilic interests and behaviors in the general population: A provincial survey. *The Journal of Sex Research*, *54*, 161–171.

Joyal, C.C., Cossette, A., & Lapierre, V. (2015). What exactly is an unusual sexual fantasy? *Journal of Sexual Medicine*, *12*(2), 328–340.

Kaylor, L., & Jeglic, E. L. (2021). Non-contact paraphilic disorders and offending. In L. A. Craig, & R. M. Bartels (Ed.), *Sexual deviance: Understanding and managing deviant sexual interests and paraphilic disorders* (pp. 171–188). John Wiley & Sons, Ltd.

Kruger, T.H.C., Sinke, C., Kneer, J., Tenbergen, G., Khan, A.Q., Bukert, A., Muller-Engling, L., Engler, H., Gerwinn, H., von Wurmb-Schwark, N., Pohl, A., Weib, S., Amelung, T., Mohnke, S., Massau, C., Kargel, C., Walter, M., Schiltz, K., Beier, K.M., & Frieling, H. (2019). Child sexual offenders show prenatal and epigenetic alterations of the androgen system. *Translational Psychiatry*, *9*, 28.

Langevin, R. (1990). Sexual anomalies and the brain. In W. L. Marshall, D. R. Laws, & H. E. Barbaree, *Handbook of sexual assault: Issues, theories, and treatment of the offender*. Plenum Press, p. 103–113.

Laws, D. R., & Marhsall, W. L. (1990). A conditioning theory of the etiology and maintenance of deviant sexual preferences and behaviour. In W. L. Marshall, D. R. Laws, & H. E. Barbaree (Eds.), *Handbook of sexual assault: Issues, theories, and treatment of the offender* (pp. 209–230). Plenum Press.

Lee, J. K. P., Jackson, H. J., Pattison, P., & Ward, T. (2002). Developmental risk factors for sexual offending. *Child Abuse & Neglect*, *26*, 73–92.

Lunde, D.T. (1976). *Murder and madness*. San Francisco Book Company.
Lussier, P., McCuish, E., & James, J. (2021). The developmental pathways of sexual deviance: More than 100 years of research in context. In L. A. Craig, & R. M. Bartels (Ed.), *Sexual deviance: Understanding and managing deviant sexual interests and paraphilic disorders* (pp. 25–40). John Wiley & Sons, Ltd.
Martin, S.F. (2016). Fetishistic disorder. In R. Balon (Ed.), *Practical guide to paraphilia and paraphilic disorders* (pp. 155–170). Springer.
McGuire, R. J., Carlisle, J. U., & Young, B. G. (1964). Sexual deviations as conditioned behaviour: A hypothesis. *Behaviour Research and Therapy*, *2*, 185–190.
Money, J. (1984). Paraphilias: Phenomenology and classification. *American Journal of Psychotherapy*, *38*, 164–179.
Money, J. (1990). *Gay, Straight, and In-Between: The Sexology of Erotic Orientation*. Oxford University Press.
Nolen-Hoeksema, S. (2004). *Abnormal Psychology* (3rd ed.). McGraw-Hill Publishers.
Ponseti, J., Granert, O., Jansen, O., Wolff, S., Beier, K., Neutze, J., Deuschl, G., Mehdorn, H., Siebner, H., & Bosinski, H. (2012). Assessment of pedophilia using hemodynamic brain response to sexual stimuli. *Archives of General Psychiatry*, *69*(2), 187–194.
Ressler, R.K. (1985). Violent crime. *FBI Law Enforcement Bulletin*, *54*, 1–43.
Ressler, R. K., Burgess, A. W., & Douglas, J. (1988). *Sexual homicide: Patterns and motives*. Free Press.
Revitch, E. (1965). Sex murderer and the potential sex murderer. *Diseases of the Nervous System*, *26*, 640–648.
Salter, A.C. (2003). *Predators, pedophiles, rapists, & other sex offenders: Who they are, how they operate, and how we can protect ourselves and our children*. Basic Books.
Scarpazza, C., Finos, L., Genon, S., Masiero, L., Bortolato, E., Cavaliere, C., Pezzaioli, J., Monaro, M., Navarin, N., Battaglia, U., Pietrini, P., Ferracuti, S., Sartori, G., & Camperio Ciani, A. S. (2021). Idiopathic and acquired pedophilia as two distinct disorders: an insight from neuroimaging. *Brain Imaging and Behavior*, *15*(5), 2681–2692.
Schlesinger, L.B., Kassen, M., Mesa, V.B., & Pinizzotto, A.J. (2010). Ritual and signature in serial sexual homicide. *Journal of American Academy of Psychiatry and the Law*, *38*, 239–246.
Scorolli, C., Ghirlanda, S., Enquist, M., Zattoni, S., & Jannini, E. A. (2007) Relative prevalence of different fetishes. *International Journal of Impotence Research*, *19*, 432–437.
Seto, M.C. (2008). *Pedophilia and sexual offending against children: Theory, assessment, and intervention*. American Psychological Association.
Shaffer, L., & Penn, J. (2006). A comprehensive paraphilia classification system. In E. W. Hickey (Ed.), *Sex crimes and paraphilia* (pp. 69–93). Prentice Hall.
Stinson, J. D., Becker, J. V., Sales, B. D. (2008). Self-regulation and etiology of sexual deviance: Evaluating causal theory. *Violence and Victims*, *23*(1), 35–51.
Storms, M. D. (1981). A theory of erotic orientation development. *Psychological Review*, *88*, 340–353.
Sullivan, J., & Sheehan, V. (2016). What motivates sexual abusers of children? A qualitative examination of the Spiral of Sexual Abuse. *Aggression and Violent Behavior*, *30*, 76–87.
Walter, M., Witzel, J., Wiebking, C., Gubka, U., Rotte, M., Schiltz, K., Bermpohl, F., Tempelmann, C., Bogarts, B., Heinze, H.J., & Horthoff, G. (2007). Pedophilia is linked to reduced activation in hypothalamus and lateral prefrontal cortex during visual erotic stimulation. *Biological Psychiatry*, *62*, 698–701.
Ward, T., & Beech, A. (2008). An integrated theory of sexual offending. In R. D. Laws and W. T. O'Donohue (Eds.), *Sexual deviance—Theory, assessment and treatment*. (2nd ed.). Guilford Press, pp. 21–36.
Wylie, R.A., & Wylie, K.R. (2016). Sexual masochism disorder. In R. Balon (Ed.), Practical guide to paraphila and paraphilic disorders (pp. 107–122). Springer.

9 Violent Non-paraphilic Crimes

Stephanie Cappadona

Introduction

Criminal profiling has traditionally been used in sexually sadistic serial murder cases to assist law enforcement in their criminal investigations. The technique utilizes case evidence to construct a sketch of the offender, containing certain psychological, behavioral, or geographic characteristics. Petherick and Turvey (2023) describe profiling as a "collection of logical inferences documenting the relevant qualities of the person responsible for committing a crime or series of crimes" (47). Several different terms have been applied to this process of criminal investigation, such as personality profiling, psychological profiling, behavioral profiling, and forensic profiling (Barrow et al., 2014). From CSA to GP and BEA, a variety of methods of criminal profiling have evolved over the past several decades. Initially, this approach was applied to particularly appalling and difficult serial homicides. More recently, investigators have also sought this technique as a tool in cases of more conventional murders and rapes (Chifflet, 2015; Douglas & Burgess, 1986; Kocsis & Cooksey, 2002). The umbrella term *criminal profiling* is used throughout this chapter to refer to the technique that analyzes crime scenes and other case evidence in an attempt to provide investigators with likely characteristics of the criminal offender (Chifflet, 2015). Instead of applying this technique to a sexually sadistic serial homicide case, the focus of this chapter is on the application of criminal profiling techniques to violent crimes such as hate crimes, bullying, stalking, robbery, and arson.

Criminal profiling methods have been utilized in serial murder cases, most famously in particularly atrocious serial homicides that contain a heinous sexual component. Bartol and Bartol (2013) explain that this process was used in more bizarre and often complicated cases, such as those with sadistic torture and mutilations, as these usually yield more useful information for constructing a criminal profile. Basically "the reasoning ... is that mentally disordered persons, ironically, demonstrate greater consistency in behavior from situation to situation than persons not so disordered" (p. 36). For crimes like arson, robbery, and hate crimes, it may be expected (correctly or incorrectly) that offenders are not as likely to suffer from a mental disorder. Therefore, would a criminal profile be useful in crimes committed by someone who does not have a mental disorder or for crimes without a sexual component?

The field of social sciences contains much debate about the effectiveness of criminal profiling in assisting with criminal investigations (Chifflet, 2015; Woodworth & Porter, 2000). Several problems have been identified in the literature, such as a lack of uniformity of terminology, inconsistency in education and credentials among profilers, type of scientific reasoning techniques employed to construct a profile, and scarcity of significant empirical evidence to demonstrate the accuracy of criminal profiling (Dowden et al., 2007; Petherick, 2014; Woodworth & Porter, 2000). Nevertheless, since the 1980s, various criminal profiling techniques have been

DOI: 10.4324/9781003366300-10

used in non-sexual violent crimes such as repeated threats, hostage situations, arson, and rape. Criminal profiles can also assist law enforcement investigations beyond determining the characteristics of an offender, such as by narrowing a list of suspects and providing guidance during suspect interviews (Douglas & Burgess, 1986). Unlike serial homicides in which criminal profiling is most frequently utilized, non-sexual violent crime scenes may not contain similar amounts of evidence. Hate crimes, bullying, and stalking may be only verbal or occur in public spaces where insufficient evidence of the crime is left behind. In a robbery, limited evidence may be left at the scene, but usually not the amount left on the victim or at the crime scene with rape and murder. In some arson crimes, considerable evidence may be destroyed in the fire. The current chapter will discuss the use of criminal profiling in non-sexual violent crimes such as hate crimes, bullying, stalking, robbery, and arson.

Hate Crimes

Definition and Nature of Hate Crimes

The term "hate" in the context of a hate crime does not refer to the general notion of hate as intense dislike of another. When referring to hate crime or incident, the term more precisely indicates "bias against people or groups with specific characteristics that are defined by law" (US Department of Justice, Hate Crime Laws, n.d., para 1). A hate crime or bias crime is any criminal act motivated in whole or in part by bias toward an individual perceived as belonging to a protected group of individuals. In America, the type of group protected varies by state. The Federal law applies to eight protected groups with respect to "race, color, religion, national origin, sexual orientation, gender, gender identity, and disability" (US Department of Justice, Hate Crime Laws, n.d., para 2). Each of the 50 United States differs in terms of class protections, levels of protection offered, and punishment for the crime. As of this writing, South Carolina[1] and Wyoming[2] are the only states without a comprehensive hate crime law.

In 1990, Congress recognized hate crimes as a social problem when they passed the Federal Hate Crime Statistics Act, which tasked the Attorney General (AG) with collecting data "about crimes that manifest evidence of prejudice based on race, religion, sexual orientation, or ethnicity" (US Department of Justice, Hate Crime Statistics 2010: para 1). The Act was amended in 2009 to include the following groups, "race, *gender and gender identity*, religion, disability, sexual orientation, or ethnicity" (emphasis in original, US Department of Justice, Hate Crimes Statistics, 2010: para 1). While the 1990 law directed a study of the scope of the issue of hate crimes, it was not specific legislation to codify certain anti-black discrimination. The United States AG asked the FBI to collect the data from all local and state law enforcement agencies and produce an annual report as to the prevalence of the crimes. Since the implementation of that Act, scholars, legislators, and law enforcement have attempted to ascertain the origins and extent of the crime. What motivates individuals to commit hate crimes, how many hate crimes actually occur each year, and exactly what is the extent of the problem?

History of Hate Crimes

Between 1865 and 1870, Amendments 13, 14, and 15 were passed by the U.S. Congress to grant freedom to enslaved African peoples, ensure constitutional protections for those born in America, and confer the right to vote to U.S. citizens (Turpin-Petrosino, 2015). In 1866, Senator Lyman Trumbull introduced the first federal civil rights bill. He posited that "the 'abstract truths and principles' of the Thirteenth Amendment meant nothing 'unless the persons to be affected … have some means of availing themselves of their benefit'" (Guelzo & Miller, n.d. Civil Rights Act of 1866, para 1). President Johnson vetoed the bill as he was vehemently opposed to the idea that black African freedmen were equal to white citizens.

Hate crimes, though not legally defined as such in the antebellum era, continued to occur throughout the nation. Extrajudicial killings, termed lynchings, occurred in the West or North, but most were concentrated in the Southern states. These were terroristic murders of mostly black men, women, and children conducted at the hands of local citizens, although Jewish people and white people who advocated for black people. They were not merely anti-black murders, which would be horrific enough. These slayings were meant to convey a direct message to other black people in the community—this is what happens to black people in this community if they "step out of place" concerning social norms and mores. Attempting to vote, interracial relationships, or inhabiting certain Sundown Towns after dark were considered punishable offenses. Lynchings were public displays of animosity entailing torture and humiliation, even advertised in newspapers for all whites in the area to attend. The Equal Justice Initiative (EJI) documented over 4,400 racial lynchings that occurred from 1877 to 1950 (EJI, 2017). Though several federal bills were proposed, the Emmett Till Antilynching Act was not signed into law until March 2022. Hate crime laws as they are known today would not take modern form until 1990.

The United States Civil Rights Act was signed in 1968 by President Lyndon Johnson (US Department of Justice, Civil Rights Division, About Hate Crimes, 2019). As stated, the 1968 Federal Statute

> made it a crime to use, threaten to use, force to willfully interfere with any person because of race, color, religion, or national origin and because the person is participating in a federally protected activity, such as public education, employment, jury service, travel, or the enjoyment of public accommodations …
>
> (para 1)

With this law, Federal District Attorneys could prosecute, among others, white supremacists for their threatening and violent acts against African Americans and their white allies. The Violent Interference with Federally Protected Rights law, while landmark legislation, lacked comprehensive protections for every American citizen.

Hate Crime Statistics

The pervasiveness of the issue of hate crimes varies depending on the source. The most widely used data is published by the Department of Justice, Federal Bureau of Investigation. The FBI publishes annual data on crime in the United States, collected from participating law enforcement agencies across the country through the National Incident-Based Reporting System (NIBRS). The Bureau of Justice Statistics (BJS) conducts a comprehensive survey of randomly selected American homes to determine the number of criminal victimizations experienced by residents, using the National Crime Victimization Survey (NCVS). Each data source has strengths and weaknesses, and often reports vastly disparate crime totals.

The most recent data available as of this writing is the FBI-Crime in the United States, Hate Crimes 2024. Hate crimes reported in the United States are at historic levels, increasing over the past few years. The most common motivations of bias included 26% anti-black, 17% anti-Jewish, and 9% anti-gay (male). The same data reported the percentage of hate crimes motivated by bias as race/ethnicity/ancestry (51.4%), religion (23.34%), sexual orientation

(17.51%), gender identity (4.25%), gender (1.05%), and disability (1.45%) (FBI Crime Data Explorer, 2024). Often in the NIBRS data, anti-religious and sexual orientation bias alternate from year to year for the second and third top target categories, while anti-black is consistently by far the most common target of bias in the race/ethnicity/ancestry category. It should be noted that both the anti-black and anti-Jewish communities are highly overrepresented in the data.[3] It is difficult to determine the percentage of gay males in the American population; males who identify as gay in 2021 are reportedly 1.5%, also indicating an overrepresentation in the NIBRS hate crime statistics (Jones, 2022: table 2).

For a more complete picture, the BJS NCVS provides statistics resulting from national self-report surveys. The 2019 NCVS data reveal a very different picture of hate crimes in the United States. Victims reported a total of 268,910 violent hate crimes and 32,540 property hate crimes in 2019 (US DOJ, BJS, Hate Crime Victimization, 2021).

Between the years 2005 and 2019, there was an average of 246,900 hate crime victimizations each year. That is a remarkable difference compared to the NIBRS data. Still, hate crimes are very underreported, so it should be no surprise that there is a vast difference in reported victimizations. Between 2005 and 2019, simple assaults accounted for 62% of hate crime victimizations, followed by aggravated assault (18%), robbery (6.6%), and rape/sexual assault (2.7%). To put those percentages into perspective, there were a total of 1,075,470 violent hate crimes reported to the NCVS survey during the years 2005–2019. Personal crimes accounted for nearly 90% of the hate crimes, while property crimes were only 10%. The NCVS data demonstrated a somewhat different bias motivation for hate crime victimization. Race/ethnicity/national origin comprised 59.5% of the targeted personal crimes, followed by gender (24.2%); association, those who reported their hate crimes were the result of associating with the targeted gender (22.5%); sexual orientation (20.3%); and religion (9.4%). The smallest percentage was for those who thought they were targeted due to their perceived characteristics or beliefs (6.9%).

Profiling Serial Hate Crimes

As the above data demonstrates, there is enormous variation in estimates of yearly hate crimes. The reported offenses also differ greatly in criminal behavior. What does seem to be consistent is the motivation for hate crimes each year. The most frequently targeted motivation for both property and violent crime is anti-black, followed by anti-Jewish, and anti-gay (male). With considerable variation in criminal behavior and the frequent scarcity of crime scene evidence, is it possible to profile a crime motivated by bias—either personal or property crime? Personal crimes motivated by bias occur in public every day, in a time when most people have cell phones and can record any confrontation. Cameras are in most public spaces, and increasingly personal "Ring" doorbells can capture crimes on camera, too. That being said, and despite training, law enforcement often has difficulty identifying hate crimes or locating evidence to prove a hate crime. It is challenging for law enforcement to identify a hate crime suspect with no video evidence or if the target and perpetrator are unknown to one another. This is especially true for property crimes and "blitz-style" attacks on an individual or group in public. Therefore, investigators may find it necessary to pursue alternatives to standard investigative procedures.

Scholars continue to research hate crimes in an effort to develop a typology of hate crime offenders. If the common character or behavioral traits of hate crime offenders can be determined, prevention, intervention, and educational policies or programs can be developed. Jones et al. (2022) suggest that typological information can also be useful for officers to investigate hate incidents and crimes—both the obvious and the inconspicuous. Levin and McDevitt et al. (2002) conceived one of the most popular classification systems for hate crime offenders. From interviews with police, victims, and offenders of hate crimes in their data set from the Boston Police Department, they constructed three types of hate crime offenders. The authors determined that bigotry was the common element in all hate crimes in the sample, but the motivation to act on that bigotry varied in the three types. The thrill offender commits a hate crime because they derive pleasure and excitement from the act and the power they wield over the target. The defensive perpetrator reacts with violence when they believe their resources and/or neighborhood are jeopardized. The smallest group of hate crime offenders, the mission offenders, consider it their duty to destroy those believed to be inferior and responsible for social problems that need to be eliminated. Nearly a decade later, the authors revisited their original study and reanalyzed 169 Boston police files (McDevitt et al., 2002). The authors found their original hate crime typology to be incomplete and added retaliatory offenders as a fourth type. While the motivation was the same for each group, the categories "differ with respect to the conditions, both psychologically and environmentally, that ultimately lead to a violent attack" (306). The retaliatory offenders, while similar to the defensive type, are driven by more than the need to protect their territory. Many of these offenders indicated the additional requirement "to avenge a perceived degradation or assault on their group" (306). This hate crime offender typology has been criticized due to a lack of empirical evidence and few or inadequate replication studies (Phillips, 2009).

However, an innovative study—the Bias Incident and Actors Study (BIAS)—was recently undertaken to address the deficiency of data and research in the study of hate crimes (Jensen et al., 2021, p 4). The BIAS study comprised 966 adult hate crime offenders—689 violent and 277 non-violent bias crime offenders randomly selected from a pool who committed their offenses between 1990 and 2018 in the United States. Researchers compiled this list of U.S. hate crime offenders by using publicly available data. The comprehensive data set contained crime, victim, and offender characteristics. Offender data covers 80 different variables, including offender education, employment, mental health, and criminal histories, as well as associations with peers and hate groups. Additionally, Jenson et al. collected 30 more data variables concerning the targets of the hate crime and the events themselves.

Results from the BIAS study revealed that "[r]egardless of hate motivation, offenders displayed significantly higher rates of low educational attainment, poor work performance, mental illness, substance abuse, and criminal histories than the general population" (Jensen et al., 2020b, p. 2). Of the offenders, data revealed that 60% had a criminal record before they committed their bias crimes. However, 81% did not include a criminal record of previous hate crimes before the one that earned them inclusion in the BIAS data set. Those offenders who held leadership positions in hate groups were 72% less likely to engage in acts of violence than individuals who did not belong to a hate group. The authors divided the correlates of hate crime offenses into positive and negative correlates of violent outcomes with hate crime offenders in the United States. The positive correlates for violent outcomes were committing the crime with peers, in a public setting, a spontaneous encounter with the target, under the influence of drugs and alcohol, with bias based on sexual orientation/gender, including a theft motive, and the mission-oriented type with a violent criminal history. Some negative correlates of the violent outcomes were, as stated above, a hate group leader and a defensive hate attack based on anti-religious bias.

Jensen et al. (2021) found that for the bias offenses, those that were based on race, ethnicity, or nationality accounted for the vast majority in the data set, followed by bias based on religion, sexual orientation, and sexual identity. These findings are consistent with findings from the FBI's previous UCR and current NIBRS data. This demonstrates further consistency in bias motivation for the attacks that occur from year to year in the United States. An overwhelming majority of the bias offenses, just over 71%, were violent in nature, "defined as the intent to injure or kill one or more individuals" (p. 10). The authors reported the remaining offenses showed that a little over 15% were acts of intimidation, and just over 13% were bias-motivated property crimes. With such extensive data, it was found that offenders in the study who committed hate crimes motivated by sexual orientation/gender identity were over 2.5 times more likely to commit violent crimes, but they were 65% less likely to commit violent crimes when they were motivated by religion.

The Jenson et al. (2021) study found some similarities and differences from the McDevitt and Levin typology discussed earlier in the chapter with the BIAS data. The classifications included mission-oriented, thrill-oriented, and defensive categories of offenders. The study did not include data on the retaliatory type but did contain the category of mixed-motive offenders. Their findings suggest that the mission offenders typically committed their hate crime offenses with others. These offenders were found to be "older than other offender types ... more likely to have a suspected or diagnosed mental illness ... and are more often members of hate groups ... and very high rates of military experience ... [and] had higher rates of criminal histories" (47).

In a unique aspect of the BIAS study concerning defensive offenders of hate crimes, the offenders were separated into "proximate" and "distant," based on whether the motive appeared to be closer to the offenders' community or a personal threat, and those that were related to a more nationally ideological focus (Jensen et al., 2020a). The proximate offenders were more likely to commit their hate crimes with others than the distant offenders. Proximate offenders who committed their hate crimes based on a philosophical belief tended to be younger than distant offenders, and their hate group membership was five times higher than the distant group. The mental illness rate was far less for proximate than for distant offenders. Results indicate that both sets of defensive offenders were more likely than other types of hate crime offenders to commit their crimes in public spaces. The authors noted that their "update to McDevitt and Levin's typology [could] ... better capture perpetrator motivations in a time of polarized mass media and political culture" (52). If the typology was used as a tool by law enforcement, the distinction between a locally focused defensive offender and the more nationally focused one could prove more useful than the original single defensive category. More research would be necessary to make that determination.

The BIAS data also included thrill-oriented offenders, who had the highest percentage of group participation of all offender categories (Jensen et al., 2020a). The thrill group of offenders was much more likely to target members of the LGBTQ community, but they had a more varied group of targets than the other offender classifications included in this study. Also consistent with McDevitt and Levin's notion of thrill offenders was the finding that this group was the youngest of all types. Thus, results from these studies could bolster the notion of utilizing criminal profiling for bias crimes. By determining similarities in offender characteristics, combined with investigation of the crime scene, it may be possible to develop a profile of an offender in bias crimes.

Lastly, for motives behind the attacks, offenders in the study whose incidents had mixed motives were 3 ½ times more likely to be violent than those offenders who were motivated solely by bias (Jensen et al., 2020a). The authors classified some of the offenders into one of the McDevitt and Levin categories and labeled it as "mixed motive." They determined that some of these could be considered defensive, but a larger number could not and appeared to not have a distinct motive. In these cases, the authors "found a substantial number ... in which the offender perceived slights on behalf of the victim and quickly escalated the conflicts with violence or threats of violence while also expressing prejudice" (51). The mixed-motive offenders maintained the highest rate of spontaneous crimes and the likelihood of attacking in public settings. In contrast, they had the lowest rates of mental illness and poor employment history. The authors state that these attacks, while motivated in part by bias, also contained another motive that was usually financial.

There appears to be some consistency between the McDevitt and Levin and the more recent Jensen et al. study of hate crime offenders. Findings concerning motivation for hate crimes from the Jensen study are also comparable to the reported annual statistics from the FBI, with bias against race/ethnicity/national origin being the top motive for hate crimes in the United States. The second and third most frequently found motives include bias against religion and sexual orientation/gender identity. Similar to other criminal typologies, the hate crime typology is not intended to identify an offender. While this classification system is not quite the same as a serial murderer criminal profile, it may still prove useful in assisting law enforcement investigations of bias-motivated crimes. It is another instrument to support law enforcement so they can identify hate crimes for what they are. By recognizing the bias motivation of a particular crime, law enforcement agencies can respond with compassion to the victim(s) of the crime and provide appropriate services. Identifying the types of hate crimes occurring in a community can enhance law enforcement responses, guide appropriate consequences and educational components to an offender's sentence, and inform prompt and proper community notifications of hate crimes occurring in a particular neighborhood. Finally, it can direct resources and proactive anti-bias policies in the targeted community.

Bullying

Definition of Bullying

Bullying has existed in this country since its inception. The behavior, while not labeled as such, took the form of physical or emotional violence. Beginning in the early 20th century, swiftly evolving technology allowed bullying behaviors to permeate the cyber world. Prior to cell phone and computer use, targets of bullying could often escape the violence at home. Now, cyberbullying, while not limited to children and teens, can permeate all aspects of the target's life. Cyberbullying is addressed in a separate chapter so that particular behavior is not directly addressed in this discussion of bullying. Bullying also occurs in the workplace, but here, the discussion focuses on childhood and youth bullying.

School bullying was not recognized as a pervasive social problem, at least in America, until around the mid to late 20th century (Allanson et al., 2015; Olweus & Limber, 2010). For decades, childhood bullying has been minimized as a "rite of passage" or "boys being boys." Today, many still view it as such. But bullying has increasingly been recognized in social science literature for what it is—disturbing and damaging behavior with lifelong negative consequences for the targets and perpetrators. Most recently, schools and communities have been concerned with preventing mass shootings in schools. Vossekuil et al. (2004) observed that while school shootings are a grave issue, they comprise merely a small fraction of the violence occurring in American schools. Bullying behaviors take a variety of forms and by its nature, bullying is considered serial behavior. Olweus and Limber (2010) describe how bullying occurs when "a student … is exposed repeatedly and over time, to negative actions on the part of one or more other students" (2010, p. 124). There is currently no consensus on the definition of bullying. Allanson et al. (2015) note that most definitions include the fact that the behavior is intentional aggression aimed at the target, repetitive and persistent, and contains the notion of inequity in power.

Huntingdon and Petherick (2014) define serial bullying "as aggressive acts characterized by persistent and recurring psychological or physical harm, oppression, or intimidation, wherein a real or perceived power imbalance facilitates distress by, or control of, one person by another" (265). Aggressive acts may be physical or verbal in nature. Physical bullying behaviors may include pushing, kicking, punching, physical intimidation, slapping, stalking, spitting, and destruction of personal property. Emotional or psychological bullying behaviors could take the form of rumor-spreading, social isolation, incessant teasing, name-calling, and demeaning the target. The authors report that research has affirmed the customary belief that bullies, both in and out of the school environment, seek to dominate and control and act impulsively and aggressively with total disregard for the pain they cause others. There does appear to be a gender difference in bullying behaviors in schools. Male youth tend to exhibit more physical aggression and violence, while females engage in social relationship bullying by excluding other girls or relentless psychological attacks (Huntingdon & Petherick 2014). Males are more likely to be the bully and be the target of more overt types of behavior. Females usually use covert bullying tactics and are less likely to be both the bully and target than males.

Bullying Statistics

Statistics on bullying behaviors rely mostly on self-reports. Huntington and Petherick (2014) state that the average percentage of bullying in public schools hovered around 30% in the first decade of the 21st century. The National Center for Education Statistics conducted two contemporary studies published by the Department of Education and revealed that students' reports of bullying behaviors in schools have decreased.

The School Crime Supplement (SCS), a supplement to the NCVS, includes self-report results from school children aged 12–18 regarding their victimization in school (Irwin et al. 2023). In 2021, the total number of non-fatal victimizations reported by students was 7 victimizations per 1,000, a reduction from 30 victimizations per 1,000 students in 2019.[4] These behaviors include robbery, aggravated and simple assault, rape, and sexual assault. Concerning bullying specifically, 22% of students reported experiencing bullying in school. The data also provided information regarding variations in bullying target victimization. The SCS results identified the following groups were more likely to report being bullied at school: females, those who identified as more than one race, those who attend rural schools, and those in middle schools were more likely to report bullying than those in high school.

The second study, the School Survey on Crime and Safety, was conducted in public schools during the school year 2021–2022 (Burr et al. 2024). Results revealed 857,500 violent incidents and 479,500 non-violent incidents reported by students. Reported bullying incidents were similar to the former study, wherein 28% of middle schoolers reported at least one instance of bullying per week, 10% in grade schools, and 15% in high schools.

Another statistical source to identify the scope of the issue about the prevalence of bullying behaviors is the Centers for Disease Control and Prevention (CDC). The Center published preliminary data in March 2024 declaring that bullying in schools is quite pervasive, with one in five high school students reporting being bullied at school (CDC, About Bullying, 2024). The report also revealed that 40% of high schoolers who identified as LGBTQ, along with 33% who were unsure of their sexual identity, reported being bullied at school or electronically.

Profiling Serial Bullying

The literature on bullying affirms the serious nature of the behavior (Donegan, 2012; Huntingdon & Petherick, 2014; Olweus, 2003; Pineda et al. 2022). As in criminology generally, bullying studies demonstrate that a small number of individuals are overwhelmingly responsible for numerous targeted peer victimizations. If schools and communities can effectively identify this smaller group of perpetrators and intervene to modify their behavior, many serial victimizations could be prevented (Huntingdon et al. 2014). Prevention and intervention of bullying can benefit the target, the bully, the school, and the community. The issue of bullying encompasses the entire environmental system, not only the target of aggression. Bullying has, for too long, been viewed as a personal issue between the target and the bully. Research has revealed that bullying behavior should be viewed in the social context in which it occurs (Swearer & Hymel, 2015). The target and the bully are both influenced by family experience, neighborhood structure, community values, and the school climate.

It is crucial to identify youth who engage in bullying so the behaviors can be modified to more prosocial behavior. Without intervention and consequences for the bully, the behavior may continue for years and have lifelong damaging effects on both the bully and the target (Donegan, 2012; Rokach & Clayton, 2023). For the targets, the result of exposure to bullying is physical, emotional, and social trauma, the effects of which they will endure throughout their entire lives. Some victims of bullying resort to suicide when they feel adults cannot help them or there is no other way to stop the pain of victimization (Cook et al., 2010). Bullies themselves are also susceptible to negative life outcomes, as their aggressive and cruel behaviors may continue throughout their lives (Donegan, 2012). Vaughn et al. (2010) discuss studies of youth who continue their bullying behaviors as adults and manifest depression, anxiety, and substance abuse. Cook et al. (2010) report that bullies experience detrimental psychiatric and relationship issues, which frequently culminate in criminal involvement and apprehension into adulthood.

While there is not specifically a profile of youth who bully, risk factors associated with bullies have been studied to identify characteristics most likely to be exhibited by them. Cooke et al. (2010) found the "typical bully" in their study had difficulty in social and academic areas, maintained negative beliefs about themselves and others, had difficulty resolving conflicts, and came from a negative family environment frequently characterized by poor parenting. Their family life was frequently characterized by parental attachment issues, coercive parents, a lack of effective adult supervision, and aggression and violence.

Huntingdon and Petherick (2014) discuss three categories of bullies from the literature—the active, the passive, and the Machiavellian types. While these are not necessarily profiles of the perpetrators, the information they provide could prove beneficial for identifying those at risk for bullying. The most frequent type, an active bully, is a narcissist who lacks compassion and establishes a relationship with the target, manipulating and intimidating them. This type of bully often enlists others to engage in the cruelty. The second type is the passive or anxious bully. This is an individual who may not necessarily have initiated the targeting of peers but is easily pressured into bullying behaviors by another more dominant bully. The passive bully is characterized by a lack of self-confidence and the need to be accepted by peer groups. The final type is the Machiavellian bully. This type appears egotistical and maintains high self-esteem. Instead of using strength and aggression, the Machiavellian bully relies on their charm and social skills to accomplish their personal goals through the victimization of peers.

Proper identification of antisocial behavior in early childhood combined with effective intervention programs may reduce the deleterious effects of bullying for both the perpetrator and the target of peer victimization. Bullying and antisocial behavior have been indicated in the research to be precursors to later criminality, especially in males (Huntingdon & Petherick 2014). Intervention and prevention of these behaviors in youth may also serve to reduce criminal behavior by these individuals in their adulthood.

Stalking

Definition of Stalking

While not defined as stalking behavior, Hollywood and other forms of mass media frequently portray the behavior of stalking as that of a love-sick person, completely consumed with passion and the need for the target of the "affection." The script typically plays out as a comedy wherein the target of the "affection" inevitably falls in love with the "admirer." One of the two scenarios plays out. In the first, the target of "affection" learns of the lengths the suitor went to and is so in awe of this that they fall in love with the "admirer" in the end. In the second, the friends of the target of "affection" appear incredulously jealous at how much the "admirer" loves the target and even attempt to convince the target to love the "admirer" back. In reality, stalking is a frightening and sometimes deadly violent crime that frequently occurs with other violent crimes like intimate partner violence and sexual assault. As this chapter will demonstrate, stalking is a complex crime that, by its very nature of patterned behavior, may make it more beneficial for law enforcement to use criminal profiling to investigate these criminal offenses.

The Department of Justice's (DOJ) Office on Violence Against Women (OVW) defines stalking as "engaging in a course of conduct directed at a specific person that would cause a reasonable person to fear for his or her safety or the safety of others or suffer substantial emotional distress" (US Department of Justice, OVW, Stalking, 2023, para 1). The DOJ Office for Victims of Crime adds to this definition by stating that

> [s]talking is a crime of power and control … a course of action directed at an individual that causes the victim to fear for their safety and generally involves repeated visual or physical proximity, nonconsensual communication, and verbal, written, or implied threats.
> (US Department of Justice, Office for Victims of Crime (n.d.), Stalking, para 1)

And, unlike hate crimes, stalking is recognized as a crime in every state in America.

In comparison to other serial crimes discussed in this chapter, such as robbery and arson, stalking, like hate crimes, has only been recognized as a social problem and criminal behavior for about three decades (Brady & Nobles, 2017). Despite being recognized as criminal behavior at the state and federal levels and receiving increasingly more scholarly research in the literature, there is still no uniform definition of stalking. Although there is variation in terminology, Brady and Nobles (2017) contend that in the last 20 years, most research on stalking has derived from victim surveys. This data has been useful in raising awareness of the appalling behaviors the targets of this violent crime often endure. Similar to hate crimes, the crime of stalking requires a specific component for prosecution—the establishment of a pattern of behavior. The authors state that "by definition, the crime of stalking entails a repeated course of conduct … [and for] offenders to engage in a *series* of acts targeted as a specific person or persons" (p. 3152). With stalking behaviors, the target is not exposed to a single act of victimization, and the crime is completed. The acts are varied and sustained, which leaves the target in extreme fear and constantly on high alert. The target is left dreading what will come next, and when, where, and how subsequent stalking behavior will occur. They often must find ways to alter their usual routines, such as taking different routes to work, school, or other social obligations. Stalking may necessitate the target switching phone numbers frequently, or even relocating their residence to avoid encountering the stalker. The authors point out that stalking also puts the onus on the target to document the various behaviors. They must deal with the stress and anxiety of potential attacks, while at the same time, they must carefully detail and compile evidence as proof of the patterns of criminal behavior.

Stalking Statistics

The crime of stalking is not collected by the FBI's NIBRS system. The scope of the problem is only reflected in the BJS NCVS data. Therefore, it is not possible to compare the disparity in the number of stalking crimes reported to the police and those reported by the targets in a survey. However, one recent study provides a snapshot of stalking behaviors. Brady and Nobles (2017) compiled police reports of stalking reported to the Houston Police Department (HPD) between 2005 and 2013. Specifically, regarding the criminal behavior of stalking, the authors reported that HPD received 3,756 calls for service, recorded 66 incident reports, and arrested 12 individuals in eight years in one of the largest cities in the nation. Considering the high numbers of underreporting for stalking generally, the authors of the study pointedly remark that examining the stalking calls for service is the "widest possible net to cast in terms of case intake and further processing throughout other stages of the criminal justice system" (3165). On a more macro scale, what do the statistics tell us about stalking?

As previously mentioned, statistics on offenders of stalking are not routinely collected at the national level—the NIBRS data set does not currently include the category of stalking.[5] For a brief history, in a 2016 Press Release, Senators Gillibrand and Ernst requested the Director of the FBI to collect more data on stalking crimes (Jodi Ernst Press Release, 2016). They acknowledge that NIBRS was implemented to obtain more detailed information on crime incidents in the United States,

> which collects more information through incident and arrest data on 32 categories of crimes, from homicide to loitering, but no data on stalking and very limited data are collected on domestic violence---two crimes that disproportionately affect women and families.
>
> (para 1 and 3)

At the time of this writing, statistics for the crime of stalking were available from the BJS for 2019 (Morgan & Truman, 2022). There were about 2.3 million individuals over 16 years of age who reported being the victim of "traditional" stalking (as opposed to cyber-based stalking, not covered in this chapter). The report further indicated that less than one-third of those victims actually reported their stalking crime to the police, and women were twice as likely to be victims of stalking as men. About 1.3 million victims of "traditional" stalking reported being followed or watched, and about 1.1 million victims reported that their stalker showed up, drove by, or rode by places where the target was. More than 70% of these victims said they did not report their victimization to the police. Of those, 43% declared that they didn't report their victimization to the police because they didn't perceive it as "important enough to report," 4% said they "dealt with it in another way," and about 34% believed "police couldn't do anything." The victim-offender relationships in these "traditional" stalking crimes knew one another in 56% of the cases, 30% were strangers, and 13% were unknown to one another (Morgan & Truman, 2022).

Profiling Serial Stalking

It is the very definition of stalking that makes it more amenable to criminal profiling than some other individual criminal acts. To profile an offense or offender, a considerable amount of information is necessary. One fundamental component of profiling a crime is the repetitive nature of the behavior. With each ensuing act of stalking, patterns of criminal behavior can be established, and further evidence can be gathered to aid in constructing a proper profile for police investigations.

One study of interpersonal stalking offenders sought to use data to develop a typology of these offenders (Wright et al., 1996). It used stalking cases to help construct a Stalking Incident Checklist. The authors describe it as "based on the nature of the relationship (non-domestic or domestic), content of communication (nondelusional or delusional), level of victim risk in terms of offender aggression (noncontact or physical contact), and outcome (court, psychiatric, not reported, suicide)" (1489). The authors conclude from their sample of 30 cases of stalking that interpersonal aggression, not financial or sexual issues, motivated these crimes, where the impetus of the stalking behavior is a function of the mental state of the perpetrators. These individuals "are compulsive … with a misperceived fixation … the result of an underlying emotional conflict that propels the offender to stalk … a target" (495).

Wright et al. (1996) classified stalkers as non-domestic and domestic stalkers. The first, the non-domestic stalker, contains two different types: the organized and the delusional. The non-domestic stalker may have met the target during a brief encounter, or the target is not even aware of the existence of the stalker. The first type of non-domestic stalker is the organized stalker. These individuals attempt communication with the target through anonymous means—letters, phone calls, where they don't respond, hang up, or leave obscene messages. This is a one-way relationship, and the target may not be aware of the stalking behaviors until the stalker chooses to reveal themselves.

The delusional non-domestic stalker is also labeled an erotomania-related stalker (Wright et al., 1996). In this situation, the offender fantasizes about the target and "is commonly expressed in such forms as fusion, where the stalker blends his or her personality into the target's … where a fantasy is based on idealized romantic love, or spiritual union of a person rather than a sexual attraction" (497). The authors state that the motivation for these stalking behaviors may be unrequited feelings, which can lead to the above-mentioned fusion with the target. The erotomania often escalates and may turn confrontational, becoming an obsession that could end in the death or injury of either party involved.

The final classification is that of the domestic stalker (Wright et al., 1996). This behavior typically occurs between those with a current or former relationship and is motivated by the "desire to continue or reestablish a relationship … [and] often culminates in a violent attack directed at the target" (p. 499). The crime scene typically involves either the parties' home or workplace and displays disorder and violence that likely escalated from a disagreement. Sometimes these attacks devolve into murder-suicide. The authors proffer that "clinicians can classify stalkers by the nature of the relationship, content of communication, level and escalation of aggression, and risk-level to the victim" (p. 500). They suggest that data like that in the study could be used to determine stalking behaviors and violence patterns that could benefit law enforcement and other criminal justice players with investigations, bail decisions, and granting restraining orders.

Wright et al. (1996) discuss how with stalking, the behaviors should be viewed on a continuum, with one end of the spectrum representing the absence of physical contact and on the opposite end deadly aggression. On one end is the delusional stalker, and on the other is the non-delusional. Somewhere in the middle of the delusion spectrum exists a mixed type. The authors explain the main difference between the behaviors, and thus the classification is the presence or absence of a factual, reciprocal relationship. The authors describe the non-delusional offender as one with whom the victim has or has had a personal relationship, albeit likely a troubled one. An individual who exhibits delusional stalking behavior is not moored in reality and has fabricated, in their minds, the presence and nature of the relationship. In actuality, this relationship is completely one-sided. The stalkers who display behaviors in the middle of the spectrum had some realistic interaction, though it seemingly took on a more significant meaning to the stalker than to the target. This interaction could have been a date or two, a casual greeting in passing, or some other familiarity through their social environment.

Robbery

Definition of Robbery

Robbery, as defined by the FBI, is "the taking or attempting to take anything of value from the care, custody, or control of a person or persons by force or threat of force or violence and/or by putting the victim in fear" (F.B.I., *Crime in the United States*, 2019, para 1). The BJS elaborates by stating that the criminal behavior of robbery "includes armed, unarmed, and aggravated robbery, carjacking, armed burglary, and armed mugging" (US Department of Justice, BJS Glossary, n.d., p. 11). Robbery necessarily includes the element of violence, and the FBI classifies it as a violent crime along with murder and manslaughter, forcible rape, and aggravated assault (US Department of Justice, FBI, Crime in the United States 2011). The FBI makes a further distinction between robbery and theft in explaining that theft involves the taking of property or money, like robbery, but there is no use of violence or fear to achieve their ends.

Robbery contains elements of both property and violent crime. Emphasized in the definition of robbery is the element of force or the threat thereof (Burrell, 2022). The end goal of a robbery is typically to obtain property or money from a target. Perpetrators accomplish this by instilling fear, often using physical violence (Fuller, 2014). Robbery targets can be either personal or commercial. Burrell (2022) found that personal robberies most frequently include physical violence, and firearms are more often used in commercial robberies. But, whether personal or commercial, robbery, especially serial in nature, is a serious social problem due to the injuries, trauma, deaths, and financial losses to the targets. Robbery has negative impacts on both the individual and society.

Robbery Statistics

In 2019, the FBI reported that the average financial loss amount reported per robbery was $1,797 (US Department of Justice, FBI, Crime in the United States, 2019). Not surprisingly, bank robberies accounted for the highest monetary loss at $4,213 per crime. In total, for 2019, the FBI reported $482 million in total losses due to robberies.

Unlike the slight decrease in overall violent crime in the United States, robbery increased slightly (1.3%), according to the FBI 2022 statistics (US Department of Justice, 2023, FBI Releases 2022 Crime …). As of this writing, the latest statistics available from the FBI come from the 2022 NIBRS report. According to FBI 2022 crime rates, the most frequently occurring violent crime was aggravated assault, with a rate of 268.2 per 100,000 people, followed by robbery at a rate of 66.1, the rate of rapes was 40.0, and homicide was 6.3 (United States

Department of Justice, FBI Crime Data Explorer, 2022). In the same year, there were 150,107 robbery incidents and offenses reported to law enforcement. As noted by NIBRS, this includes 75% of the United States as reported by 13,293 law enforcement agencies. FBI data show that for offenders, the two largest percentages of robberies reported to law enforcement were committed by those whose ages were unknown and those 20–29 years old. As to the sex and race, robberies in 2022 were overwhelmingly committed by black (57%) and white (29%) males (79%). Offenders used either a firearm, handgun, or rifle in the robberies (41%) or personal weapon (28%) in the majority of the robberies, and were linked to weapon law violations (23%) and destruction/damage/vandalism of property (13%). While this data can provide a snapshot of the typical American robbery, it cannot be considered a profile of an offender.

For another view of the scope of robberies in the United States, the NCVS can provide information on personal robberies. The BJS' 2022 NCVS published survey data revealing 694,860 robberies. The BJS data calculate the crime rate per 1,000 people. The robbery rate for 2022 was 2.5, which was an increase over the rates recorded for 2018–2021: 2.1, 1.9, 1.6, and 1.7, respectively (Thompson et al., 2023).

The U.S. Sentencing Commission, which focuses on Federal sentences and court policy, posits that their research reveals perpetrators of robbery were more violent, had a higher recidivism rate than other violent offenders, and had more severe offender histories (Christine et al., 2022). They further found that dangerous weapons and threats of violence were prevalent in most of the robberies, while 77% included the use of a dangerous weapon. Of those crimes where weapons were used, firearms accounted for nearly 80% of robberies where a weapon was used, and about 90% of the federal robberies investigated included threats to use physical force.

Profiling Serial Robbery

Due to the violent and pervasive nature of robbery, the likelihood of a robbery offender recidivating, and the high financial costs of the crime, it is in society's best interest to solve serial robberies as quickly as possible. Also, since the FBI reports robbery has the lowest clearance rate of violent crime in the nation, criminal profiling is one tool that law enforcement should consider when investigating serial robberies.

Most previously proposed typologies focused on the characteristics and motivations of the offender (Fuller, 2014). Gabor (1988) identified four categories of robbers from their sample of 39 convicted robbery offenders in Canada. From their sample, the authors classified them as chronic (28%), professional (41%), intensive (10%), and occasional (21%). The chronic and professional types reportedly committed their offenses over a long criminal career. The chronic offender did not plan the crimes well, nor profit much from their robberies. However, the professional was well-prepared and achieved lucrative earnings. The occasional and intensive types were similar in that they achieved small rewards through their crimes and maintained criminal behavior for a short time. The authors described how perpetrators differed in that the intensive offender committed a quick series of impulsive robberies. The occasional type of robbery offender also hastily planned their crimes, but robbery was a sliver of the types of crimes committed in those cases.

Matthews (2002) constructed a classification of robbery offenders based on their motivations, expertise, preparation, and other characteristics. Data were collected from 340 convicted armed robbers serving time in prison in the United Kingdom between 1992 and 1995. The author reports that 90% of the offenders were males who came from under-resourced neighborhoods and ranged in age from 20 to 40 years old. Matthews termed the types amateurs, intermediates, and professionals. The amateurs, as the label suggests, committed more spontaneous and chaotic robberies than the other two groups. They were also less likely to actually complete their robberies and more likely to have substance abuse issues or use drugs during their crimes. The second group, the intermediates, maintained more proficiency in their robberies and planned more than the amateurs. Matthews divided the intermediates into two groups—diversifiers and developers. The diversifier group committed other crimes, such as burglary and drug dealing. The developers shifted into more expert professional armed robbers. The last group, the professionals, were career criminals who committed well-planned robberies, often with firearms, and focused on higher reward targets.

Woodhams and Toye (2007) investigated characteristics of robbery styles in 160 solved serial commercial robberies committed by 80 perpetrators. The authors defined serial robbers as those who committed more than two commercial robberies. They included the most recent two robberies from each of the robberies in solved cases. There were no fundamental differences among the robberies with respect to the distance traveled to commit the crime and the age, ethnicity, employment status, or criminal history of the perpetrator. Researchers examined 71 offender characteristics across four behavioral domains—target selection, planning, control, and property. Three classifications of serial robbers derived from the analysis were violent opportunists, organized risk-takers, and bladed nocturnal planners. Violent opportunists were characterized by impulsive violence directed at a retail shop, but lacking a weapon, to obtain the desired property. Organized risk-takers were endowed with more expertise and focused on financial institutions, planned their crimes, and used a weapon. The authors state that this appears to be more for compliance than intent to injure any person. Both of these types committed their crimes during daylight hours. The authors categorized the bladed nocturnal planners as existing between the other two types. These robbers planned their crimes, behaved aggressively, and even brandished a knife in some cases. But, like the violent opportunists, they committed their crimes at night, targeting retail shops. The results of this study produced consistent results with other studies regarding serial crimes (Woodhams & Toye, 2007). They found support for their offender behavior consistency and behavior distinctiveness hypotheses. The authors deduced from their results that "pairs of crimes committed by the same offender were found to show greater similarity in target selection, planning, and control and were characterized by shorter intercrime distances than pairs composed of crimes perpetrated by different offenders" (p. 77). The authors found that serial commercial robbery offenders exhibited similar behaviors in successive repeated robberies across varying behavioral domains. This lends credibility to the development of a profile of a serial robbery offender because it demonstrates similarities in behaviors that may be due to personal characteristics. In this way, determining behavioral consistency is more likely to assist in identifying a potential type of suspect.

Fuller (2014) used location to characterize armed robberies in Australia to more effectively capture the association between the perpetrator and the environment during these crimes. The author utilized 627 armed robbery reports submitted by police to the National Armed Robbery Monitoring Program at the Australian Institute of Criminology. The author classified four types of robberies as either armed robberies committed against individuals or businesses. The personal armed robberies were committed either in private spaces (residences) or public spaces (private and public transportation and streets). The commercial armed robberies included insecure (retail, private businesses) and secure (financial institutions, hotels, bars, and post offices) locations. In this study, Fuller found that 12% of the robberies occurred in private spaces. A fundamental difference between the private space robberies and the others in the sample was that the perpetrator and target were either friends or acquaintances. These crimes also included violence in 55% of the cases, with 22% involving a knife. The authors noted the fact that in cases where a weapon was present during the robbery, the offender used other physical violence (pushing, kicking, etc.) and not the weapon. It appears the weapon was intended as a threat or device to gain compliance, not to cause harm to the target. The next group of robberies was termed public spaces and accounted for 41% of the cases. Results from the study indicated that the offenders frequently committed crimes of opportunity, were less likely to plan their crimes, and were more likely to involve either an individual or a team of males using a knife. About 41% of the public space robberies included violence. So while the private space robberies included more overall violence than private space ones, the violence inflicted on the target was less lethal in private spaces.

Next, Fuller (2014) studied two commercial classes of robberies—the secure (8%) and the insecure businesses (37%). The secure commercial robberies appeared well-planned and involved a firearm and a targeted victim. These armed robberies were more likely than the others to be committed by several individuals. The insecure commercial robberies involved only 3% of violence against employees, although Fuller reports they also contained elevated levels of aggression and low levels of planning, and most often occurred at the end of the business day.

Arson

Definition of Arson

According to Brogan (2014), arson is "the setting of a deliberate, malicious fire to damage property, generally that of another person ... with arson for fraud ... [and] the target is usually the property of the arsonist" (p. 373). Because it may be difficult to determine at first glance whether a fire is accidental or intentional, fire investigators must be well-trained with substantial experience in the field. Brogan asserts that, initially, the fire investigator is responsible for utilizing their skills to investigate a blaze to ascertain the cause of the fire. The first determination is whether the fire has an accidental or intentional cause. Once this is established, police may be brought in to collaborate on the investigation, where forensic investigators trained in collection techniques and CSA can preserve and collect evidence to determine a cause. Understandably, due to the nature of the crime, investigating arson can be challenging because much of the evidence may be destroyed in the fire itself. Even if a fire investigator can establish a link between arson scenes, identifying the perpetrator(s) may be extremely difficult. To this end, Brogan emphasizes the importance of arson investigators maintaining knowledge of recent psychological literature to assist with possible motivations for the crime.

Arson Statistics

Quite a bit of discrepancy exists regarding fire data in the United States. The data presented here are from several different sources to provide a more complete picture of the scope of the issue. First, the federal criminal data from the FBI NIBRS reports 30,400 incidents and offenses of arson in America (US Department of Justice, FBI Crime Data Explorer). The age of the offenders was 30–39 (22%), unknown (17%), and 10–19 (17%). Arsons were committed by white (55%) and black (22%) males (64.9%). Offenders' ages were 30–39 (22%), 20–29 (16%), 10–19 (17%), and the same number was of an unknown age. A majority of the reported arsons occurred in personal residences (47%). Data indicated that relationships between perpetrator and target were unknown (35%), committed by strangers (14%), or by an acquaintance (11%), and 10% were unknown (10%).

Another source of arson can be found in the Bomb Arson Tracking System (BAT) data (US Department of Justice, ATF, US Bomb Data Center [USBDC], Arson Incident Report, 2023). The USBDC compiles "information and intelligence about the investigation of bombings, arson, and the criminal use of explosives to support interagency criminal cases" (US Department of Justice, ATF, USBDC Fact Sheet, 2020, para 1). The Arson Incident Report records incidents in the BAT system from 2,100 interagency affiliates reporting fire-related incidents. The fire incidents recorded include "arson, undetermined, accidental, threats, natural and wildlife" (p. 1). The BAT data included a reported total of 21,750 incidents. Of those, 5,440 were categorized as arson with 37 suspects and 117 victims, and financial costs were estimated at over $171,700,000. Arson motives were not recorded in this incident report.

The US Fire Administration maintains a database of reported fires from 23,000 fire departments. In 2022, there were an estimated 374,300 residential building fires, causing 2,720 deaths, 10,250 injuries, and over 10 billion dollars in financial losses. There were 129,500 non-residential building fires, causing 140 deaths, 1,300 injuries, and over $3.7 billion in financial losses (US Fire Administration, n.d.). Reports of residential fires from 2021 increased by over 20,000 incidents and over $1 billion in financial losses, but deaths and injuries decreased. The reports of non-residential building fires increased by over 10,000 incidents, injuries increased by 200, and deaths increased by 20 instances, while the amount of financial loss decreased by $300,000 from 2021 to 2022.

Profiling Serial Arson

As one of the first developers of methodical contemporary criminal profiling, the FBI developed one of the most widely recognized profiles of arson offenders (Douglas et al., 1992). The National Center for the Analysis of Violent Crime at the FBI posits that investigators can use arson motivation to deduce perpetrator attributes, and offender profiles can be constructed to prioritize suspects to identify or exclude perpetrators. In their *Crime Classification Manual*, Douglas et al. (1992) identify the offender's motive as the fundamental component of crime analysis. Through research reviews, investigations of arson cases, and interviews with convicted perpetrators, the authors identified the following six classifications for motives of arson along with some of their distinguishing attributes. These types have been recognized as successful when attempting to deduce the characteristics of arson offenders.

1. *Vandalism-motivated arson*: usually targets a structure out of opportunity, derived from a malicious and mischievous motive; commonly committed by juveniles, often in groups acting impulsively with little planning, who live within a mile of the target.
2. *Excited-motivated arson*: these fires are set by those seeking thrills or who wish to garner attention, or satisfy sexual feelings; committed by socially inadequate lone or multiple juveniles or young males between the ages of 18 and 30 who may linger after the fire set to watch the response; set near inhabited properties (though there is usually no intention to harm anyone), dumpsters, woods and brush; often serial arsonists.
3. *Revenge-motivated arson*: usually committed in retaliation for a real or imagined injustice as perceived by the offender against another person, institution, group, or society; when it occurs as a single event, it is often well-planned, but when committed by a serial offender there may be little planning; most frequently committed by adult males with a blue-collar position who maintains short-term or unstable relationships with others, who flees the scene and does not usually return.

4 *Crime concealment-motivated arson*: these fires are set to cover up another crime, often murder, suicide, breaking and entering, embezzlement, larceny, or destroying records; typically not well-planned, and may be rushed due to the offender's emotional state; alcohol and recreational drug use by the perpetrator is common, and they frequently have a history of law enforcement interactions; usually committed by a young adult who lives close, leaves the scene, and does not return; this is generally a singular event.
5 *Profit-motivated arson*: these fires are set intentionally for material gain, usually by fraudulent means, or may be hired by another to commit the crime; it is a more organized approach to arson including methodical planning using incendiary devices; the offender is usually an adult male with no police record who lives more than a mile away from the target and leaves the scene of the crime.
6 *Extremist-motivated arson*: committed to further social, political, or religious causes, set for reasons of terror, civil unrest, and discrimination; the target of the fire represents opposition to the offender's beliefs (animal rights groups, abortion clinics, etc.); when the intention is to send a symbolic message to society, there is often a claim of responsibility and these fires tend to be set by younger offenders; these are organized and sophisticated crimes that are well-planned, usually committed by multiple offenders who may leave a message at the scene and may have prior interactions with law enforcement.

The authors define a serial arsonist as "involved in three or more separate firesetting episodes, with a characteristic emotional cooling-off period between fires" (p. 187). They note that this is the most dangerous type of arsonist due to the seemingly random time between fires and the indiscriminate nature of the selected target. Serial arson commonly occurs in arson motivated by revenge, excitement, or extremism.

Serial arson has been classified by instrumental or expressive motivations (Canter et al., 1998). The authors conducted an empirical test of categorizations of arson incidents and behavioral offender characteristics. They describe an expressive crime as internal, which communicates the perpetrator's emotions. An instrumental crime is one in which an action is taken to explicitly achieve the individual's goal. Canter et al. (1998) hypothesized they would find differences between incident and perpetrator characteristics of fires committed for either instrumental or expressive purposes. They further subdivided these categories into those directed at a person or object to determine if any variations exist. Data consisted of 175 solved arson cases in England, from which they derived crime and offender behavioral variables. The findings indicated that the first type, expressive arson directed at a person, is likely intended to assuage the intense feelings of the perpetrator. The authors say this type of arson derives from an internal position. A few of the arson cases in this group appeared to be "parasuicidal" in nature, with the offender either attempting to set themselves or targeted objects near them on fire. The second is an instrumental arson directed at a person. These crimes were the result of a conflict between individuals, with arson being targeted externally. There is usually a precipitating event that catalyzes a vengeful arson. Third is the expressive object fire, which was inclined to be serial in nature. The authors posited that this behavior contains some form of "intrinsic fascination with fire which relates to the internal emergence of the behavior" (p. 82). These fire-setters targeted public buildings expected to be the center of attention, where they frequently returned to or stayed at the scene. The fourth and final type was the instrumental object fire. These fires were usually set by youth, sometimes in groups who entered the targeted building illegally and often committed theft in the process of arson. These were crimes of opportunity, originating externally.

Next, Canter et al. (1998) tested four similar models for fire-setting offender characteristics. The hypotheses were supported, indicating that specific characteristics of the offender were exhibited in their acts of arson. For expressive persons and expressive object types of perpetrators, the act of arson reveals intense emotional responses; the first is usually demonstrative of a mental illness, and the second targets a structure on which to take out their feelings. The third and fourth types are the instrumental person and instrumental object. The instrumental person type reflects the fire-setters' emotional reactions regarding their associations or bonds with other individuals. Lastly, the instrumental object showed how the perpetrator utilized fire setting to achieve criminal outcomes.

Kocsis et al. (1998) conducted a direct test of the FBI organized and disorganized model of serial crimes using arson offenses occurring in New South Wales, Australia, from 1991 to 1994. Using the records of convicted arsonists, the authors chose only those arsons known to be motivated by vandalism or profit. The purpose of this narrow selection was due to the FBI BSU research suggesting that these are the two arson motives determined to be "most strongly representative of the organised and disorganised behavior syndromes" (p. 121). The authors hypothesized that their chosen arson offenses would fundamentally correspond to the two types of serial crime classifications and reveal an association with specific offender characteristics. The investigation yielded 45 arson incidents, of which 14 were established to be motivated by vandalism, and 31 were financially motivated. The authors examined the demographic variables of the offenders, including offender grooming habits, distance from residence to the crime scene, and indications of a prior criminal record. They also included 14 evidentiary factors from the crime scene, such as the use of accelerant, target and entry method, ignition method of the fire, damage, evidence of theft at the scene, physical evidence at the scene, etc. After analyzing the data, Kocsis et al. determined that their results supported their hypothesis that the FBI serial crime model was present in their arson offenses. Further, they posited that the "typology can be imposed on the crime scene structure of crime scene characteristics in cases of arson … [and found] the organised/disorganized distinction to be an intrinsic feature of the crime scene characteristics" (p. 129). The authors concluded from their results that organized arson offenders planned their crimes, choosing their targets carefully, and were willing to travel to achieve their ends, which was motivated by profit. This classification type was organized in their criminal endeavors and their personal lives. The second classification was the disorganized group, who committed their crimes intending to vandalize the chosen property. Offenders did not plan well for their crimes, with the targets more residential than commercial, not bringing an accelerant to the scene, that tended to be near their home base, and not requiring travel. This group appeared to be disorganized in their personal lives as well as their criminal behavior.

In the final study included in this chapter section, Brogan et al. (2014) investigated gender differences in serial arsonists. Their findings determined that male fire-setters were more likely than females to have a diverse criminal history, while females had experienced more sexual abuse. The authors determined that the behavior of committing arson seemed to fulfill separate needs for each gender. This information, combined with other arson classification systems, may provide more useful information when constructing a profile of arson offenders. Brogan cautions that these classification systems should not be considered discrete, fixed categories, but only one of several tools and application methods utilized in crime investigations.

Conclusion

The current chapter includes a review of the nature and extent of such crimes and studies that focus on categorizing non-paraphilic serial crimes. The criminal behaviors included hate crimes, bullying, stalking, robbery, and arson. While the literature investigating each criminal behavior includes sometimes contradictory results regarding classification systems for these crimes, additional research is required to further substantiate specific typologies of non-paraphilic crimes.

As this chapter reveals, non-sexual serial crimes are a serious social issue with detrimental and widespread effects. While the public is captivated by serial sexual crimes, non-sexual serial crimes occur more frequently and create far more damage. These crimes cause serious injuries, deaths, and immense financial costs to individuals and society.

Classification systems are utilized to facilitate humans' understanding of the phenomena in the world around them. While behavioral patterns can be established, humans are still individuals and won't always fit nicely into a certain type. Criminal profiles can assist law enforcement in focusing on suspects for inclusion or exclusion in the commission of an offense.

The criminal profile literature still indicates mixed results concerning its effectiveness as a tool to assist with law enforcement investigations in serial homicides. Future research can advance the classification systems of serial crimes by studying the criminal behavior displayed during various serial crimes, combined with risk and protective factors. Problematic antisocial behaviors that can be identified during early childhood may help to prevent or reduce bullying and stalking behaviors, possibly even hate crimes, arson, or robbery committed in adulthood.

Notes

1 South Carolina does have a Bill in the Legislature regarding penalty enhancements for victims chosen "based on certain factors." The Act reads as follows: "

> The Clementa C. Pickney Hate Crimes Act … so as to entitle the article 'Penalty Enhancements for Certain crimes,' to provide additional penalties for persons who commit certain delineated crimes when the victim was intentionally selected based on certain factors, and to provide victims of a violation of the article may bring a civil action for damages sustained
>
> (South Carolina Legislature, Session 125 (2023–2024), (https://www.scstatehouse.gov/billsearch.php?billnumbers=3014&session125&summary=B)

2 Wyoming does have an anti-discrimination law, but it is a:

> Lower-level misdemeanor to deny a person access to public accommodations and facilities or 'the right to life, liberty, pursuit of happiness, or the necessities of life,' based on their race, religion, color, sex, or national origin … sexual orientation, gender and gender identity are not included … in Wyoming, misdemeanors are generally not punishable by more than one year in jail, so **hate crime offenders are generally subject to federal firearm restrictions only if they are convicted felons**.
>
> [bold face type in original] (Gifford's Law Center, 2024: para 1)

3 Recent statistics estimated that African/black Americans represent about 14.4% of the population (Moslimani, Tamir, Budiman, Noe-Bustamante, and Mora, 2024, "Facts About the U.S. Black Population"). Jewish people make up about 2.4% of the U.S. population (https://www.pewresearch.org/religion/2021/05/11/the-size-of-the-u-s-jewish-population/).

4 Note that the data covers the time span 2019–2021 during the Coronavirus pandemic, which disrupted in-person attendance at American public schools.

5 The current NIBRS Data Tool includes the Violent Crimes of Homicide, Rape, Robbery, and Aggravated Assault; Property crimes include Arson, Burglary and Motor Vehicle Theft, and Individual Crimes include an array of crimes from Animal Cruelty, Embezzlement, Fondling, Human Trafficking, Pocket-Picking, Sports Tampering, to Wire Fraud among others. Stalking is not included in any categories (https://cde.ucr.cjis.gov/LATEST/webapp/#/pages/explorer/crime/crime-trend).

References

Allanson, P. B., Lester, R. R., & Notar, C. E. (2015). A History of Bullying. *International Journal of Education and Social Science*, 2(12), pp. 31–36.

Barrow, L., Rufo, R., & Arambula, S. (2014). *Police and Profiling in the United States: Applying Theory to Criminal Investigations*. CRC Press, Taylor & Francis Group

Bartol, C. R., & Bartol, A. M. (2013). *Criminal and Behavioral Profiling*. Sage Publications, Inc.

Brady, P. Q., & Nobles, M. R. (2017). The Dark Figure of Stalking: Examining Law Enforcement Response. *Journal of Interpersonal Violence*, 32(20), pp. 3149–3173. https://doi.org/10.1177/0886260515596979

Brogan, R. (2014). Serial Arson, In Petherick, W (ed). *Profiling and Serial Crime: Theoretical and Practical Issues*. (3rd edition), Elsevier/Academic Press, Ch 17, pp. 373–392.

Burr, R., Kemp, J., & Wang, K (2024). Crime, Violence, Discipline, and Safety in U.S. Public Schools: Findings from the School Survey on Crime and Safety: 2021-2022. (#NCES 20240-43). *National Center for Education Statistics*, Institute of Educational Sciences, U.S. Department of Education. Washington, D.C.

Burrell, A. (2022*). Robbery: The Tipping Point between Theft and Violence*, Palgrave Macmillan

Canter, D., & Fritzon, K. (1998). Differentiating Arsonists: A Model of Firesetting Actions and Characteristics, *Legal and Criminal Psychology*, 3(1), pp. 73–96 https://doi.org/10.1111/j.2044-8333.1998.tb00352.x

Centers for Disease Control and Prevention (2024). About Bullying, National Center for Injury Prevention and Control. https://www.cdc.gov/youth-violence/about/about-bullying.html

Chifflet, P. (2015). Questioning the Validity of Criminal Profiling: An Evidence-based Approach. *Australian & New Zealand Journal of Criminology*, 48(2), pp. 238–255 https://doi.org/10.1177/0004865814530732

Christine, A., Semisch, C. Ray, C., & Russell, A. (2022). *Federal robbery: Prevalence, trends, and factors in sentencing*. United States Sentencing Commission, https://www.ussc.gov/sites/default/files/pdf/research-and-publications/research-publications/2022/20220818_Robbery.pdf

Cook, C., Williams, K., Guerra, N., & McCoy, S. (2010). Predictors of Bullying and Victimization in Childhood and Adolescence: A Meta-analytic Investigation, *School Psychology Quarterly*, 25(2), pp. 65–83.

Donegan, R. (2012). Bullying and Cyberbullying: History, Statistics, Law, Prevention and Analysis, *The Elon Journal of Undergraduate Research in Communications*, 3(1), pp. 33–42. https://eloncdn.blob.core.windows.net/eu3/sites/153/2017/06/04DoneganEJSpring12.pdf

Douglas, J. E., & Burgess, A.W. (1986). Criminal Profiling: Viable Investigative Tool Against Violent Crime. *FBI Law Enforcement Bulletin*, 55(12), pp. 9–13.

Douglas, J.E., Burgess, A.W., Burgess, A.G., & Ressler, R.K. (1992). *Crime Classification Manual*, Macmillan.

Dowden, C., Bennell, C., & Bloomfield, S. (2007). Advances in Offender Profiling: A Systemic Review of the Profiling Literature Published over the Past Three Decades, *Journal of Police Psychology*. 22, pp. 44–56.

Ernst, J. (2016). Press Release, Senators Gillibrand and Ernst Urge FBI to Collect Crime Data on Stalking and Domestic Violence, https://www.ernst.senate.gov/news/press-releases/senators-gillibrand-and-ernst-urge-fbi-to-collect-crime-data-on-stalking-and-domestic-violence

Equal Justice Initiative, (2017). *Lynching in America: Confronting the Legacy of Racial Terror*, (3rd edition). https://eji.org/reports/lynching-in-america/

Federal Bureau of Investigation. Crime in the United States 2011 https://ucr.fbi.gov/crime-in-the-u.s/2011/crime-in-the-u.s.-2011

Federal Bureau of Investigation. FBI Crime Data Explorer, Hate Crimes, 2024, retrieved 9/2/25. https://cde.ucr.cjis.gov/LATEST/webapp/#/pages/explorer/crime/hate-crime

Fuller, G. (2014). Where and when: A profile of armed robbery by location, *Trends & Issues in Crime and criminal Justice*. No 479. American Institute of Criminology, Australian Government.

Gabor, T. (1988). Armed Robbery Overseas: Highlights of a Canadian Study. In D. Challenger (Ed.), *Armed Robbery*. No. 26 Proceedings from a seminar, March 22-24, 1988. Australian Institute of Criminology, pp. 13–24 https://www.ojp.gov/pdffiles1/Digitization/119997-120009NCJRS.pdf

Guelzo, A.C. & Miller, D.A.H. (n.d.) Civil Rights Act of 1866, "An Act to protect all Persons in the United States in their Civil Rights, and furnish the Means of their Vindication", Selected Summary

of the Civil Rights Act of 1866, National Archives, Washington, D.C. (https://constitutioncenter.org/the-constitution/historic-document-library/detail/civil-rights-act-of-1866-april-9-1866-an-act-to-protect-all-persons-in-the-united-states-in-their-civil-rights-and-furnish-the-means-of-their-vindication#:~:text=Summary,would%20eventually%20resolve%20the%20issue.)
Gifford's Law Center (2024). Hate Crimes and Gun Laws in Wyoming, https://giffords.org/lawcenter/state-laws/hate-crimes-guns-in-wyoming/#:~:text=Wyoming%20is%20one%20of%20the,happiness%2C%20or%20the%20necessities%20of
Huntingdon, Y., & Petherick, W. (2014). Serial Bullying and Harassment, (ed) Wayne Petherick, *Profiling and Serial Crime* (3rd edition), Academic Press
Irwin, V., Wang, K., Cui, J., & Thompson, A. (2023). *Report on Indicators of School Safety: 2022*. (NCES 2023-092/NCJ 307328). National Center for Education Statistics, U.S. Department of Education, and Bureau of Justice Statistics, Office of Justice Programs, U.S. Department of Justice. Washington, DC. https://nces.ed.gov/pubsearch/pubsinfo.asp?pubid=2023092
Jensen, M., Yates, E., & Kane, S. (September 2020a). A Pathway Approach to the Study of Bias Crime Offenders 1990–2018, National Consortium for the Study of Terrorism and Responses to Terrorism (START), University of Maryland, https://www.researchgate.net/publication/349236494
Jensen, M., Yates, E., & Kane, S. (2020b). Motivations and Characteristics of Hate Crime Offenders, National Consortium for the Study of Terrorism and Responding to Terrorism (START) College Park, MD, https://www.start.umd.edu/sites/default/files/publications/local_attachments/START_BIAS_MotivationsCharacteristicsOfHateCrimeOffenders_Oct2020.pdf
Jensen, M., Yates, E., & Kane, S. (2021). A Pathway Approach to the Study of Bias Crime Offenders, National Criminal Justice Reference Service (NCJRS) Office of Justice Programs, Document #300114.
Jones, J.M. (2022). "LGBTQ Identification in U.S. Ticks Up to 7.1%," Gallup, https://news.gallup.com/poll/389792/lgbt-identification-ticks-up.aspx
Jones, L.M., Mitchell, K.J., Turner, H.A. (2022, April). U.S. *Hate Crime Investigation Rates and Characteristics: Findings from the National Hate Crime Investigation Studies (NHCIS)*. U.S. Department of Justice
Kocsis, R., Irwin, H., & Hayes, A. (1998). Organised and Disorganized Criminal Behaviour Syndromes in Arsonists: A Validation Study of a Psychological Profiling Concept. *Psychiatry, Psychology and Law*, 5(1), pp. 117–131.
Kocsis, R., & Cooksey, R. (2002). Criminal Psychological Profiling of Serial Arson Crimes, *International Journal of Offender Therapy and Comparative Criminology*, 46(6), pp. 631–656.
Matthews, R. (2002). *Armed Robbery*, Routledge
McDevitt, J., Levin, J., & Bennett, S. (2002). Hate Crime Offenders: An Expanded Typology, *Journal of Social Issues*, 58(2), pp. 303–317.
Morgan, R.E., Truman, J.L. (2022). Stalking Victimization, US Department of Justice, Bureau of Justice Statistics. NCJ301735, https://www.justice.gov/d9/2023-06/2022%20Report%20to%20Congress%20on%20Stalking.pdf
Moslimani, M., Tamir, C., Budiman, A., Noe-Bustamante, L., & Mora, L. (2024). Facts About the US Black Population, Pew Research Center. https://www.pewresearch.org/social-trends/fact-sheet/facts-about-the-us-black-population/
Olweus, D. (2003). A Profile of Bullying Behavior in School. *Educational Leadership*, March. Association for Supervision and Curriculum Development, pp. 12–16.
Olweus, D., & Limber, S. P. (2010). Bullying in School: Evaluation and Dissemination of the Olweus Bullying Prevention Program. *American Journal of Orthopsychiatry*, 80(1), pp. 124–134.
Petherick, W.A. (2014). *Profiling and Serial Crime: Theoretical and Practical Issues* (3rd ed.). Elsevier/Academic Press.
Petherick, W.A., & Turvey, B. E. (2023). *Criminal Profiling* (5th ed.). Elsevier Ltd.
Pew Research Center (2021). Report, Jewish Americans in 2020, https://www.pewresearch.org/religion/2021/05/11/the-size-of-the-u-s-jewish-population/
Phillips, N. D. (2009). The Prosecution of Hate Crimes: The Limitations of the Hate Crime Typology. *Journal of interpersonal violence*, 24(5), pp. 883–905. https://doi.org/10.1177/0886260508317190
Pineda, D., Rico-Bordera, P., Martinez-Martinez, A., Galan, M., & Piqueras, J. (2022). Dark Tetrad Personality Traits Also Play a Role in Bullying Victimization, *Frontiers in Psychology*, 13–984744. https://doi.org/10.3389/fpsyg.2022.984744?
Rokach, A., & Clayton, S. (2023). Adverse Childhood Experiences and Their Life-Long Impact, https://doi.org/10.1016/B978-0-323-85853-3.12001-4

Swearer, S., & Hymel, S. (2015). Understanding the Psychology of Bullying: Moving toward a social-ecological diathesis-stress model, *American Psychologist*, 70(4), pp. 344–353.
South Carolina Legislature, Session 125, (2023-2024). *Clementa C.* Pickney Hate Crimes Act, https://www.scstatehouse.gov/billsearch.php?billnumbers=3014&session125&summary=B
Turpin-Petrosino, C. (2015). *Understanding Hate Crimes: Acts, Motives, Offenders, Victims, and Justice*, Routledge
Thompson, A., & Tapp, S.N. (2023). Criminal Victimization 2022, September, NCJ 307089, https://bjs.ojp.gov/document/cv22.pdfs
United States Department of Justice, Alcohol, Tobacco & Firearms, US Bomb Data Center (2020). United States Bomb Data Center Fact Sheet, https://www.atf.gov/resource-center/docs/undefined/usbdc-fact-sheet-june-2020/download
United States Department of Justice, Alcohol, Tobacco & Firearms, US Bomb Data Center, (2023). Arson Incident Report 2023, https://www.atf.gov/resource-center/docs/report/2023arsonincidentreport pdf/download
United States Department of Justice, Bureau of Justice Statistics, (n.d.). "Glossary," https://bjs.ojp.gov/glossary?page=11
United States Department of Justice, Bureau of Justice Statistics, Special Report- "Hate Crime Victimization 2005-2019". September 2021, NCJ 300954. https://bjs.ojp.gov/sites/g/files/xyckuh236/files/media/document/hcv0519_1.pdf
United States Department of Justice, Civil Rights Division (2019). About Hate Crimes, https://www.justice.gov/crt/hate-crime-laws#:~:text=The%201968%20statute%20made%20it,or%20the%20enjoyment%20of%20public
United States Department of Justice, Federal Bureau of Investigation (2010). Hate Crime Statistics, 2010. https://ucr.fbi.gov/hate-crime/2010/resources/hate-crime-2010-about-hate-crime
United States Department of Justice, Federal Bureau of Investigation (2019). Crime in the United States, http://ucr.fbi.gov/crime-in-the-u.s/2019/crime-in-the-u.s.-2019/topic-pages/robbery
United States Department of Justice, Federal Bureau of Investigation (2022). Crime Data Explorer, https://cde.ucr.cjis.gov/LATEST/webapp/#
United States Department of Justice, Federal Bureau of Investigation (2023). FBI Releases 2022 Crime in the Nation Statistics, https://www.fbi.gov/news/press-releases/fbi-releases-2022-crime-in-the-nation-statistics
United States Department of Justice, Hate Crimes (n.d.). Learn About Hate Crimes, https://www.justice.gov/hatecrimes/learn-about-hate-crimes#:~:text=a%20%22crime.%22-,Hate,are%20defined%20by%20the%20law
United States Department of Justice, Office for Victims of Crime (n.d.). Stalking, https://ovc.ojp.gov/topics/stalking
United States Department of Justice, Office of Violence Against Women (2023). Stalking, https://www.justice.gov/ovw/stalking
United States Fire Administration, National Fire Incident Reporting System (n.d.). Federal Emergency Management Agency, https://www.usfa.fema.gov/statistics/
Vaughn, M., Fu, Q., Bender, K., DeLisi, M., Beaver, K., Perron, B., & Howard, M. (2010). Psychiatric Correlates of Bullying in the United States: Findings from a national sample, *Psychiatric Quarterly*, 81, pp. 183–195.
Vossekuil, B., Fein, R.A., Reddy, M., Borum, R., & Modzeleski, W. (2004). *The Final Report and Findings of the Safe School Initiative: Implications for the prevention of school attacks in the United States*. United States Secret Service and the Department of Education
Woodhams, J., & Toye, K. (2007). An Empirical Test of the Assumptions of Case Linkage and Offender Profiling with Serial Commercial Robberies, *Psychology, Public Policy, and Law*, 13(1), pp. 59–85.
Woodworth, M., & Porter, S. (2000, December). Historical Foundations and Current Applications of Criminal Profiling in Violent Crime Investigations, *Expert Evidence*, 7(4), pp. 241–264. https://doi.org/10.1023/A:1016655103536
Wright, J., Burgess, A.G., Burgess, A.W., Laszlo, A., McCrary, G., & Douglas, J. (1996). A Typology of Interpersonal Stalking, *Journal of Interpersonal Stalking*, 11(4), pp. 487–502.

10 Cybercrime, Cyberspace, and Cybersecurity

Binneh S. Minteh and Kevin Borgeson

Introduction

The problem of cybercrime is one of the most consequential security challenges of modern times. Cybercrime comprises of a myriad of crimes committed in the changing arena of information technology and computer network infrastructure. Cybercrime is refer to as "any crime that involves a computer and a network, where a computer may or may not have played an instrumental part in the commission of the crime" (Moore, 2014). A computer can become an instrument of crime when it is used to commit a crime, such as malware, denial of service attacks, fraud, extortion, or pornography. Computers can also become the object of a crime when there is theft of hardware or software (Kremling and Parker, 2019) The prefix "cyber" is commonly understood as the realistic or virtual attachment to a computer or a network (Kremling and Parker, 2019). The terms cyberspace and cybersecurity are now commonly used as a prefix to mean that the following word is computer or computer network related. Cyberspace is the virtual environment in which we interact (Kremling and Parker, 2019).

Cyberspace consists of four layers: the physical layer, consisting of physical devices such as computers, networks, and wires; the logic layer, consisting of the platform nature of the internet and its components providing interactive spaces such as social media, shopping, and content; the information layer, consisting of the production and consumption of information such as websites, social media sites (Facebook, Twitter), books, pictures, and videos; and the personal layer, referring to the people who make websites, tweets, etc. To better understand cyberspace in operational terms, Kremling and Parker (2019) further looked at cyberspace in the context of surface webs, the Deep Web, and Darknets. The surface web refers to all websites accessible to anyone with an internet connection, and hosted by browsers such as Internet Explorer, Firefox, and Google Chrome. The deep web consists of all data behind firewalls. The dark web is just a small portion of the deep web—both the deep and dark webs are inaccessible from the surface web. The term cybersecurity is often used broadly and vaguely—the definition varies across individuals, governments, the private sector, which can be confusing. Some definitions focus on cyberspace, while other definitions focus more on security and protection. From a criminal justice perspective, cybersecurity encompasses understanding the tactics of perpetrators, protection practices, and the jurisdiction in which the criminal operates. The prevalence and accessibility of computers and the internet give cybercriminals a wide range of tools to humiliate, attack, harass, steal, and commit other crimes.

In the past decade, cybercrime has increased considerably in the Gambia. The character, nature, and frequency of occurrence across our social, political, and economic spaces have

DOI: 10.4324/9781003366300-11

changed dramatically. The expansion of the internet and the emergence of new forms of technology make some crimes easy to detect and other crimes difficult to understand. Crimes such as theft, fraud, and destruction of data files are easily identified. Other cybercrimes, such as pornography, extortion, cyberstalking, and gambling, are difficult to detect.

With Africa increasingly becoming a haven for online criminals, Gambian law enforcement institutions are inadequately equipped with the capacity and resources to combat cybercrime. The only two national policies with the language of protection include the Public Utilities Regulatory Authority and the National Telecommunications Act. Other developments include the commissioning of a National Cybersecurity Strategy Proposed Formulation and Action Plan by the West Africa Regional Communication Infrastructure Program (WARCIP). The program was designed to provide the Gambia Government a Cyber Security Strategy to contain the threats of cybercrime. In December 2019, the Ministries of Justice and Information and Communication of the Gambia prepared a draft Cybercrime Bill, which was finalized in December 2019 and open for public consultation until January 2020. Similarly, in June 2020, the Gambia, along with 12 other African nations, participated in a U.S. Department of State and the Council of Europe (COE) hosted webinar on "Challenges of International Cooperation on Cybercrime and Electronic Evidence in the Africa Region." Notably, the nations represented at the webinar include Benin, Burkina Faso, Cabo Verde, Ivory Coast, the Gambia, Ghana, Kenya, Liberia, Mauritius, Morocco, Nigeria, Senegal, and Tunisia. The purpose of the webinar was to look at the challenges of international investigations on dark web markets and relevant case studies, international law enforcement cooperation, and international cooperation in codifying and adjudicating cybercrime. Despite all these efforts to harmonize cybercrime legislation, no legislative action has been taken to domesticate regional and international instruments into the laws of the country to facilitate the criminalization of cybercrime.

This chapter provides an assessment of cybercrime, cyberspace, and cybersecurity in the Gambia to inform policy on adopting a National Cyber Security Strategy to address the threats of criminal actors. The study looks at national and regional legislation formulated to protect citizens from vulnerabilities and associated risks of cybercriminals. Furthermore, the study provides suggestions for the Gambia Government to develop a National Cyber Security Task Force composed of representatives from respective cybersecurity units of security and armed institutions, and stakeholders in the private and public sector.

We proceed with a theory and literature review of cybercrime in the first section. The second section explores typology of cybercrime in West Africa and the Gambia in particular. In this section, law enforcement response to cybercrime will be discussed using two cases investigated by the police. The third section will discuss policy implications by looking at the impact of legislative action and other regional instruments on combating cybercrime. We provide concluding remarks in the final section. I will first provide a brief overview of the history and background information of the Gambia.

Case Study: The Gambia

History and Background

Since attaining independence on February 18, 1965, the Gambia has enjoyed relative peace and stability under the country's first republic. President Dawda Jawara, the country's founding president, laid out modest development goals and a moderate foreign policy, and adhered to principles of democracy, human rights, and an open economy. This has won the Gambia much respect in Africa and internationally, as the nation's general image was projected as a beacon of peace and the smiling coast of West Africa. Hence, the Gambia became home to the African Center for Democracy and Human Rights Studies in 1989. With the same historic, cultural, and traditional ties, Senegal and the Gambia have generally maintained peaceful relations and embraced human rights and the rule of law.

In 1994, a military coup led by Yahya Jammeh ushered in the Second Republic. President Jammeh was elected three consecutive times in elections that were regionally and internationally recognized as neither free nor fair. In the Second Republic, Jammeh has controlled and used state security apparatus to maintain a repressive environment in which citizens are routinely jailed, tortured, forced to flee, and sometimes extrajudicially executed. The government interfered with the electoral process, harassed and abused citizens, and enforced disappearance of citizens. Government officials routinely used various methods of intimidation to retain power. Prison conditions were kept poor; citizens were denied due process; pretrial and incommunicado detentions were prolonged; privacy and freedoms were restricted; and violence against women and girls increased.

In December 2016, Yahya Jammeh was defeated by an alliance of opposition parties led by President Adama Barrow. Tension grew in the Gambia after Yahya Jammeh's attempt to overturn the results of the election. Yahya Jammeh's reversal of his initial acceptance of the election results sparked ECOWAS response and subsequent intervention to uphold the legitimate aspiration of the people. President Barrow was sworn in on January 17, 2017, in Dakar, Senegal, after West African leaders evacuated him for security concerns. Some semblance of peace, freedom, and rule of law has since then returned to the Gambia. Under President Barrow, "GDP growth exceeded 6 percent during the two years before COVID-19 struck, supported by rebounding confidence, investment, low interest rates, and growing tourism. Investment accounted for over 22 percent of GDP in 2019." While there has been some moderate economic growth, crime has increased significantly under the Barrow government. Prominently among the crimes that spiked include murder, rape, robbery, theft, and the targeting of computers and the weaponization of data to commit fraud, sextortion, money laundering, drugs, arms, and human trafficking, and to use malware against targeted network spaces.

The Gambia has six licensed internet service providers and four GSM providers. Prominent among the service providers are Africell, the leading firm, with approximately 1.4 million subscribers in 2014, followed by the national firms Gamtel and Gamcel, Comium (Luxembourg), and Qcell (Dib, Grimsland, Muller, Dolele, and Kibuuka (2021), the Gambia is connected to the rest of the world by an ACE cable with over 100GB capacity (Ministry of Trade, Industry, Regional Integration and Employment 2022). Similarly, a study by the Ministry of Trade (funded by the European Union) in collaboration with the European Union recorded

> 1.4 million unique GSM subscribers, a penetration rate of 66.6%, which is the second-highest in West Africa after the Republic of Ghana (66.7%) and far ahead of Senegal (60.5%) and the Federal Republic of Nigeria (45.4%).
>
> (Ministry of Trade, Industry, Regional Integration and Employment 2022)

To put it into context, the Gambia's "penetration rate of 21.3% for data Subscribers and 27.5%" (Ministry of Trade, Industry, Regional Integration and Employment 2022) for Smart phones has shown increased interconnectedness, more actors, and greater vulnerabilities of networks and network architectures across cyberspace.

The Gambia's national backbone is a total land area of 10,000 square kilometers with about 1,300 kilometers of fiber (Ministry of Trade, Industry, Regional Integration and Employment 2022). The national telecommunications firm Gamtel is one of the shareholders in the fiberoptic cable established in 2012 that runs across the country and controls its connection to the internet through the Africa Coast to Europe (ACE) submarine cable system (Ministry of Trade, Industry, Regional Integration and Employment 2022). In May 2013, private telecommunication operators began leasing access to the gateway for data services in the Gambia (Ministry of Trade, Industry, Regional Integration and Employment (2022). The first internet exchange point was also launched in 2014 to increase speed, security, and affordability of internet access (Ministry of Trade, Industry, Regional Integration and Employment 2022). While these developments are significant in the nation's ICT agenda, it is important to understand the opportunities technological advances provide for criminals. Majid and Kevin (2023) has postulated that "Technology acts as a 'force multiplier', enabling individuals with minimal resources to generate potentially huge negative effects." Technological advances in modern Gambia have led to an expansion of organized criminal activities, including drugs, arms, and human trafficking, as well as cybercrime.

Organized Crime—Cybercrime and Drugs Trafficking in the Gambia

The expansive reach of criminal actors driven by technological advances has provided opportunities for new actors in the Gambia, including the pervasive intrusions of cybercriminals, drugs, arms, and human traffickers. Over the years, the Gambia began to experience cybercriminal activity in the form of cyberbullying, pornography, bank fraud, money laundering, and cybertheft. In 2010, over 2 tons of very pure cocaine were seized behind a false wall of a warehouse basement, an hour's drive from the capital Banjul—the operation started following reports that the concerned import/export fishing company may have been involved in bank fraud. In July 2020, Benin cybercriminals demanded 500 euros from Lamin Bojang, leader of the Gambia Action Party, threatening to leak his alleged pornographic video. In all cases, the police were unable to track the criminals, and the nude photos of the victims were circulated on social media. On January 8, 2021, drug enforcement authorities made the largest drug seizure in the history of the country, seizing 3 tons of cocaine at the seaport with an estimated street value of about $90 million (The Maritime Executive, 2021). There are also growing concerns of rising corruption of public officials, declining moral standards, and the weaponization of data against citizens and the state. To ensure that our interactive cyber spaces are secure and protected, the government must adopt a National Cyber Security Policy informed by theoretical and empirical reasoning to better protect, prevent, and adjudicate cybercrime.

Theory and Explanations for Cybercrime

Rational Choice Theory

The relevant theories explaining the causes of cybercrime have evolved considerably in the past decades. There is the rational choice theory with the view that individuals commit crime, including cybercrime, because they have made the rational choice to do so after weighing the risks and benefits. It argues that crime is committed by rational, calculating individuals, and only by punishing offenders can crime, including cybercrime, be deterred. The rational choice theory presupposes that humans are hedonistic (maximize pleasure and minimize pain), and policy should focus on making the risk of committing cybercrime higher than any gains from the crime (Taylor et al., 2019). In sum, the rational choice perspective assumes that the use of punishment to control crime can deter criminal acts if the risk outweighs the gains. The rational choice theory explains cybercrime as a product of strategic choice, involving the criminals planning and making logical choices to succeed.

Drawing on the rational choice theory, the deterrence theory presupposes that cybercriminals commit crime because they make a choice based on perceived risks and benefits in committing the crime (Taylor et al., 2019). The central assumption is that if the risk outweighs the benefit, the crime is prevented. The general deterrence theory seeks to discourage would-be offenders from committing crimes through the threat of punishment, while specific deterrence imposes sanctions on convicted offenders to prevent recidivism. While there is limited evidence supporting assumptions of the deterrence theory, the applicability of deterrence for software and music piracy was validated in a study using samples of college students (Taylor et al., 2019). The study suggests that the certainty of being caught by an IT administrator or fellow student did not reduce the likelihood of being caught; however, the severity of punishment helped reduce hacking activity (Taylor et.al, 2019).

Routine Activity Theory

Developed by Lawrence Cohen and Marcus Felson, the RAT argues that crime occurs when there is the convergence in time and space, a motivated offender (hacker), a suitable target (vulnerable computer system), and the absence of a capable guardian (weak or poor software protection). Cohen and Felson therefore opined that "rapid expansion of the use of computers and internet services has increased the number of targets for motivated offenders such as hackers, fraudsters, pedophiles, and other illicit activities online." An empirical study by Holt, Bossler et al. (2019) found that RAT can be used to explain online harassment. Similarly, Taylor, Fritsch, Liederbach, Saylor, and Tafoya (2019) opined that the millions of computers and smart devices connected online at any point in time and space create a large number of targets available for motivated offenders such as hackers and malicious code writers.

Psychological Theories

Proponents of psychological theories have looked at moral development and personality disorders. Moral development theory suggests that there is a difference between moral beliefs of criminals and non-criminals while personality disorder looks at personality characteristics that are prone to criminal behavior (Taylor et al., 2019). Kohlberg looked at cognitive development in sequential stages that individuals go through, and decisions on what is right and wrong at each stage are made for varying reasons (Taylor et al., 2019). An empirical study observing 500 delinquent and non-delinquent boys over time found that certain personality characteristics were conducive to crime. This included extroversion, impulsivity, lack of self-control, hostility, resentment, suspicion of others, destructiveness, reduced fear of failure, ambivalence toward authority, assertiveness, and feelings of being unappreciated (Taylor et al., 2019, in Glueck and Glueck, 1950). These terms are referred to as ASPD, which is defined as the lack of empathy and regard for other people and the lack of regard for right or wrong. In view of these personality characteristics, it is generally argued that certain computer criminals meet the criteria of ASPD (Taylor et al., 2019).

Strain Theory

In a social structural context, Merton's strain theory suggests that there is a discrepancy between a person's desire to obtain economic success and their ability to do so. This means individuals lacking equal opportunity to succeed are strained and more prone to commit crime.

In retrospect, social process theories look at socialization and crime in a cultural context. It explores the influence of peer and family relationships on crime and performance. The central premise of the social process is learning by differential association or through family and peers. It presupposes that individuals commit crime, including computer crime, because they learn the skills, techniques, attitude, and reasoning required to commit the crime. Taylor et al (2019) posited that learning theories can be applied to our understanding of cybercrimes such as music and media piracy, hacking, and virus writing. In a subcultural context, hackers and virus writers are defined by sets of norms, rules, and values that inform continuous learning. There is strong evidence linking the hacker and the virus writer to a learning process before they become experts.

Summary of Theoretical Perspectives

The general conclusion drawn from the theoretical analysis is that there is no one single theory that can help us understand cybercrime. Given the variations in capacity and challenges to deal with cybercrime as a new phenomenon, a multidimensional approach informed by digital literacy and exchange of good practices between nations and intergovernmental organizations is important in helping our efforts to protect our cyberspaces from becoming a haven for criminal groups.

Profile of Cybercrime in West Africa

Cybercrime is a new criminal phenomenon for sub-Saharan Africa and the developing world. It is different from the traditional crime, since most cybercrime does not require any physical proximity of the criminal to the victim. Cybercrime can be committed across transnational boundaries, making questions of jurisdiction a challenge for law enforcement. It is estimated to cost Africa €3.5bn. As Cassim (2011) puts, "it can be committed, in specific jurisdictions without the offender being physically present." Such abysmal situations make it difficult to investigate and gather evidence against criminals for purposes of prosecution. As such, sub-Saharan African nations, including the Gambia, are confronted with a problem of weak legislative and law enforcement capacity to criminalize and punish cybercrime. To understand cybercrime in the Gambia requires a careful analysis of the common types of cybercrime committed in sub-Saharan Africa. The common types of cybercrime across sub-Saharan Africa include:

- Hacking: It is generally referred to as the unauthorized access to computers or computer systems.
- Online Harassment: Refers to the "sending of repeated threatening or harassing electronic communications via email, websites, or other digital media that cause another person to be harmed or deeply disturbed" (Kremling, Parker, 2019).
- Cyber Bullying: It is a form of online harassment defined as "the intentional and repeated harm inflicted upon another by use of a computer, cellular telephone, or other electronic device (i.e., a social networking site)" (Kremling, Parker, 2019).
- Cyber Stalking: It is a form of online harassment defined as "the process in which electronic communications, such as e-mails, instant messages, and any other form of electronic communications, contain psychologically threatening remarks that harass a recipient or cause victims to fear for their lives" (Kremling, Parker, 2019).

- Malware and Banking Scripters: West African Cybercriminals began using banking Trojans to gather credentials of targets in 2013. As fraud became lucrative, the collaborative work of Interpol and member states found that RAT and keyloggers began to be widely used instead of banking Trojans. For example, in August 2016, "Nigeria cybercriminals were arrested as a result of a joint effort between INTERPOL and security vendors, including Trend Micros" (Flores et al., 2017).
- Pornography, sextortion, fraud, and phone scams.

Cybercrime in the Gambia: The Case Studies

Case #1: Sextortion against Former Gambia Action Party Leader

In July 2020, Benin cybercriminals demanded 5,000 euros from the Gambia Action Party Leader, Lamin Bojang, threatening to leak his alleged pornographic video. Despite collaborative efforts by the Gambia Police Force and Interpol, the Benin scammer could not be located or traced. The scammer appeared to have used a virtual cam whore that tricks victims to think they are interacting with a beautiful woman.

A report in July 2020 stated that nude photographs of Gambia Action Party leader and presidential aspirant Lamin Bojang were leaked online, in a pornographic video and still photos showing Bojang in a comprising position. He immediately claimed that the video was fake and part of a smear campaign, stating, "it is a doctored video. It is a faked video. That was not me. There are scammers, who are out to tarnish my image. I am innocent."

Mr. Bojang contacted Interpol and reported that a friend in the United Kingdom told him that he should pay 5,000 euros to the person who posted the video. According to the report, Interpol was given multiple messages supplying them with information that would allow them to identify the individual who was responsible for the video. Unfortunately, this person has not yet been identified despite efforts to track the perpetrator down.

It appears that this incident is in no way unique, as videos purporting to depict Gambian political figures in compromising sexual acts and positions have been common. Louise Dewast reported in 2019 that a 23-year-old former Gambian beauty queen, Fatou Jallow, charged former President Yaha Jammeh with rape. The woman has repeatedly spoken out but has yet to receive any compensation or to have her case brought to court. As Dewast also reported, the Gambia Action Party has expressed frustration regarding the regular accusations of sexual crime of some type or another by an elected party official. This has been facilitated by the internet, which makes videos and still photographs accessible to the general public and prohibits a meaningful response by the accused.

Case #2: Bank Fraud of Former Human Resource Manager of the Gambia Teachers Union (GTU) and Others

A major salary fraud was uncovered at Gambia's Foreign and Defense Ministry and its Treasury Department. This multifaceted scandal involves not only bank fraud committed by the former manager of the GTU but also members of the military and the government. The amount of fraud has been extensive, particularly under the presidency of Yaha Jammeh, who ruled Gambia for 20 years between 1994 and 2014 (Rahman, 2019).

In many of these cases, bank fraud was commonplace, with people in positions of power using government funds for personal purchases and expenses. The challenge is that it is difficult at best to obtain accurate evidence that supports such cases, which cannot otherwise be addressed legitimately. However, this report indicates that over $100 million, or more than one-third of the annual budget, has been diverted from government programs in the Gambia into private hands. A major part of the problem is that police officers themselves "have been judged to be the most corrupt political officials in the Gambia.... Impunity and abuse of office by law enforcement officials was common under the Jammeh regime" (Rahman, 2019).

Case #3: Scamming via Keylogging

The Interpol report on West African cybercriminal activities offered an excellent example of an actor who installs keyloggers on victims' corporate computers, using email credentials that have been stolen, and then hijacking business transactions and direct funds to his or her own personal account. In the process of installing keyloggers on others' computers, the actor mistakenly installed the keylogger he was using on his own machine, which allowed Interpol to access his logs and to obtain his identity, leading to his arrest. Once a cybercriminal gains control of a victim's machine, he or she is able to log in and remotely manage it, stealing passwords, hijacking email conversations, and ultimately even creating online communities wherein cybercriminals in West Africa share technical skills and know-how. This underground criminality is all too common in much of West Arica, including the Gambia.

Law Enforcement Response

Due to the broad extent of corruption in Gambia's government under former President Yahya Jammeh, which involved not only criminal activity such as embezzlement, looting of state resources, and illicit arms and drug trafficking, the Gambian police were themselves deeply involved in all forms of criminal activity in the country, including cybercrime (kaunain, 2019). There has, however, been a more proactive response by the new Gambian leaders, particularly with the training of police officers under the Gambia Cyber Security Alliance (GCSA), which is

> a civil society professional organization with a view to promote, advocate, and create awareness on cybersecurity, positive information communication technology (ICT) policies, regulations, unrestricted access to information, net neutrality, Internet governance, and by extension provide technical and theoretical assistance to civil society organizations, including police training in cybersecurity (Gambia Cyber Security Alliance, 2021).

According to a news report in *The Point*, GCSA President Amadou A. Bah said that the organization has trained 30 police officers from the Police Information Technology, Major Crime, Serious Crime, Interpol, and Fraud-Squad on practical cybersecurity. The concept behind the training is technology driven, and the GCSA has begun collaborating with the Gambia Computer Security and Incident Response Team to introduce "incident response command and will be monitoring social platforms and any fake news found would be filtered out and a deep investigation and fact check done" (Bah, 2020).

This effort is a significant start and is undertaken in part as a response to studies which have revealed that Africa, in general, and the Gambia in particular, are not fully prepared for cyberattacks. The "2019 *KnowBe #4 African Report* collated insights from more than 800 respondents across such countries as South Africa, Kenya, Nigeria, Ghana, Egypt, Morocco, Mauritius, and Botswana to determine their understanding of the growing cyber threats" (Biz community, 2020).

Both personal and business internet users in this survey indicated that they were concerned about cybercrime but did not know how to properly identify ransomware or other threats. The researchers concluded that "people cannot protect themselves because they don't realize the extent of the cyber threat or how it presents itself.... Most users are not aware of how cybercrimes operate and the tools they use" (Biz community, 2020).

Due to awareness in the Gambia as well as elsewhere about the growing problem of cybersecurity and cybercrime, specific legislation related to cybercrime in the country has been mandated. As described by Jallow (2021), the Gambia has an internet penetration rate of 70% and a mobile penetration rate of 147%. It is connected to the rest of the world through the ACE cable with over 100GB capacity. What this means is that a substantial portion of the Gambian population—in terms of personal, governmental, and business uses of the internet—are vulnerable to some type of cybercrime.

The GCSA is taking the lead role in training police on cybersecurity and cybercrime. It is doing so in association with the Gambia Cyber Security Incidence Response Team, but is experiencing some difficulties in terms of providing training throughout the country. That noted, Gambian law enforcement is in fact learning a great deal through cooperative ventures with other West African and sub-Saharan countries. Part of the problem is that most of Africa "has no control over cybercrime and one of the reasons cited for the prevalence of cybercrime is the promotion of cyber capacity without concomitantly planning for cybersecurity" (Andoh-Baidoo, Osatuyi and Kunene, 2014).

The cybersecurity system in the Gambia, as elsewhere in Africa, depends to a large measure on the effectiveness of a knowledge management (KM) framework and cybersecurity awareness and enforcement frameworks. Researchers are of the view that "awareness is a critical antecedent to effective knowledge management" and "stakeholders can benefit from knowledge management architecture only when they are made aware of the threats of cybercrime and how they can use the knowledge from the architecture to mitigate those effects" (Sallah, 2020).

Far from having a KM architecture in place, the United National International Telecommunications Union reported that "Gambia does not have any officially approved national and sector specific cybersecurity frameworks for the certification and accreditation of national agencies and public sector professionals." (UN, 2014). Gambia's cybersecurity strategy, as described by Mussa Sallah, was commissioned by the WARCIP (Sallah, 2020). Sallah contends that as of 2020, the Gambia National Cybersecurity Strategy was still very much in the proposal or draft stage. This essentially means that "in the Gambia, every day that goes by, many victims on the commonly utilized social media platforms are approached by cybercriminals." Emails are flooded with messages from modern day criminals attempting to extort individuals of their hard-earned money (Sallah, 2020).

Even police officers, who are charged with protecting the public from various types of cybercrimes that have been identified above, do not possess the education, training, or skills that are necessary to ensure that citizens are informed as to the kinds of vulnerabilities they face. The next section of this study examines policy implications, specifically with respect to legislative action that criminalizes cybercrime and the draft of the National Cybersecurity Strategy.

Policy Implications

As described by the United Nations Institute for Disarmament Research, the Gambia National Cybersecurity Policy, Strategies, and Action Plan to be implemented between 2020 and 2024 has the following goals:

- Identify and manage the critical information infrastructure of The Gambia;
- Develop and enhance cybersecurity-related capacity, infrastructure, legal, regulatory and other related frameworks;
- Promote awareness, information sharing and collaboration on cyber security;
- Enable and continuously improve the safety of vulnerable groups in cyberspace, especially the safety of children;
- Enhance and coordinate the fight against all forms of cybercrime;
- Promote the use of cyberspace to drive social and economic development.

UN Institute of Disarmament Research (2020)

Further, the identified mission of this policy is "to develop and deliver effective cybersecurity capacity, services and infrastructure that instills confidence in cyberspace." Within this mission scope, it is the Ministry of Information and Communications and Infrastructure that will be charged with establishing and overseeing a proposed National Cybersecurity Commission, which will serve as the primary advisor to the national authority regarding all aspects of cybersecurity strategy while ensuring that "relevant public and private stakeholders are identified, mobilized and leveraged" (UN, 2020).

The purpose and objectives of the draft cybersecurity strategy, as identified by Gambia's Ministry of Information and Communication Infrastructure, consist of the following:

- Lays the foundations and inform the development of institutional and legal framework for data protection and privacy to safeguard personal data and associated rights of individuals, and in particular the right to privacy.
- Establishes internationally recognised best practices in data protection and privacy law, including fair, transparent and lawful processing of personal data, existence of explicit, specified and legitimate purpose for processing personal data, data protection and privacy by design and default among others.
- Ensures appropriate safeguards for the processing of special categories of personal data, especially personal data about children and other vulnerable groups of individuals.
- Establishes individuals' rights concerning their personal data.
- Provides a framework for assessment of the existence of appropriate level of protection for cross-border transfer of personal data.
- Proposes the requirement for the establishment of an independent and impartial National Supervisory Authority that will be mandated to oversee, monitor and enforce compliance and safeguarding of personal data and privacy rights of individuals.

UN Institute of Disarmament Research (2020)

Fundamental to the development of a successful strategy for securing the Gambian cyberspace must necessarily include securing each of its ICT systems, critical infrastructure, and networks. This places a special demand on each owner and operator of ICT systems, whether it be an individual, a for-profit or non-profit entity, or a public sector agency, who has a direct responsibility for contributing to the success of the strategy. However, a study conducted by Expertise France in 2016 found that the challenge is that

> securing ICT systems requires specific skills that most owners and operators do not have, which results in a need for cybersecurity products and services. It is therefore important for the success of the strategy that the private sector can respond to this need and that The Gambia can foster the development of a cybersecurity ecosystem.
>
> (Expertise, France, 2016)

Additionally, the same organization contends that it is essential for the success of the strategy that the Gambia develop the capacity for investigation, arrest, and prosecution of cybercriminals. This in turn will necessitate ongoing education and training programs, awareness activities, and the development of a national cybersecurity governance scheme that will be fully coordinated and operational. From a policy perspective, Enterprise France identifies the Gambia National Cybersecurity Strategy as being based on six key elements, which are schematically represented in Figure 10.1.

A key driver of the NICI is the Gambia's Vision 2020, which has the goal of transforming the country into a technologically advanced and information-rich society that leverages its ICT and infrastructure to achieve economic growth and development. It also requires that those who commit attacks against ICT systems be brought to justice by strengthening law enforcement authorities and ensuring that a cross-disciplinary approach to public policy and mobilization of all stakeholders occurs (Expertise, France 2016).

In its discussion of the proposed Gambian National Cybersecurity Strategy, Expertise France 2016) also identified a number of principles that should be integrated into such a strategy. These include a recognition of public policy inclusiveness, which means that cybersecurity is everyone's responsibility. It calls for a cross-disciplinary approach as well as a lifestyle approach, which acknowledges that technology itself is constantly changing and cybercrime

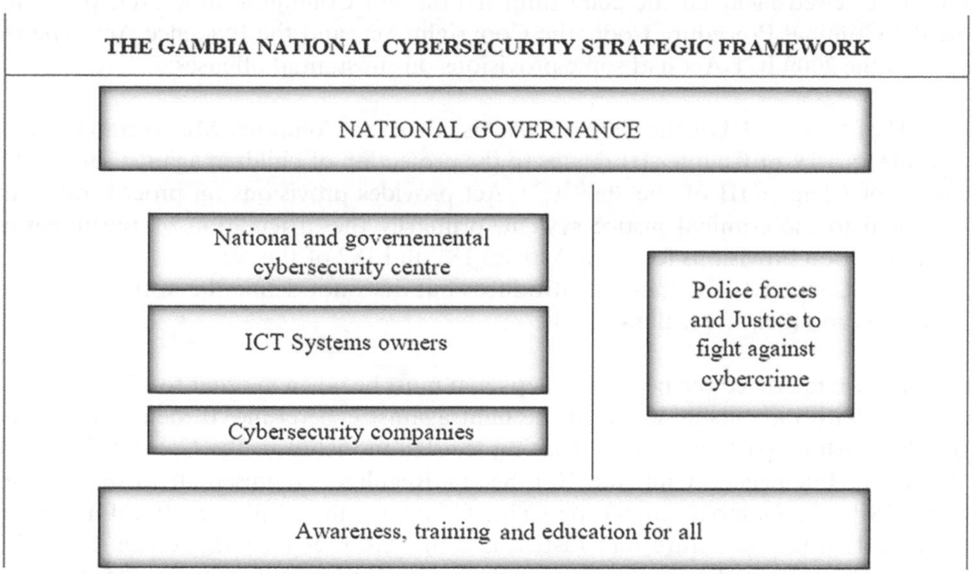

Figure 10.1 The Gambia National Cybersecurity Strategic Framework (Expertise France, 2016).

changes along with it. The strategy must also be action-oriented rather than abstract, provide for clarity of roles and responsibilities, and ensure a balance between security and privacy (Expertise France, 2016). The strategy is admittedly quite complex and will require the participation of multiple government and private sector organizations as well as the creation of new, highly sophisticated, and well-trained cybersecurity professionals.

In December 2019, the Ministry of Justice and the Ministry of Information and Communication prepared a draft Cybercrime Bill, which was finalized in the same month and was open for public consultation until January 2020. This particular piece of legislation, to be discussed below, is characterized as a comprehensive strategy for building cybersecurity into the everyday activities of ITC users in the Gambia (Sallah, 2020). The next section of this report discusses the details of the currently pending cybercrime legislation in the Gambia.

Cybercrime Legislation

As noted above, the internet penetration rate in the Gambia is at 70% with a mobile penetration rate of 147%. Until the formation of the Cybersecurity Policy, Strategies, and Action Plan, it was recognized that the Gambia currently has insufficient detection mechanisms, that investigation of cybercrimes is deterred by the lack of legislation on what constitutes e-evidence, and thus far, prosecutions against cybercriminals have been undertaken under the aegis of economic crime law (Jallow, 2021)

The legislation was introduced in recognition of the fact that the Gambia was .identified as vulnerable by the West Africa Cybersecurity Index and Readiness Assessment Report. The 2016 National Cybersecurity and Action Plans called for urgent formulation of legislation on cybercrime. Some reforms included in this recommendation are underway as a change of government. This includes a review of the Information and Communication Act of 2009 (Jallow, 2021).

The process of this legislation is worth examining. In 2018, an advisory mission from the COE assessed the laws of the Gambia in comparison with the Budapest Convention. Laws that were reviewed included the 2009 Information and Communication Act, the Criminal Code, the Criminal Procedure Code, the Copyright Act, and the Evidence Act. The review found that the 2009 ICT Act had some provisions on substantial offenses:

> Part III of Chapter III of the 2009 ICT Act is related to Computer Misuse and Cybercrime while Part IV of Chapter III relates to the protection of children against sexual abuse.
> Part V of Chapter III of the 2009 ICT Act provides provisions on procedural elements related to the criminal justice system, primarily the articulation of the retention of information provisions found in Articles 181 and 182 of the Act.
> Part V of Chapter III of the Act introduces but does not define the notion of electronic records and their use (Jallow, 2021).

The report also identified the necessary steps that must be taken in order to assist the Gambia in engaging with the outside world in the fight against cybercrime. It identified as relevant stakeholders whose participation in drafting legislation included: the Gambia Police Force, the Financial Intelligence Unit, the ICT Sector Regulator, representatives of the telecom industry, ISPs, the Gambia Submarine Cable Company, the Ministries of Information and Communication Infrastructure, and Justice, and the Attorney General's office. The Office of the National Security Advisor and a civil society representative from the Information Technology Association of the Gambia, and a human rights representative from the Gambia Bar Association were also included in a three-day workshop to draft the bill (Jallow, 2021).

The draft bill that was produced at the workshop, which was overseen by the Ministry of Information and Communication Infrastructure, was shared online for public comments over the course of a full month. Next, a team from the COE joined in the foregoing Gambian participants in a validation workshop to provide for the legislation that is now going to be considered. The bill was submitted to the Cabinet, which was in turn asked to incorporate cybersecurity-related provisions such as the establishment of a formal, government-funded cybersecurity agency. Plans are underway to submit the bill to the National Assembly of the Gambia in November and December of 2021 (Jallow, 2021).

The bill is still being considered as of this writing. Nevertheless, it has already begun to exert an impact in the form of collaboration with local stakeholders, participation in international meetings and seminars on cybercrime and cybersecurity, and enhanced awareness and exposure of cybercrime and cybersecurity strategies in the country. Jallow maintains that there are a number of changes that remain to be addressed before the legislation takes effect. These include: (1) problems with internal processes, (2) insufficient capacities locally, and (3) deficiency in awareness (Jallow, 2021).

The primary lesson that has been learned from the process thus far is that it is vital to establish from the beginning a public-private sector partnership that will work together to ensure that once legislation is finalized, it is fully implemented. There are plans for an engagement workshop with the National Assembly Select Committee on ICT, as well as a series of capacity-building activities and the formulation of additional legislation that is focused on data protection and privacy. The Internet Communications Act of 2009 will be further subjected to review and will be expanded to include new cybersecurity laws for the protection of cyberspace in the Gambia (Jallow, 2021).

Conclusion

It is vital to recognize that the legislative and policymaking efforts that are occurring at this time in the Gambia are in part due to the involvement of the COE. In July 2020, the COE and the United States Department of State hosted a webinar titled "Challenges of International Cooperation on Cybercrime and Electronic Evidence in the Africa Region." Attended by 60 participants from 13 countries (Benin, Burkina Faso, Cabo Verde, Ivory Coast, the Gambia, Ghana, Kenya, Liberia, Mauritius, Morocco, Nigeria, Senegal, and Tunisia), this webinar was focused on expanding the Budapest Convention on Cybercrime, which speaks to law enforcement, judicial proceedings, e-evidence admissibility, and transborder cybersecurity and cybercrime (Sallah, 2020).

Patryk Pawlak, the head of the Brussels office of the European Union Institute for Security Studies and the Institute's Cyber-Related Activities, stated that the Budapest Convention is designed to cover a broad range of online activities, including electronic commerce, data protection, and cybercrime, with a special focus on racism, xenophobia, child pornography, and national cybersecurity. Pawlak argued that there is no single "good" model for securing cyberspace (Pawlak, 2020).

What matters, in the view of Pawlak and Josep Borrell Fontelles, who is the EU's Diplomat-in-Chief, is a commitment to multilateralism in tandem with digital sovereignty, which would maintain and develop a rules-based international order, including cyberspace. Strategic autonomy and digital sovereignty are not about protectionism but are about the willingness and ability of sovereign states to defend mutual interests and values by acting multilaterally when possible, but "being ready to act autonomously whenever we must," which is accomplished by protecting "key technological sectors from falling under excessive control by potential third parties and to ensure the security of vital sectors such as digital, energy, raw materials, and health" (Pawlak, 2020).

There is certainly a recognition, as explained herein, that there are differing levels of development across the world with respect to all of the issues involved in cyberspace—from rules to law enforcement to defining crime, and to punishing crime and criminals. Nevertheless, the realities of a global internet and a global economy are such that countries like the Gambia will benefit from participating in multilateral activities of the type that have been described in this report. It will be interesting to see the results of the finalized National Cybersecurity Strategic Legislation that should be finalized by the Gambian National Assembly by the end of 2021.

References

Andoh-Baidoo, Osatuyi, & Kunene (2014), "Architecture for Managing Knowledge on Cybersecurity in Sub-Saharan Africa," *Information Technology for Development*, 2(2014): 140.

Bah, A. (2020), "GCSA Trains Tallinding Police on Cybersecurity Crime." *The Point*, (July 2020); 1. Retrieved from https://thepoint.gm/africa/gambia/national-news/gcsa....

Biz Community (2020) "Report Reveals Africa is not Fully Prepared for Cyber Attacks." 1. Retrieved www.bizcommunity.com

Cassim (2011), Addressing the Growing Spectre of Cyber Crime in Africa: Evaluating measures Adopted by South Africa and other Regional Role Players, *The Comparative and International Law Journal of South Africa*, 44(1), 3.

Dewast (2019), *Beauty Queen 'Raped by Gambia's Ex-President Jammeh'*. BBC News, June 26, 2019, p. 1. Retrieved www.bbc.com/news/world-africa-48757981

Dib, Grimsland, Muller, Dolele, and Kibuuka (2021), *The Gambia - Digital Economy Diagnostic*, World Bank Group 2021.

Expertise France (2016), *The Gambia National Cybersecurity Strategy: A Proposed Formulation*, Commissioned by West Africa Regional Communication Infrastructure Program (WARCIP) - The Gambia Project, July 2016): 6.

Flores, Ryan, Matsukawa, Bakuei, Remorin, Lord Alfred, and Sancho, David (2017), *Trend Microsecurity News*, Cybercrime in West Africa, Poised for an Underground Market accessed March, 7, 2021 at https://documents.trendmicro.com/assets/wp/wp-cybercrime-in-west-africa.pdf

Gambia Cyber Security Alliance (2021). "About Us." 2021, 1. Retrieved from https://gamcyber securityalliance.com/about-us

Holt, Thomas J. Bossler, Lee, Jin R, Liggett, Roberta, Holt, Karen M. (2019) Examining Perceptions of Online Harassment among Constables in England and Wales, *International Journal of Cybersecurity Intelligence &Cybercrime*, 2(1), 24–39.

Jallow, M. (2021), "Cybercrime Legislation in the Gambia." *Council of Europe*, 2021, p. 4. Retrieved from https://rm.coe.int/cyber-eu-coe-webinar-africa-en-july-2020-momodou/16809ef01e

Kremlin, J. & Parker, A. (2019), In Kremling, Parker, *Cyber Space, Cyber Security, and Cyber Crime*, Sage Publications.

Majid, Y., & Kevin, F. S. (2023). Cybercrime and Society, 4th Edition, Thousand Oaks, CA, Sage Publication.

Ministry of Trade, Industry, Regional Integration and Employment (2022), "Youth and Trade Roadmap of the Gambia Information and Communication Technologies Sector 2018-2022" Youth Empowerment Project/International Trade center 2022. Retrieved from https://yep.gm/tools

Moore, R. (2014), *Cybercrime*, 2nd *Edition*, Taylor & Francis, [Milton ParkAbingdon, Oxon OX14 4RN]. Available from: VitalSource Bookshelf.

Pawlak. P (2020), "EU's Cyber Diplomacy," (September 25, 2020): 1. Retrieved https://directionsblog.eu/navigating-the-eu-cyber-diplomacy/

Rahman, Kaunain (2019), "The Gambia: Overview of Corruption and Anti-Corruption." January 22, 2019, pp. 1–3. Retrieved https://knowledgehub.transparency.org/assets/uploads/helpdesk/gambia

Sallah, M (2020), Cyber Security in The Third Republic, *The Chronicle accessed on March*, 15, 2021, at https://www.chronicle.gm/cyber-security-in-the-third-republic/

Taylor et.al (2019), In Glueck, S. and Glueck, E. (1950), *Unravelling Juvenile Delinquency*, New York Common Wealth Fund.

Taylor, Fritsch, and Liederbach, Saylor, Tafoya (2019), *Cybercrime and Cyber Terrorism*, Pearson Education Inc., USA.
The Maritime Executive (2021), Gambia's Largest Cocaine Seizure: Nearly 3Tons Destined for Europe, The Maritime Executive. https://maritime-executive.com/article/gambia-s-largest-cocaine-seizure-nearly-3-tons-destine-to-europe
UN Institute for Disarmament Research (2020), "Gambia: Cybersecurity Policy," (2020): 1. Retrieved from https://gid.gov.gm/wp-content/uploads/2023/10/CYBERSECURITY-POLICY-2024.pdf
UN International Telecommunications Union (2014), "*Cyberwellness Profile*: Gambia," (2014): 1.

Conclusion

Limitations, Successes, Failures: Future Considerations for Criminal Profiling

Limitations of Criminal Profiling

Social science models in profiling, such as those used in criminology, psychology, and sociology, are often subject to various limitations. One key weakness is their reliance on generalized assumptions. Most BEA profilers believe that profiling types usually rely too heavily on broad patterns and statistical data when developing their profiles, which may fail to account for individual nuances and experiences. Human behavior is complex and influenced by a complex set of cultural, environmental, and emotional factors that vary significantly among individuals. As a result, profiling models may fail to predict or explain specific behaviors or actions accurately. A model that works well in one context or with one group may not apply to another, making it less effective and potentially misleading.

While criminal profiling has provided valuable in predicting some behavior and motivations of serial offenders, it has several notable weaknesses. One of the primary criticisms of profiling is its subjectivity. Profilers often rely on experience, intuition, and interpretation of evidence, which can vary widely among different individuals. This subjectivity means that two profilers could come to different conclusions based on the same evidence (Petheric & Brooks, 2020). Another important weakness included in many inductive profiles is the lack of real-world observational evidence supporting the effectiveness of profiling. While profiling has been successful in some cases, studies show that its accuracy is often no better than random chance. A study in the early 2000s by Dr. Richard Kocsis (2006) revealed that criminal profiles produced by trained profilers were correct about 15% of the time. These findings raise numerous questions regarding the validity of profiling as a reliable investigative tool.

Successes

Profiling has proven to be highly effective in some high-profile cases. One of the most famous examples is that of the Unabomber. The FBI employed a combination of behavioral and forensic analysis to identify Ted Kaczynski as the individual they were seeking. The FBI's profile described the Unabomber as a white male, brilliant, isolated, and a victim of social and political oppression. The psychological profile led investigators to Kaczynski, who had already been a suspect. The case of the Green River Killer is an example of where profiling helped narrow the suspect pool. The FBI's criminal profiling team identified that the offender was likely a sexually motivated serial killer targeting women in a specific area. The profile suggested that the offender was familiar with the area and possibly had a history of interpersonal issues. Profiling eventually led investigators to Gary Ridgway, who committed the crime scene.

DOI: 10.4324/9781003366300-12

The FBI's profile described the killer as methodical, with a history of family relationships and an affinity for control. Although Rader eluded investigators for a long time, profiling provided investigators with critical insights into the nature of the crimes and the potential characteristics of the offender, ultimately aiding in his identification and subsequent arrest in 2005 (Hutnyan, 2022).

Failures

Despite its successes, criminal profiling has also faced significant failures. One such instance is the case of the Washington, D.C., Sniper Attacks in 2002. Law enforcement initially used profiling to suggest that the sniper was a white male, likely acting alone. The profile for this crime relied on attack patterns, which appeared to be carefully planned and executed (Koen & Bowers, 2018). However, when the actual perpetrators, John Allen Muhammad and Lee Boyd Malvo, were apprehended, it became clear that the profile was inaccurate. Muhammad and Malvo were both African American, and the profile did not match their age, behavior, or motivations.

Another failure occurred in the case of the Atlanta Olympic Bomber (Eric Robert Rudolph). Profilers initially mischaracterized the bomber as a left-wing radical or environmental extremist whose political motivations inspired the attacks. However, it turned out that Rudolph was motivated by anti-abortion and anti-government sentiments, which were not in the profile they created at the time.

These cases highlight the inherent risks associated with profiling, particularly when profiles are created based on limited or biased data. The accuracy of profiling is contingent on the quality of the information used to construct the profile, and flawed assumptions or biases can lead to false leads and misguided investigations.

Improvements to CAPS Theory Research

While the CAPS theory, introduced by Walter Mischel and Yuichi Shoda in the 1990s, offers a comprehensive framework for understanding personality, future research should focus on this critical theory and its application to profiling methods. One strength of CAPS theory and its application to criminal profiling suggests that personality is not stable but rather a dynamic structure influenced by factors such as self-concept and rational strategies, all of which can adapt to different conditions. While CAPS has made significant contributions to the understanding of personality and its application to criminal profiling, further research is needed. Below are important areas researchers should focus on.

As pointed out in Chapter 3, an essential aspect of the CAPS model is its focus on the stability of personality across different situations rather than across time. Longitudinal research could focus on how stable the affected personality is across the criminal's lifespan, as well as how it might evolve. By tracking individuals over extended periods, researchers may be able to identify patterns of personality development in response to changes in life experiences and emotions as they evolve throughout an individual's criminal career.

CAPS has been widely researched in Western cultures, leaving out how this theory may be applied to third-world countries. An investigation is needed to assess its applicability across various social situations. As previous research has demonstrated, cultural values influence personality, and consequently, CAPS may be observed differently across societies. Examining different societies may reveal the prevalence of specific personality traits and identify areas where societal influences conflict, ultimately enhancing the theory's acceptance in the social sciences field (Office of the Surgeon General (US); Center for Mental Health Services (US); National Institute of Mental Health, 2001).

References

Hutnyan, M. (2022). BTK: A case study in psychopathy. *SMU Journal of Undergraduate Research*, *7*(2), Article 5. https://www.ncbi.nlm.nih.gov/books/NBK424857

Kocsis, R. (2006 July). Validities and abilities in criminal profiling: A critique of the studies conducted *International Journal of Offender Therapy and Comparative Criminology*, *50*(3), 344–360. https://doi.org/10.1177/0306624X05277660

Koen, C., & Bowers, S. (2018). *The Psychology and Sociology of wrongful convictions* (pp. 1–43). Academic Press.

NA. Office of the Surgeon General (US); Center for Mental Health Services (US); National Institute of Mental Health (US). Rockville (MD): Substance Abuse and Mental Health Services Administration (US); 2001, Aug. Available at: https://pubmed.ncbi.nlm.nih.gov/20669516/. Retrieved on July 26, 2025.

Petherick, W., & Brooks, N. (2020 December 10). Reframing criminal profiling: a guide for integrated practice. *Psychiatry Psychology and Law*, *28*(5), 694–710. https://doi.org/10.1080/13218719.2020.1837030. PMID: 35571594; PMCID: PMC9103349

Index

Page numbers in *italic* indicate figures, page numbers in **bold** indicate tables and page numbers followed by "n" indicate notes.